I0893444

THE LEGACY OF LOUIS RIEL

THE LEGACY OF LOUIS RIEL

LEADER OF THE MÉTIS PEOPLE

John Andrew Morrow

Baraka Books

Montréal

All rights reserved. No part of this book may be reproduced or transmitted in any form or by any means, electronic or mechanical, including photocopying, recording, or by any information storage and retrieval system, without permission in writing from the publisher.

© John Andrew Morrow

ISBN 978-1-77186-315-5 pbk; 978-1-77186-328-5 epub; 978-1-77186-329-2 pdf

Cover and book Design by Folio infographie
Editing and proofreading: Robin Philpot, Daniel Rowe, Anne Marie Marko

Legal Deposit, 2nd quarter 2023
Bibliothèque et Archives nationales du Québec
Library and Archives Canada

Published by Baraka Books of Montreal

Printed and bound in Quebec

Trade Distribution & Returns
Canada – UTP Distribution: UTPdistribution.com

United States
Independent Publishers Group: IPGbook.com

We acknowledge the support from the Société de développement des entreprises culturelles (SODEC) and the Government of Quebec tax credit for book publishing administered by SODEC.

Société de développement des entreprises culturelles Québec

Funded by the Government of Canada
Financé par le gouvernement du Canada
Canada

"Resistance to tyrants is obedience to God." Louis Riel

TABLE OF CONTENTS

A NOTE ON NOTES

In the hope of making this work more accessible to more readers, traditional, academic, in-text references have been removed from the book's main body. The result is a work not cluttered with brackets, names, and page numbers that annoy the eye and intimidate some readers. To satisfy university students, scholars, and researchers, all references can be found at the end of the book in a section titled "Notes on Chapters." When citations are translated into English, their original French is found in the notes. French speakers, especially academics, will appreciate having the original citations made available to them. While dates and places of composition may appear fastidious, they allow readers to view Riel's ideological evolution chronologically. Despite being richly researched, every reasonable effort has been made to ensure that this study reaches as many Métis people as possible regardless of their educational level. It is always a struggle to reach a mixed audience of lay readers and scholars. All shortcomings are those of the author.

Disclaimer

Except for the prologue and the conclusion, the views expressed in this work are those of Louis Riel and not those of the author. The role of the literary critic is to explain and interpret the writings of the subject and to expound upon them, placing them in the context of their time, and relating them to the pressing issues of our age. Consequently, my religious and political views are immaterial. Those of my subject are all that matter. Some nineteenth-century terms, which were acceptable in those times, have been replaced by terms that are viewed as more appropriate in ours. Neither Riel nor the author, nor many of the sources cited for that matter, intend any offence by using terms such as Indians, savages, Half-Breeds, Negros, coloured people, or lunatics. While Riel's views will please some, they will displease others. It would be wise to remember the adage: don't kill the messenger. That being said, as the author of this work, I refuse to misrepresent the views of Riel because they might hurt somebody's feelings. That would be an act of academic, intellectual, and historical dishonesty. I find some of his views to be deeply offensive; however, I refuse to censor them and respect his right to hold them and to share them. *Pro deo, patria et libertate in perpetuum.*

PREFACE

> *"My people will sleep for one hundred years, but when they awake, it will be the artists who give them their spirit back."* Louis Riel

Louis Riel has been the subject of scores of articles and books. As Jennifer Reid, the author of *Louis Riel and the Creation of Modern Canada*, notes, "more histories, biographies, novels, and poetry have been written about Riel than any other Canadian figure." Most of the works, however, are biographical or concentrate on his role in the Métis uprisings of 1869-1870 and 1885, namely, the Red River Rebellion and the Northwest Rebellion, respectively. In short, while they deal with his life, sometimes superficially and others more meticulously, they primarily address his political and military actions. Few, however, focus on Riel's radical and provocative thoughts, namely, the theoretical, social, political, philosophical, and religious foundations of his emerging and evolving ideology. In fact, the four volumes of writings that Louis Riel left behind—works of great significance, featuring poetry and prose, and a vast assortment of genres, which make a seminal contribution to French and English Canadian literature—have been largely ignored by both scholars and laypeople. This is like relating the lives and actions of Fidel Castro or Che Guevara with little consideration of their speeches and writings. Many studies on Riel suffer from this severe shortcoming or even fatal flaw. Thoughts and actions are symbiotic. Ideally, one should not be considered without the other as they inform one another and are complimentary, like the yin and the yang.

To understand a person as fully as possible, one must strive to paint a complete picture based on the available and accessible material to the best of one's ability. Since the life of Louis Riel has been duly documented and examined in reasonable detail, this work, though biographical in part, is not a biography. It falls squarely in the field of literary criticism, exegesis, and hermeneutics. In an attempt to fill the gaps left by previous authors and scholars, some of which are chasms and gorges, this study examines the literary legacy of the Franco-Indigenous luminary in question. It explores his nuanced views on a variety of vital subjects, which remain relevant in our day and time, including the term *Métis*, Métis identity, Indians, Jews, Islam, Quebec, French-Canadians, the French language, the Irish, the United States, women, liberalism, and Métis unity, some of which have been sidelined or ignored and which are sure to stoke considerable controversy in our current socio-political context. In so doing, this study will increase our understanding of Louis Riel, his thought, and his writings, and hopefully stimulate lively debate. It is also hoped that it will help create greater cohesion among Métis communities throughout North America when attempts are being made to divide them into Western and Eastern Métis to further weaken and dispossess them. Most importantly, this humble but arguably ambitious work answers the critical question: "Why does Louis Riel matter?"

Louis Riel mattered to his family and his community. He mattered to the Métis people, French-Canadians, and First Nations. He counted to Irish Catholics in North America. He mattered to traditional, conservative, anti-secular, Christian believers who opposed liberalism. He mattered to republicans and anti-imperialists of all origins who opposed colonialism, oppression, despotism, and exploitation. And he mattered to the poor, persecuted, disenfranchised, and oppressed from all walks of life, from ethnic to religious groups to entire peoples and nations.

Although he could have passed for white and benefitted from colonialism, the status quo, and the imposed order, perhaps even obtaining free land stolen from dispossessed First Nations as a homesteader, Riel insisted on identifying as a Métis French-Canadian, honouring his ancestors from all sides, and assuming the role of the Indigenous David against the Imperial Goliath. For British and Canadian colonizers, who viewed opposition to imperial power in the same fashion, none but a madman would rise against their rule. In their imperial eyes and materialistic minds, which greedily yearned for world domination, fighting for freedom was futile while insubordination against subjugation was insanity. For Riel, however, resistance was both a right and a duty.

A man of many worlds, dimensions, and depths, the multifaceted Louis Riel bridged the Indigenous and the European, the past and the present, Tradition and Modernity, not to mention monarchy and republicanism. His traditional, religious, biblically based morality, which was instilled by radical ultramontane priests—who rejected modern secular ideals in favour of Catholic religious supremacy in both personal and public life—merged, in his later life, with some modern, arguably liberal, principles of participative democracy and human rights.

Riel's personal and ideological evolution, growth, and maturity were marked by conflict, turmoil, and contradiction. He could be conservative and liberal, old-fashioned, and progressive, as well as reactionary and revolutionary. He internalized and embodied the troubles of his times. Inspired and illuminated, the Prophet of the Prairies was the product of his messianic and millenarian times, the end of an era, and the dawn of a new age. He was, in his words, the Daniel of the Christian era, and the Elijah of the age.

Unlike other rebels and revolutionaries, who committed excesses of all kinds to obtain their political objectives, Riel, though fierce and fearless, was mostly a man of mercy who strove to be human and humane. His qualities, the foremost of which were courage, compassion for others, and the quest for justice, were admirable and worthy of emulation. Like any human being, he had his faults. However, unlike many others, he did his best to learn from them and not to repeat them. Diplomatic and pragmatic, he attempted to adjust his ideas to changing circumstances and the needs of his people. He could present the same content using an attorney's tone, if the occasion suited it, or deliver it using a prophetic tone, if the situation called for it.

Not only was he a prophetic preacher and a charismatic spiritual and mystical leader, but Louis Riel was also an Indigenous activist and a warrior, an anti-imperialist, a French-Canadian nationalist, and a forefather and precursor of Quebec separatists and sovereigntists. He played a fundamental role in shifting voting trends in Quebec from Conservative support to Liberal support, thus paving the way, unbeknownst to him, toward increased secularization and, ultimately and fatefully, to the Quiet Revolution and the quest for Quebec independence in the middle half of the twentieth century.

Though immersed, throughout his life, in Indigenous and Catholic thought and culture, through his contact with numerous First Nations, the Métis, and the French-Canadians, Riel was an admirer of the Founding Fathers, a proponent of republicanism, and a believer in democracy in its American manifestation. He was a pivotal, articulate, and passionate political activist who established the Provisional Government of the Red River, founded the province of Manitoba, and spearheaded two militant armed resistance movements against the Government of Canada.

A man of words and action, Riel fought for the sovereignty of the Métis people, First Nations, and French-Canadians, to protect their languages, cultures, and lands. He was committed to social justice for all. Multiracial and multilingual, Riel, the Catholic Christian Métis, was the living embodiment of opposition to white Anglo-Saxon Protestant supremacy. Although the British and English Canadians were his avowed enemies, and the Orangemen wanted him dead, Riel did not want to dehumanize or demonize them.

While he condemned the faults of his white Anglo-Saxon Protestant foes, and vituperated them, he also praised their qualities, the foremost of which were their administrative skills, namely, the art of effective and efficient government. Able to admire even his enemies, Riel stood for tolerance at a time of generalized, systemic, institutionalized intolerance, racism, bigotry, and discrimination. Although he was a fervent and zealous Christian, an ultra-conservative one to be precise, Riel broke from the bounds of dogma and doctrine to proclaim himself the Prophet of the New World with an Indigenous neo-Catholic Christian religion that, in his mind, was more aligned with the needs and aspirations of its people. And it was an evolving religion at that.

Louis Riel has had a lasting effect on Canadian history and remains relevant. Despite numerous ideological differences, he stands on the same pedestal of socio-political significance as Imam Husayn, Joan of Arc, Toussaint L'Ouverture, George Washington, Thomas Jefferson, Túpac Amaru II, Omar Mukhtar, Simón Bolívar, José Martí, Tecumseh, Crazy Horse, Geronimo, Chief Joseph, Sitting Bull, Benito Juarez, Augusto César Sandino, Ernesto "Che" Guevara, Fidel Castro, James Connolly, Emiliano Zapata, Éamon de Valera, Michael Collins, Frantz Fanon, Martin Luther King, Malcolm X, Nelson Mandela, and Ayatollah Khomeini, among many other revolutionaries, ranging from the famous to the infamous. After all, one man's terrorist and traitor is another man's freedom fighter and patriot, while one woman's madman is another woman's saint, prophet, or messenger of God. It all depends on perspective and the side on which one stands.

While many ideological movements have attempted to appropriate him for political purposes, some rightly and others wrongly, we must strive to honour the memory and legacy of Louis Riel as accurately as possible. He may have been a proponent of pluralism; however, it was a very narrow one, a pluralism of origin and not of outcome. He may have been an anti-racist; however, he supported a temporary ban on Asian immigration for socio-cultural and political reasons instead of racial ones. He may have encouraged Europeans of all origins to settle in the Americas; however, as an assimilationist, he expected them to merge with the Métis people. He may have espoused French and English bilingualism; however, he expected all immigrants to adopt them as their languages.

As progressive and pluralistic as Louis Riel may sound when cited out of context, it must be stressed that he was a proponent of multiple melting pots: the Aboriginal, namely, the Métis, as he was convinced that all First Nations would eventually become Métis, the French, who were the cousins of the Métis, and the English, whom he recognized were here to stay, could not be supplanted, and with whom co-existence on this continent was inescapable. While this might sound like a paradox, it is not. It was the philosophy that "from many, we are one," namely, that many people of different origins can come together to create a common people and culture.

Louis Riel's attitude toward immigration did not resemble that of contemporary Canadian multiculturalism. It was more closely connected to the situation in Mexico and other parts of Latin America, where a plurality of racial and ethnic origins posed no problem so long as one integrated, racially, linguistically, and culturally, into the dominant Hispanic culture. Whether one was of Indigenous, Spanish, African, Lebanese, or other origins was immaterial so long as the result was the same. Discrimination in Mexico, for example, is not based on origin: it is based on one's current identity. People who decide to remain Indigenous are subject to considerable discrimination. The same applies to any other race or ethnicity. They are all expected to become Mexicans, a single, predominantly Mestizo people, regardless of race or origin, who share a common language, culture, history, and identity. The origin of their ancestors is immaterial. It is nationality and current identity, not genetics, that matter. Obviously, Riel was not anti-First Nations. He was convinced, however, due to their dire situation, that they would disappear as distinct tribes and nations and merge with the Métis to become a larger mass of Aboriginal people. He continued, however, to defend their rights and sovereignty to the end of his life with prophetic passion and revolutionary fervour.

Riel's attitude toward immigration contrasts sharply with the current Canadian multicultural philosophy which, for some, signifies "from many, we remain many." Since Canada, as a nation, was created and built by the combined efforts of Aboriginal people, the French, and the British, Riel expected newcomers to integrate into one of the original, founding, or heritage cultures. He did not believe in empowering newcomers to create ethnic enclaves or bringing them in such numbers that they would overwhelm Aboriginal people and the first European Christian settlers of predominantly French and English origin. This nationalistic and patriotic view stands in sharp contrast to the official multiculturalism policy that was instituted by Prime Minister Pierre Elliott Trudeau in 1971 and sounds, in our times, decidedly more American than Canadian.

While Canadians prepared a salad bowl, with distinct ingredients co-existing side by side, remaining independent but theoretically enhancing each other, Americans cooked up a melting pot in which all elements fused into one to create a single dominant culture. The point here is not to take sides. It is simply to describe Riel's ideas and place them in a broader context. His colonization project, which he conceived as a confederation, was not multicultural, nor was it intercultural. It was assimilationist.

One could claim that what Riel proposed for immigrants was what was done to the Métis, namely, an attempt to assimilate them. That was not the case. The Orangemen who were settling in the West were intent on displacing, eliminating, and replacing the Métis and the French Canadians. They were opposed to them racially, religiously, and linguistically. The Métis, both Francophone and Anglophone, and both Catholic and Protestant, had co-existed harmoniously since their formation. The fanatical Freemasons and Protestants, many of whom were Ulster-Scots, arrived with a violent, racist, scorched-earth policy. They wanted to do to the French-Canadians and the Métis, and to the Catholics for that matter, what Oliver Cromwell (1599-1658) and William III (1650-1702) of England did to Irish Catholics. "All Mighty God!" prayed Louis Riel, "Protect the Métis whom the English have almost annihilated."

Since Riel and his people were faced with a relentless flood of foreigners—primarily from Great Britain, who were coming to the Northwest of Canada like a biblical plague of locusts, but who were not integrating into First Nations, Métis, and French-Canadian culture, focusing on usurping their land and resources—Riel's position was the polar opposite of the state-sponsored doctrine and dogma of multiculturalism. As Louis Riel and Gabriel Dumont described them, these Orangemen were racist white Anglo-Saxon Protestant supremacists. They were unlike the French, Scottish, and Irish, who had married First Nations women and created the Métis people in the process. Since this invasion posed an existential threat, Riel wanted to secure an existence for his people, the First Nations, Métis, and French-Canadians, and a future for their children.

If Riel encouraged immigration, it was on the condition that immigrants integrate into the founding nations, not diluting them, turning them into minorities in their land, and imposing outside cultures, customs, and incompatible values. When in Rome, he thought, do as the Romans. There was no doubt in his mind that North America was Indigenous, that the French had made an alliance with the First Nations to share resources in a process of collaboration and co-existence as opposed to conquest, and that the French had encouraged intermarriage with the First Nations, thus leading to the creation of the Métis people. The First Nations and the French depended on one another as the fur trade was an integral part of the economy. In much of North America, many of the French had "gone Native." Their way of life was not tangibly different than that of the First Nations. For Riel, the only conquerors and colonizers were the British who took Acadia by force in 1710 and New France in 1760. The French had settled North America promoting inclusion; the British had conquered it imposing exclusion.

"We will not be replaced" may be a right-wing, twenty-first century, rallying cry that, for the left, is racist and white supremacist. However, it was also the call of the First Nations, the Métis, and French-speaking North Americans who were conquered by the British, the Americans, and the Anglo-Canadians. The situation had become so dire for the survival of the First Nations, Métis, and French-Canadians that Riel had his militants swear an oath to "save our country by taking up arms if necessary." Some current right-wing Europeans, Euro-Canadians, and Euro-Americans complain about white genocide and the Great Replacement, ideas that are dismissed as racist, white-supremacist, conspiracy theories by the left. For critics, the demographic decline that they whine about is the result of immigration policies put into place by their very people, their very politicians, and their refusal, as men and women, to reproduce sufficiently to survive and prevail as a race, culture, and civilization.

As far as the left is concerned, white people have nobody to blame but themselves and the sooner that they become minorities, the sooner white supremacy will fade, and the better it will be for everyone. This supports the claim of right-wing whites that liberal and left-wing whites who suffer from suicidal ideation wish to wipe them off the face of the earth. Unlike current white people, the First

Nations, Métis, and French-speaking North Americans were faced with actual genocide through conquest, colonization, deportation, and extermination. In addition, the descendants of the survivors were faced with cultural genocide that would continue for centuries through government policies. Comparing the so-called plight of white people to that of Aboriginal people is like comparing apples to cacti.

The *Grand Dérangement* or the Great Upheaval, namely, the Expulsion or Deportation of the Acadians, which took place between 1755 and 1764, involved the forcible relocation of nearly twelve thousand people from Acadia to Louisiana and elsewhere. Over five thousand Acadians died due to disease, starvation, and shipwrecks. This was a classic example of so-called ethnic "cleansing" that was enacted by British colonialists and imperialists. Many of the Acadians happened to be Métis who were terrorized by the British invaders and subjected to scalping like their relatives from the First Nations. DNA analysis of Louisiana Cajuns demonstrates that many of their ancestors were of mixed French and Indigenous ancestry. The conquest and colonization of North America, the American Indian Wars, which took place between 1609-1924, Indian Relocations, starvation, and epidemics caused by diseases brought from Europe, resulted in the deaths of millions of Indigenous Peoples, primarily First Nations but also Métis.

In light of historical horrors and darkness, comparing the demographic decline of Europeans and Euro-descendants to the physical genocide of Aboriginal peoples and the theft of their continent is unfair and unjust. The attempt, on the part of the right, along with occasional First Nations and Métis leaders, to appropriate Indigenous figures to serve their racist, xenophobic, and Islamophobic agenda, and compare the self-imposed plight and political choices of white people to the cataclysm that was brought upon Native peoples, is tasteless, dishonest, and disingenuous. For some critics, it is a white pity party in which Indigenous Peoples should not partake. Historically, First Nations, Métis, and French-Canadians remember far too well that "white rage" was always associated with racism, the Ku Klux Klan, and acts of anti-Indian, anti-Métis, anti-French, and anti-Catholic violence. They may be opposed to the burning of churches in retaliation for past abuse; however, they remember vividly who was burning down their homes and stringing them up on trees. These right-wing whites complain that they are becoming minorities, but their ancestors were the ones who turned First Nations, Métis, Acadians, and French-Canadians into minorities.

While some First Nations and Métis might empathize with those who currently claim that they are being replaced as part of a globalist capitalist plot, as they themselves were indisputably replaced, they must ask themselves where the ancestors of these white people were all along during the conquest, colonization, and genocide of Indigenous Peoples. And where are they today? What have they done for the First Nations and the Métis? Did they ever stand by their side and defend their rights? Why should First Nations and Métis people come to the defence of the descendants of white settlers and later white immigrants, who are now neighbours, when they never built any bridges of friendship and solidarity, much less alliances with Indigenous Peoples?

Other First Nations and Métis are perfectly fine with a nation where we are all minorities. However, this is not the demographic future that is projected. At current rates of immigration, some Western European countries will become predominantly Asian, while others will become primarily North African, Middle Eastern, and African. The United States will become a majority Hispanic nation while Asians, mostly Chinese and Indo-Pakistanis, will dominate Canada. Neither Canada nor the United States will have populations equally divided between minorities from around the world. So-called whites were once twenty percent of the world population. They are now down to nine percent. Understandably, some of them are frightened and feel that their survival is at stake. They fear that others will do to them what their ancestors did to others.

World power is shifting, leaving Europeans and Euro-descendants in the lurch while Asians rise to global power. To rejoice that "WASPS are ... becoming a minority and losing a great deal of their power," as Bill Wilson apparently does, is like playing Russian roulette in the minds of some Aboriginal people. They do not know if the new non-white majorities will treat Indigenous Peoples the same, better, or worse than the whites. Considering the dominant perceptions of the cultures from which they come—namely, dismal traditions of democracy, civil, and human rights, where tribalism and racism are seen to be rampant, and where genocides are said to have been perpetrated—some Aboriginal people believe that placing hope in them is perilous. After all, Canada tends to welcome people who have been their allies in some of the worst atrocities committed by imperialists.

Do Aboriginal people have a greater chance of obtaining justice from European heritage Canadians or from Asians? These are questions that Indigenous people ask themselves as the reins of power are shifting over to people from the so-called Third World. After centuries of waiting for justice from whites, some Aboriginal people are willing to give other ethnicities a chance. As much as they may worry, they have little to no power to influence Canadian immigration policy. Many just shrug their shoulders and state that so long as immigrants do not try to impose their ways on Aboriginal people, or steal their land, then they are willing to share the country with them.

Aboriginal people were willing to share the land with newcomers. However, they were left with nothing of substance or nothing at all. They were disinherited. The settlers were not interested in sharing. They were interested in taking. They had no intention of living as neighbours. These right-wing white people complain that they are being replaced by people from the developing world when they replaced Indigenous Peoples. Call it karma. What goes around comes around. What goes up must come down. Ensure that justice is done to the Indigenous inhabitants of Turtle Island, and then they might ensure that justice is done to you. So far, however, with rare exceptions, it is not white people but a tiny number of immigrants, victims of Western imperialism, who have shown some signs of solidarity with Indigenous Peoples. It is ironic that right-wingers, many of whom are overtly racist against the original inhabitants of the Americas, compare their decline and demise to that of Indigenous Peoples.

The Aboriginal people of Canada did not appreciate being replaced by Europeans. If Asians, and others, replace white people, many First Nations and Métis will not like it much more. They feel like the whites stole their lands only to give them away to others. If whites want to give away Canada and the United States, why not give them back to their Original Peoples? Right a wrong, they reason. Do not compound it. Rather than bring in millions upon millions of foreigners every few years, to counter population aging and decline, many of them would prefer that the government support Aboriginal people to increase in numbers as they have some of the largest families of all Canadians. As they ask: Why invest in foreign immigrants instead of Aboriginal Canadians? As far as many Indigenous people are concerned, Canadians, original Canadians, should come first. Although people of European ancestry in Canada remain the majority for the moment, and white people will become a minority by 2036, at the latest, there has been no watershed movement or political awakening that would alter the current status quo concerning immigration and multiculturalism. As for the United States, non-Hispanic whites will become a minority by 2045.

While Indigenous Peoples hold a full spectrum of views on the subject of immigration, many of them feel that they are stuck between a rock and a hard place. "It's a bit late to ask," answered the late Chief Ken Baird from the Tsawwassen First Nation when a journalist inquired about his feelings towards Canada's immigration policy. As Bonita Lawrence from the Mi'kmaq Nation noted, Indigenous people become implicated in anti-immigration rhetoric or "support struggles of people of colour that fail to take seriously the reality of ongoing colonization."

Except for Quebec, which involves Indigenous Peoples in decisions pertaining to immigration policy, neither the Canadian nor American governments ever asked Aboriginal people how they felt about large-scale immigration and the settling of foreign people on their ancestral lands. This led the Assembly of First Nations of Canada to demand a freeze on all immigration "until the federal government addresses, commits, and delivers resources to improve housing conditions, education, health, and employment in First

Nations communities." As far as Bill Wilson, an Indigenous leader from British Columbia, is concerned, most new immigrants "are basically oblivious to Indigenous issues." Some Indigenous people feel that Canada's policy of multiculturalism ignores the special status of Aboriginal people. As far as many Aboriginal people are concerned, the Americas are not countries of immigrants. They are sovereign Indigenous nations that were conquered and upon whom waves of immigrants were imposed in a process of continued colonization. For the sake of justice, they argue, this is a conversation that must be had. In their view, Aboriginal people must not only be consulted but they must be given decision-making powers in matters that directly impact them. They feel that the people of the land must be able to determine their destiny.

Louis Riel was a nationalist and a sovereigntist, but he was no racist, unless one accepts the liberal notion that questioning or opposing immigration is inherently racist. In fact, he praised the Republican Party of his time, the Party of Lincoln, "for having freed all races and having situated them all on a perfect footing of equality." And, as Glen Campbell noted, Riel was particularly sensitive to racial prejudice. In the view of many Native people, like Riel, nation-states are not required to accept immigrants. It is a choice they make and one that must have a mandate from the majority of their citizens. In their view, there is nothing racist about saying "We have too many immigrants" any more than it is racist to say, "We need more immigrants."

As Indigenous people reason, the owner of a house can allow people to move into his house. The owner of the land can sell his land to others. However, an outside party has no right to do so. For many Aboriginal people, any government can increase, decrease, or completely halt immigration based on the wishes, interests, and needs of its population: not the needs of immigrants and refugees. They believe that nations must act in their own best interest and the interest of their citizens, not the interests of other nations and their people, and most certainly not the interests of globalist capitalists. As far as many Indigenous and non-Indigenous people are concerned, a nation that cannot secure and protect its borders, control immigration, and ensure socio-cultural and linguistic integration through acculturation or assimilation is neither sovereign nor independent. For the whites on the right, diversity is death. It is just a code name for conquest. Such people seem oblivious to the diversity of Europeans and other so-called "White" or "Caucasian" people. Ironically, they belong to the same body of people who were violently racist against the Irish, the Italians, the Poles, and other Europeans. Placing all Europeans or "Caucasians," as some like to call themselves, in the same category, treating them as a monolithic mass, and denying them their diversity, is ignorant, racist, and reductionist.

Although some of Riel's views might offend certain sensitive people in the twenty-first century, who will claim that they are politically incorrect, racist, and xenophobic, his views must always be contextualized and historicized. The image we wish to remember is that of a compassionate man. Riel cared about blacks in his opposition to slavery, and praised the "United Moral States" for having broken and destroyed that evil institution. He believed that "coloured people" made significant contributions to the country, not the least of which was their "obedient and warm-hearted disposition." Unlike some of the "civilized" Indians, who had enslaved blacks, Louis Riel, the Métis, and the "savage" First Nations from which they came, opposed the abominable practice. Unlike the secular liberals, who viewed black people as sub-human or second-class citizens devoid of human and civil rights, Riel viewed them as fellow human beings and citizens with full rights. Riel was also concerned about struggling European settlers who were not at war with Indians and Métis, so long as they integrated into Aboriginal, French, or English culture. There was enough land for all of them, so long as it was shared equitably and the First Nations, the Métis, and the French-Canadians were not left in the lurch, landless and homeless, continually fleeing from westward expansion in search of a land-base to call their own. This care for the weak and the oppressed, regardless of their origins, led him to support the Jewish people who had been persecuted for nearly two thousand years. This generous support and offer, which included a Jewish State for the wandering, nationless Jews, was genuinely unprecedented. However, it came with a considerable caveat.

Although Riel, who once identified as a Jew, was a defender and supporter of the Jewish people, at a time when many secular, liberal, and conservative politicians were openly and overtly racist, supremacist, and antisemitic, the Métis leader demanded that they embrace the Christian faith in return for a homeland in the Americas. And while he called for freedom, which one would presume included religion, Riel was opposed to Islam, spiritually and geo-politically, as were many Christians and Westerners at the time. While this hostile attitude toward Islam might be viewed negatively by some in our times, it would have been viewed positively by many in his times. The Christian West, with whom the Roman Catholic Riel identified, was still very much at war with Islam and the Ottoman Empire. For him to have sided with the enemy, even the enemy of his Protestant enemies, would have been unconscionable. This position, however, should not be falsely equated with modern, twentieth- and twenty-first-century Islamophobia.

Finally, as much as Riel was chivalrous towards women and was, to a degree, positively influenced by Aboriginal attitudes of respect towards women, he wanted to keep them in the kitchen, barefoot, chaste, pious, and pregnant, in contrast to First Nations mores and customs which granted them considerably greater liberty and agency. Once again, these were the dominant values of the day, at least among the French, English, and others, that were shared and transmitted by men and women. People are the product of their time. Women had few rights. And most cultures of the time had clear gender roles that were not meant to be breached. While some might view him as misogynistic from our current perspective, in his time some more conservative men would have viewed him as being pro-women. Change comes by degree, and change is not always perceived as being positive. Case in point, these traditional, conservative values, which are viewed as retrograde by secular liberals, are still upheld by groups today, including some Jews, Christians, and Muslims, who equate secular liberalism with degeneracy.

Viewed from our current vantage point, Riel's ideology combined elements that are liberal and left-wing with others that are conservative and right-wing. In this regard, for some, he resembles thinkers like Juan and Evita Perón, Liberation Theologians from Latin American, various right-wing Christian or Identitarian movements, and certain Islamist ideologues, the foremost of which would be Ayatollah Khomeini. Admittedly, comparing Riel to certain controversial political and religious figures might offend some. I am not, however, stating that he was a carbon copy of others, simply that he shared some ideological similarities and affinities with them. Although he was influenced by many conflicting schools of religious, political, economic, and philosophical thought, Riel was his own man and was never stagnant. Most importantly, this man of revolution was in a state of constant evolution. Consequently, Riel can function as both a unifying and a polarizing figure.

Whether we agree or disagree with any of Riel's thoughts and views, some of which were arguably traditional, conservative, and even retrograde, while others were progressive, liberal, revolutionary, and radical, we must, out of fairness, honesty, and objectivity, focus on the universal values that he embodied and espoused. While we must consider him warts and all and recognize that some of his positions clash with contemporary values and convictions that many people deeply cherish, it is nobler, more befitting and dignified to focus on his fairer human features. As the saying goes, "If you have nothing good to say, why say it at all?"

The portrait painted in this work is not intended to undermine its subject. It combines praise and criticism, as well as positives and negatives. It does not promote a cult of personality that falsely portrays Riel as some sort of saint, nor does it drag him through the dirt as others have done. It is a scholarly study of the subject that strives to be objective. It is a representation that should unite rather than divide. We can disagree when it comes to politics, even passionately so; however, we should strive to agree on fundamental ethics and universal principles.

When it comes to studying the works and thoughts of Louis Riel, critical thinking is imperative. His works are not a catechism to be accepted based on blind faith. Reason is the order of the day. Riel himself criticized his writings and statements. He altered and changed his views, and rejected many of them. Nothing prevents us from doing the same. We must prune and trim the branches, not chop down the entire tree. Otherwise, we destroy our roots. His is a tree whose fruits can nourish generations.

Riel's creativity was uncontrollable and undisciplined. It overwhelmed him and overpowered him. He took his inspiration, dreams, auditory hallucinations, and visions far too literally and most dangerously so. However, he was conditioned to do so by Indigenous culture, with its vision quests, his Catholic education, and his biblical framework and worldview. He wrote everything down, even works that most artists and writers would have torn up and thrown away out of embarrassment. He never had the time, nor apparently the desire, to edit his work, keeping his best writings, and tossing the rest into the trash. That editorial work, however, has been left to literary critics and historians. All great artists write bad songs. We do them a disservice to release them. We should focus on the works that met their standards, that they agreed to publish publicly, and that became hits and classics. Riel wrote down every dream he had and every thought that crossed his mind. If any of us did the same, and other people read them, they would indeed conclude that we were all insane as well. The fact that Riel seems to have suffered from bipolar 1 disorder with psychotic features calls for empathy, compassion, and understanding: not condemnation. His creative process was not always pretty; however, it produced botanical gardens of beauty. With roses come thorns.

As the struggle for justice, liberty, and dignity is one that never ends due to the very nature of people, Riel's message resonates in all times and places. His voice needs to reach First Nations, Métis, French-Canadians, and other peoples who have suffered from historical injustices, including imperialism, colonialism, and violence, as well as systemic racism, discrimination, marginalization, and persecution. Riel's words of wisdom remain relevant on and off Indian reservations and Métis settlements. They are a rallying call for Métis people who continue to struggle for recognition and rights from coast to coast. For many, Riel's inclusive conception of Métis identity should be central in the identification, recognition, membership, and citizenship process. His cry for unity, and his warning against division, should be heeded by all those engaged in political infighting, fraternal rivalry, family feuds, and internecine strife.

In light of generational trauma, the wise, soothing, and healing words of Riel are medicine to many survivors of the Indian, Métis, and French-Canadian residential and boarding school system, victims of language suppression, subjects of forced assimilation, and the families of missing or murdered Indigenous girls and women. They provide solace to Native people who have lost loved ones to overdoses, alcohol, and suicide. The teachings of Louis Riel are a source of inspiration to all Aboriginal and non-Aboriginal peoples who struggle for their rights, justice, equality, and liberty, enlightening many, including black people. What is more, Riel's extensive academic studies, and his incredible scholarly and literary output can motivate First Nations, Métis, French-Canadians, and others to pursue higher education and to make meaningful and impactful contributions to a variety of fields and to society as a whole.

Louis Riel matters more than ever. His thoughts, however controversial as some may be, remain relevant in our days and times and should play a role in public debates on matters of national and international policy. Hence, this humble effort to expand our understanding of his ideas and ideals and encourage further scholarship and reflection on this most meaningful and manly man. Let us honour Louis Riel, the Métis elder, and let his people be proud, for they have survived against all odds. Despite having lost political power, virtually all of their land, and turned into minorities where they were once majorities, the Métis were not wiped off the face of the earth. They live on, as does the spirit, memory, and message of Louis Riel.

Chapter 1

LOUIS RIEL AND THE NAME *MÉTIS*

"Je désire que ce nom distinctif soit le nom Métis que nous avons toujours porté." Louis Riel

1.1 Introduction

Louis Riel referred to himself, and to his people, as aboriginals, original Half-Breeds, aboriginal Half-Breeds, French, French-Canadians, *Bois-Brûlés* [Burnt Wood], *Métis Canadiens* [Canadian Métis], Halfbreeds, *Métis Français* [French Métis], and Métis. To these ethnonyms, he could have included the French terms *métif, michif, gens libres* [Free People], *hommes libres* [Freemen], and the English terms Freemen, Country-Born, Mixed-Blood, Flower Bead Work People, and the Cree term *Apihtawikosisan*, "the half people," *Otipeymisowak*, "the independent ones," *Wissakodewinmi*, "the Burnt-Sticks" or the Algonquian *Makwa* which was Gallicized as *Magua*. Other French ethnonyms for the Métis include: *Acadien, Canayen, Gaspésien, Hivernant* [a voyageur who wintered in First Nations camps], *Malouidit, Sang-mêlé* [Mixed-Blood], *Sauvage, Voyageur,* and *Rat-musqué* [Muskrat]. They were also known in English as Breed, Bungee, Burnt-Stick, Half-Blood, Half-Caste, and Pork Eaters, among other terms peculiar to specific places and periods. While Riel only used a dozen of these ethnonyms, he was likely familiar with most, if not all of them, due to his travels and interaction with Métis people throughout North America.

1.2 Métis, the First Name of a New First People

If French-Canadian was a family name, the New First People also needed a first name. After considering all available options, Riel opted for the name *Métis*. As for the reason for using this ethnonym, Riel reasoned as follows: "I want that distinctive name to be the 'Métis' name that we have always carried. I believe the name 'Métis' is likely to favour the founding of a powerful nationality in Manitoba and the Northwest."

Although Riel's people bore many names throughout their history and ethnogenesis, the name "Métis" was the most constant and the most all-encompassing. He believed he could rally his people around the name in question to create a new nationality in Manitoba and the Northwest. This vision, however, did not exclude the Métis from other regions. They were also Métis by ethnicity. However, since the Métis were the majority in Manitoba and the Northwest at the time, this region was the most logical choice for creating a political Métis nation, namely, a sovereign and independent state that was not subject to British, American, or Anglo-Canadian rule. Explaining the meaning of the word "Métis," Riel wrote:

> It's a name that means mixture. Until now it has been used to designate the race produced by the mixture of European and Indian blood. However, it is also suitable to name a race of human beings, created by the mixture between all bloods but which, while passing through the French-Canadian mold, would retain the memory of its origin, by calling itself Métis.

Riel explains that the word *Métis* means mixed and that, until his time, it was used to describe mixed-race people, in the Canadian case, namely, those of mixed European and First Nations blood. He distinguishes between Métis people in terms of racial admixture and those who belong to the Métis people who came out of the French-Canadian mold. More than the product of admixture, the Métis had become a distinct people with a distinct identity and culture as a result of a historical process.

Although they had branched off from the trunk of the French-Canadian tree that was rooted in the soil of Acadia and Quebec, and which spread throughout North America, Riel believed that it was important for the Métis, regardless of where they were located geographically, to remember, remain connected with, and celebrate their French-Canadian origins. The Cajuns of Louisiana, for example, some of whom are Métis by genes, culture, and identity, have always retained a strong connection to their ancestral homeland of Acadia. Likewise, the Métis of the US Midwest, the Prairies, the Pacific Northwest, and northern Canada should not forget their origins in Lower Canada, Acadia, and ultimately, France. As for selecting the ethnonym *Métis*, Riel reasoned as follows:

> The name "Métis" would be agreeable to everyone because it is not exclusive and has the advantage of properly referring to the contingent for which each nation would help found the new people. And, from this point of view, I believe that it would be difficult to give as a basis for our nationality in Manitoba and the Northwest a broader and stronger idea than the Métis idea.

After the failure of the Métis rebellions and the execution of Louis Riel in 1885, "the Métis dispersed and submerged." They kept a low profile for the sake of self-preservation. They were hiding in plain sight. Since they had "nowhere ... to retreat," some Métis scholars suggested that "most modern-day Métis and non-status Indian people have little choice but to integrate as quickly as possible into White society." Consequently, many of the Métis were assimilated to varying degrees into Anglo-Canadian or French-Canadian culture.

"Although all Métis are by definition persons who consider themselves Métis," notes Richard Slobodin, "this does not mean that all Métis call themselves 'Métis,' or any equivalent thereof, under all circumstances." For example, when applying for commercial fishing licenses at Hay River between 1959-1963, Slobodin noted that 46 percent of Métis applicants failed to enter "Métis," opting for terms such as "Cree Half-Breed, "Half-Breed," "Non-treaty Indian" and "Native (non-treaty)." He also pointed out that the people from the Red River used the terms "Métis," "Breed," and "Half-Breed" to describe themselves. In contrast, the Northern Métis did not self-identify as readily as "Métis" and were more prone to use the terms "Breed" and "Half-Breed." "This difference," he notes, "derives from differences in histories of the two subgroupings." As Slobodin notes,

> The Northern Métis have little tradition appertaining specifically to their Métis status. This is in keeping with the shorter family lines since the original miscegenation and the shallow genealogies of Northern as compared with Red River Métis.

Writing in 1973, Terry Lusty noted that "many Métis do not identify themselves as such." Some identified as non-status Indians. Others as French-Canadians. And yet others as Canadians. Regardless of the terms they used to identify themselves, the Métis existed and could not be disregarded. Since their status had been officially recognized, the same applied to their heritage.

Due to backlash, racism, discrimination, exile, economic disadvantage, and territorial dispossession, not to mention the traumatic impact of residential schools and forced assimilation policies, it would take generations for the Métis people of Canada to start regrouping and reasserting themselves. Following the execution of Louis Riel, writes Sébastien Malette and Guillaume Marcotte,

> Many Métis families hid their cultural heritage for fear of reprisals. The mounting racism toward all things Indigenous also pressed the Métis to dissimulate their identity, historically associated with having some "Indian" ancestry... One of the first historians commissioned by the Métis, Auguste-Henri de Trémaudan ... certainly felt that pressure when he suggested in a rehabilitative manner that the Métis assimilated easily to "civilization," to such an extent that it is hard, if not impossible, to distinguish them from White settlers.

Like the First Nations, the Métis "adopted whatever identity would offer them a better chance to survive, including joining Indigenous bands, becoming Treaty Indians or hiding their identity to their children."

Although it took a considerable amount of time for the term "Métis" to be adopted collectively, the signified exists in the absence of the signifier. Whether they were called Negros, Blacks, or African

Americans during various historical periods, these terms all refer to the same people. The same goes for the names used by the Métis, and others, to refer to themselves. Riel's vision was finally realized in the late twentieth- and early twenty-first century when most of his people rallied around the term "Métis." While many came from families that had always identified as Métis or Half-Breeds, others had previously identified themselves publicly as French-Canadians or Acadians due to discrimination. Some who were darker coloured even claimed to be Spanish, Hispanic, or Latino to avoid the stigma of being "Indian." As Katie K. MacLeod reasons,

> Hiding one's identity in response to racism and colonialism can be viewed as a "defence mechanism" that many Métis individuals use to cope with their identities in a white society... The Mi'kmaq were faced with insurmountable hardships from the British. Living in British-controlled Nova Scotia meant living in fear of the blood one possessed, and if fitting in was possible, disguising oneself as European was a safer option for many... These tactical responses enabled the Métis to pass for white in public while maintaining their culture in secrecy.

As Kristina Fagan and her co-authors have noted,

> "Métis" is a term that still has a shifting and contested meaning, and that is used and rejected by various groups depending on their situation... Yet there is an ongoing effort by organizations such as the Métis National Council to define and stabilize the meaning of the word so that it can be used in the pursuit of political goals.

Unlike Riel, who viewed the term as inclusive, the Métis National Council and most of its provincial branches treat it as an exclusive ethnonym that is limited to descendants of the Red River Métis, thereby dispossessing the vast majority of Métis people in Canada and the United States. As Sébastien Malette points out,

> Accusations of recent opportunism by "fake" Métis can easily be flipped on their head by suggesting that the political creation of more restrictive criteria to assess Métis identity is the result of political opportunism of a number of western Métis organizations that decided in the 1980s to sever from more inclusive Indigenous organizations.

Although this exclusionary vision of Métis identity is espoused by some, Kennedy, Rivard, Gagnon, Chrétien, McNab, Foxcurran, Marcotte, Bouchard, Malette, and Pulla are among those who use the term "Métis" in a more inclusive manner. "It should be noted," write Malette and Marcotte, "that not all western Métis people endorse this now exclusionary ideology regarding Métis identity." On the contrary, "many Métis in the Red River believe that there are Métis in different parts of Canada with their own cultures." In fact, the leaders, and members of various Métis organizations in Eastern Canada are Red River Métis.

As Peter Larivière notes, "there are no universal pan Métis definitions of Métis identity that would be acceptable to all political Métis organizations, the state... or by Métis people themselves." As he warns, the term Métis, like the term Aboriginal, "may be... used from a position of power to limit, redefine, and possibly destroy the identity of many nations and peoples into one neatly packaged group that then has to appear before the courts with some form of unified history to argue its universal rights." However, the fact of the matter is that "Indigenous peoples of mixed Aboriginal and non-Aboriginal ancestry need to be provided the opportunity to identify themselves as they see fit." As far as Larivière is concerned, "Who the Aboriginal peoples of Canada are must be reopened to accept and acknowledge all Aboriginal communities." As Robin White puts it, "Recognition of the Métis Nation in Historic Homelands is imperative and just, but so too are the separate and distinctive histories, culture and memories of self-identifying Métis across Canada."

1.3 Conclusions

Although they described themselves variably as Aboriginals, original Half-Breeds, Aboriginal Half-Breeds, French, French-Canadians, *Bois-Brûlés*, *Métis Canadiens*, Halfbreeds, *Métis Français*, *métif*, *michif*, *gens libres*, *hommes libres*, Freemen, Country-Born, Mixed-Blood, Flower Bead Work People, *Apihtawikosisan*, *Otipeymisowak*, *Wissakodewinmi*, *Magoua*, *Acadien*, *Canayen*, *Gaspésien*, *Hivernant*, *Malouidit*, *Sang-mêlé*, *Sauvage*, *Voyageur*, *Rat-musqué*, Breed,

Bungee, Burnt-Stick, Half-Blood, Half-Caste, and Pork Eaters, the people these terms described were one and the same: the Métis. Consequently, Louis Riel rallied them around a central racial, ethnic, cultural, and linguistic identifier. If his people were indeed a nation and not solely an ethnic group, they needed not only a common origin, language, culture, and landmass but a name that would transcend time, space, and borders. For Riel, *Métis* was the unifying term to describe his people in all their diversity and diaspora.

Chapter 2

LOUIS RIEL AND MÉTIS IDENTITY

"Rester Métis, devenir plus Métis que jamais!" Louis Riel

2.1 Introduction

Louis Riel is a towering figure among the Métis of Canada and the United States. While he was not the first Métis, as there were Métis communities in Canada since at least the seventeenth century, and possibly as early as the sixteenth century, he was one of the first to speak of the Métis as a nation, as opposed to a race, a people, an ethnic group, a tribe, or a band. And while he does not have the final say when it comes to defining Métis identity, as identity is fluid and evolving, and the living should have as much a voice as the dead, Louis Riel holds an enormous amount of sway in matters of self-identification. How, then, did Louis Riel define himself? What were, in his mind, the markers of Métis identity? And how are they relevant in the early twenty-first century, when Métis identity has become so contentious? A comprehensive study of the *Collected Writings of Louis Riel* can shed light on this controversial and divisive subject.

2.2 *Sauvages* [Indians / First Nations]

As shocking as it may seem to some and as offensive as it may be to their sensibilities, Louis Riel referred to the Indigenous inhabitants of the Americas as *sauvages* when writing and speaking in French. At the time, *sauvage* was the antonym of "civilized." Savages were wild people, nomadic or semi-nomadic, who were not fully sedentary or civilized according to the standards of the Old World. In many cases, this was in line with the myth of the "noble savage," which is commonly attributed to the philosopher Jean-Jacques Rousseau (1712-1778).

In most cases, Riel used the word *sauvage* without pejorative intent, the same way African Americans and others used the word "Negro" in the past. At times, however, Riel described some particularly fierce Indigenous people as *sauvages* in a more negative sense. This brings to mind the American distinction between so-called noble and civilized Indians like the Five Tribes of the Cherokee, Choctaw, Muscogee (Creek), Chickasaw, and Seminole, as opposed to the supposedly ignoble and savage Indians comprised of anyone who resisted racist, colonialist, and imperialistic plans. Ironically, while Riel and the Métis viewed themselves as "civilized," as compared to the Indians, they were perceived as savages by Anglo-European colonizers, occupiers, invaders, and authorities. There is no question, however, that when John A. MacDonald (1815-1891), the first prime minister of Canada (1867-1873 and 1878-1891), referred to the First Nations and the Métis as "savages," it was an expression of racist, white supremacist sentiments.

In his "Revelations against Beauport," written on May 22, 1876, Louis Riel described himself in the following terms: "Know me: most of my blood comes from France; I have some from Ireland; and I also have Indian blood." He had no qualms with claiming to have Indian ancestry. In fact, he took great pride in the matter. As he wrote in a poem, written in French between 1874 and 1878, "Indian blood shines in me / and I praise my ancestors."

In his "Petition to Alexander Morris," written in St. Vital, Manitoba, on May 5, 1875, and addressed to a Canadian politician who served in the cabinet of Prime Minister John A. Macdonald, Riel wrote that, "We are doing everything possible to communicate in the best fashion with all the Indian nations to act rightly and justly." As people of European and Aboriginal ancestry, the Métis acted as intermediaries between both worlds and cultures. Their role, however, was both positive and negative. Their legacy is therefore mixed.

In his "Letter to Paul Proulx," written in Beauport, Quebec, on May 10, 1877, Riel described Indigenous people as *sauvages*. In "While the Métis Planted," a poem written in Beauport, Quebec, on May 13, 1877, Louis Riel claimed that the Métis had been scattered abroad so that they could be enslaved like a *peuple sauvage*, a primitive people, likening the Métis to the Hebrews who were reportedly displaced and enslaved in Egypt. While in Montana between 1881 and 1884, he also wrote about the *sauvages* in his "Notes on the Intermarriage of People."

In "The French-Canadian Métis People," written in St. Peter's Mission, Montana, in August of 1883, Riel wrote about the need to borrow words from the *langues sauvages* or Indian languages. He also spoke of the *sang sauvage* or Indian blood of the Métis. Although they were both Indigenous, Riel insisted that the Métis were distinct from the First Nations. He felt that "The Métis and the Cree treat each other like good friends and relatives should treat one another."

In "Memorandum Prepared by Riel and Shown to Monseigneur Grandin," written in St. Laurent, Quebec, on September 5, 1884, he spoke about the *sauvages*. In his "Notebook," authored in St. Laurent between October of 1884 and March of 1885, Louis Riel mentioned the *tribus sauvages* or Indian tribes. In his "Letter to the English and French Métis from Rivière Bataille and Fort Pitt and the Surrounding Area," which dates from March of 1885, he speaks about the *sauvages*. He also refers to "our relatives, the *sauvages*" or Indians in another letter authored in late March 1885. In his "Journal," written in Batoche, Saskatchewan, between September and May of 1885, he used the term *sauvage*, both singular and plural, on numerous occasions.

In his "Statement to G.H. Young's Diary," written in Batoche between May 15 and May 16 of 1885, Riel wrote about "Indians." In his "Letter to R.B. Deane, Edgar Dewdney, and John A. MacDonald," written in Regina on July 6, 1885, Riel spoke of the *chefs sauvages* or Indian chiefs. Edgar Dewdney (1835-1916), who was addressed in the letter, served as an Indian commissioner (1879-1888) and Lieutenant Governor of the Northwest Territories (1882-1897). He was a proponent of starving Indigenous Peoples into submission to facilitate depopulation of the land and its resettlement with Europeans. Although he was warned that Indians and Métis were starving, he ignored calls to come to their aid, preferring to let them die. In Regina, Saskatchewan, a major thoroughfare is named after him.

Riel also used the term *sauvages* in his "Essay on the Northwest," written between August and November of 1885 while in Regina, Saskatchewan. He also spoke of the *sauvages* in his "Manifesto to My Fellow Americans," written at the same time and place. And in "Revelation Regarding the American Annexation of the Northwest," he called upon the US government to place the *sauvages* or Indians in the Northwest.

2.3 Natives / Indians

Louis Riel referred to himself as a native on one occasion, namely, in his "Petition to Grover Cleveland [1837-1908]," the president of the United States (1885-1889 and 1893-1897), which was written between August 23 and September 10 of 1885 while he was in Regina, Saskatchewan. Speaking of himself, he wrote that "he is a native of the Northwest Territory and connected by his origin with the Indian race." It is not clear what he meant by "native." It could have meant a "Native Person." However, it could simply have meant that he was born in the Northwest. And while he asserted that he was "connected by his origin with the Indian race," Riel did not describe himself as an Indian or a member of the Indian race or people. It was a matter of ancestry, not racial, cultural, ethnic, or tribal identity.

While Riel was proud of his Indigenous ancestry and spoke of "Indian righteousness," he also spoke of "the shortcomings of our Indian blood" in self-deprecation. He believed that interracial, interethnic, and intercultural marriage came with positive and negative qualities. However, in the case of marriages between First Nations and Europeans, primarily French, but occasionally Scottish or otherwise, he felt that the positive aspects would prevail. Although he was an Aboriginal Person, he appears to have been directly or indirectly impacted by some of the ideas disseminated by racial biologists and eugenicists.

Riel acquired these notions of racial characteristics and genetic determinism through his Eurocentric education and contact with white, Anglo-American thought and culture. What is now viewed as racist pseudo-science was then viewed as mainstream science. For biologists and social scientists, there was a hierarchy of races, some superior, and others inferior. Riel did not buy into such supremacist foolishness; however, he did believe that, despite individual differences, the members of each race tended to share specific characteristics in common, namely, some sort of national character.

While Western scholars and scientists of the nineteenth century viewed mixed marriages or "miscegenation" as they called it as detrimental to both races, Riel turned their theories on their heads and argued that such racial mixing was mostly beneficial. Though he was Métis, thus part First Nations, Riel was not immune to some of the prevailing stereotypes of his times. Although genetics play a role in personality development, socio-cultural factors arguably play a greater role. Communities, it must be remembered, are not monolithic. Individuals of different races, haplogroups, or ethnicities cannot be placed into distinct categories. Diversity disallows such simplistic categorization. Human beings are not homogeneous. Moreover, education, economics, social class, and opportunities play a considerable role in levelling the cultural playing field and improving outcomes. In fact, children who are moved from educationally impoverished environments to enriched ones show a significant increase in IQ. There is no such thing as racial and social determinism. Obstacles can be overcome. The case of Malcolm X is a prime example.

2.4 Aboriginals

In his "Political Fragments," authored between October and November of 1885, Louis Riel spoke "as [an] aboriginal, as an American, as anyone would, but principally as prophet of the New World," a term he would repeat again in the same segment. In short, although his prophethood superseded his ethnicity and nationality, he recognized that levels and layers of identity existed. He was not merely a Métis. He was an Aboriginal. He was an American. And, yes, he was also a Canadian. One thing did not exclude the other. He represented a spectrum.

2.5 Original Half-Breeds / Aboriginal Half-Breeds

While it may be pejorative in particular times and places, John C. Jackson notes that "the fur traders used the term *half-breed* without negative implications." The same can be said of Louis Riel. In his "Letter 'To the English Half-Breeds of Red Deer Hill, St. Catharine & St. Paul," written in St. Anthony, Saskatchewan, on March 21, 1886, Louis Riel described his people as the "Original Half-Breeds." He asserted that "the Aboriginal Half-Breeds are determined to save their rights or to perish at once." Although he was always a Métis, at times, Louis Riel emphasizes his Aboriginal side while, at others, he emphasized his French-Canadian one. As bridges between two races and cultures, Métis people can stand in the middle, walk to one side, or walk to the other. They can be Indians among Indians and French-Canadians among French-Canadians. It is not hypocrisy. It is cultural dexterity. It was one of the benefits of being bilingual and bicultural, if not multilingual and multicultural. It was an asset and not a liability. They had various points of reference. It made them culturally competent.

2.6 Whites

Although he was phenotypically white or European, according to stereotypical standards, as are many Métis and Indians, Louis Riel never identified as such while in Canada. In *A Language of Our Own: The Genesis of Michif, the Mixed Cree-French Language of the Canadian Métis*, Peter Bakker describes the use of the term "white" by the Métis:

> White people in general, except French-Canadians, are called *les blancs*... or, more commonly, *les Anglais*... Some people also know the Cree word *mu:njas:s* "white person"... French-Canadians are called *les Canadiens*. This word never refers to English Canadians... This... shows once more that the Métis consider themselves to be a group distinct from Europeans and Indians.

In his "Letter to the Editor of the Helena *Herald*," written in Carroll, Montana, between September 1882 and November 7, 1882, Riel noted that "the white men married to Indian women in Montana are counted by hundreds, their Half-Breed sons entitled to vote are themselves twice as numerous as the heads of families." In his "Letter to James Isbister, Gabriel Dumont, Moïse Ouellette, and Michel Dumas," written in St. Peter's Mission on June 5, 1884, he made the following remark:

> Montana has a pretty numerous native Half-Breed element. If we count with them, the white men interested in the Half-Breed welfare by being themselves heads of Half-Breed families, or related to them in any other way, I believe it safe to assert that the Half-Breed element of Montana is a pretty strong one.

Although they were of European ancestry, primarily French, so long as they were concerned with the cause of the Half-Breed community, the white husbands of Indigenous women could be considered part of the Métis community. Their tie was by blood and by bond. They shared a common way of life. In North America, the Métis identified as Indigenous. In Mexico, and other parts of Spanish America, the Mestizos identified as Spanish, Hispanic, or Latino. They integrated socially, religiously, and linguistically into the culture of power. They were Half-Breeds genetically; not culturally. They did not identify as Indigenous people. In fact, they generally held them in contempt, persecuted them, and massacred them. However proud many of the Métis were of their French ancestry and language, as well as their Catholic faith, they were equally proud of their Indigenous ancestry, however humble, asserted their Aboriginal rights, and defended their Indian relatives. "While it can be said that Métis culture was syncretic in essence," writes Michael Barnholden, "there is no question that its predominant elements were native."

Being part Spanish, the Mestizos identified with Spain, the Spanish language, the Spanish culture, and the Spanish Catholic religion. However proud they were of their French language, culture, and heritage, the Métis identified as Aboriginal People and sided with the First Nations when faced with the Anglo-European onslaught. The Mestizos were imperialists. The Métis were anti-imperialists. It would take centuries before the Mestizos of Spanish America decided to oust the Spanish, break away from Imperial Spain, and assert their independence. For some Mestizos, this included a new-found pride in their Indigenous ancestry.

Had France continued to rule over much of North America, it is possible that the Métis would have integrated or assimilated into French North American culture. As a result of British and Anglo racism, which refused to recognize the French and Irish as being white or equals, as chronicled by Noel Ignatiev in *How the Irish Became White*, and by David Vermette in *A Distinct Alien Race: The Untold Story of Franco-Americans*, the Métis and the French-Canadians had no other option but to remain in the racial and racist categories that were imposed upon them. Although the Métis in Quebec and Acadia were part and parcel of the French-Canadian community, the Métis in English Canada were prevented from fully integrating into English Canadian culture, even when they appeared to be assimilated. Like oil and water, the English would not allow the Métis to merge with them. They viewed them as an inferior race that followed a false faith. They believed that all Catholics were part of some grand Papist plot. The history of anti-Irish, anti-Catholic, anti-French-Canadian, anti-Métis, and anti-First Nations bigotry runs long and deep. The racism of the British and the Americans was unequalled.

For most of his life, Louis Riel was committed to the cause of the Indians and the Half-Breeds, particularly the French-speaking ones. As a result of his contact with European settlers in the United States, Louis Riel grew to admire their drive, determination, industriousness, and resilience. He felt that the Métis and Indians had much to learn from the positive qualities of white settlers. As he expressed in his "Address to the Jury," delivered in Regina on July 31, 1885, "I remembered that Half-Breed meant white and Indian, and while I paid attention to the suffering Indians and the Half-Breeds, I remembered that the greatest part of my heart and blood was white, and I have directed my attention to the whites to the best of my ability." Louis Riel was not anti-white. He was anti-occupation and oppression. As whites were human beings, he cared about them as well. He never dwelled so low as to dehumanize and demonize them.

While in the United States, however, Louis Riel identified as a white man. Although some would condemn him for doing so, his options were limited to those available. In 1860, 1870, and 1880, the racial categories used by the American government included Indian, Chinese, Black, Mulatto or White. Identifying as Indian would have made citizenship impossible. He would have had no right to vote. He could have been forcibly placed in an Indian reserve.

Refusing to tie his noose, and cast himself into destruction, Riel noted that he was White, which, as a Métis, he most certainly was, at least, in part. Even in the twenty-first century, Métis people in the United States face a predicament as racial categories include Native and White, but not Métis. Some select Native. Some choose White. While others check both boxes. Whichever ones they select, they are not lying. They are indeed part Native, and they are indeed part White. They are not "race-shifting." They are biracial. When racial constructs are imposed by governments, people are compelled to adopt them despite their aversion.

In contrast to the situation in the United States, had Louis Riel been required to identify his origins on the 1871 Canadian census, which covered Ontario, Quebec, New Brunswick, and Nova Scotia, the options, while broader, were still limited to European, with choices of English, Scottish, and other; French, Dutch, German, Italian, Russian, Scandinavian, and other; Hebrew, Native Indian and Inuit, Black, various, and unspecified. Riel could only have picked between French, Irish, and Native Indian as there was no Métis category.

Historically, the Canadian census has treated "Indian and white as mutually exclusive and diametrically opposed." "Prior to 1981," notes Matt Hiltermann, "Métis were only enumerated as Métis in the 1870 Manitoba census, the 1901 census of Canada, and the 1941 census of Canada." The fact that the number of people self-identifying as Métis has increased since 1981 should not come as a surprise and should not cause alarm as it was neither possible nor socially acceptable to identify as such for much of Canadian history.

When presented with a choice of identifying as Indian or French, many Métis who could, identified as French. Selecting Indian could come with severe consequences. Can one blame a Jewish person for claiming to be Spanish, French, Belgian, or German while under fascist occupation? Millions of blacks, Hispanics, and other ethnicities have passed for whites to secure employment, avoid segregation, discrimination, violence, and murder, and provide greater opportunities for their children. Rather than blaming them for the sin of self-preservation, and engaging in victim-blaming, critics should condemn the racist societies and systems that compelled them to act as such.

As Matt Hiltermann has shown from his study of census records, cross-checking them with Métis script archives, Hudson's Bay Company Archives, Indian band records, and local/community histories, many Métis treated themselves as default Métis. In the 1882 census of Alberta, for example, 95 percent of those who checked the "French" category were Métis. One-third of the "English" and approximately 40 percent of those who checked "Scottish" and "Irish" were Métis. They were not just Métis by race but members of Métis communities. When they marked "French," "Irish," or "Scottish," they were answering the question: what kind of Métis are you? The same process that occurred in Western Canada also took place in Eastern Canada. So, when Riel describes himself as French, it should be understood as a Métis of French ancestry.

2.7 French

In his "Public Notice to the Inhabitants of Rupert's Land," issued in Fort Garry on November 6, 1869, Louis Riel stated that he represented the interests of "the French-speaking population of Rupert's Land" and described the English-speaking population as "invaders." In fact, the "Incomplete Report on the Convention of November-December of 1869," which dates from between November 11, 1869, and December 1, 1869, describes the Red River Rebellion as a conflict between the French and the English. It was a revolt that pitted French-Canadians and English Canadians. In fact, in "The French-Canadian Métis People," written in St. Peter's Mission, Montana, in August of 1883, Riel described French as "the language of our dear ancestors." In fact, in one poem, he boasts that "My mother belongs to a warrior race / She is pure French of blood / Her name is Lagimodière," and claims that she descends from Louis XI.

Although Louis Riel spoke Cree, there is no record of him describing it as the language of his ancestors. French was the language of his family home. His parents were French speakers, and his grandparents were French speakers. It was only his paternal grandmother, Marguerite Boucher (c. 1792-1890), a Franco-Métis, whose mother was Chipewyan, who potentially spoke Denesuline. Due to the diverse origins of the Indigenous women who were married to French-Canadian men, French became the *lingua franca* among the Métis. As far as Louis Riel was concerned, his mother tongue and the tongue of the French Métis was and would always be French. This loyalty of the Métis towards all things French was the natural product of the French policy to rely "on the respect and cooperation of the Indians." The Métis were that policy personified.

2.8 French-Canadians

While Louis Riel commonly described himself as a French-Canadian Métis, he was not in the habit of identifying exclusively as French-Canadian. In his "National Program of the French-Canadian Métis," produced in 1873, Louis Riel spoke of

> [T]hose generous French-Canadians, our fathers, and our brothers, who are the friends and the force of the Métis nation and who, when they are among the Métis, seem more Métis than the Métis themselves, we support with all our united strength the noble efforts that our representatives made in the winter of 71, demanding that each of them, along with the early settlers of non-Métis blood, receive a grant of 160 acres of land.

For Riel, French-Canadians were the fathers and brothers of the Métis people and the friends and force behind the Métis Nation. He even asserted that French-Canadians were more Métis than the Western Métis themselves, perhaps alluding to the fact that some of them were being assimilated linguistically and culturally into Anglo-European culture, a phenomenon that would eventually encompass many of the Métis of the Prairies, the US Midwest, and the West who became diluted into the dominant society. In fact, many of those who maintained a Métis identity were Métis by ancestry or heritage, having lost their French language, an essential source of culture, along with many, and in some cases, most of the tangible aspects of their ancestral culture and worldview.

Consequently, having maintained their language, music, songs, literature, and cuisine, along with their customs, fishing, and outdoor survival skills, some French-Canadians are currently more Métis than many of the assimilated English Métis from Western Canada. Grey Owl (1888-1938) and Honoré Jaxon (1861-1952) may not have had a drop of Indigenous DNA; however, they were more immersed in Indigenous and Métis culture than many of their contemporaries from such communities. Many of the French-speaking Eastern Métis, who have ancestral connections to traditional Métis families and communities as demonstrated by *bona fide*, certified, and verifiable genealogical records, are more deeply connected to their culture than some of the English-speaking Métis with roots in Western Canada, namely, those who have become assimilated. Obviously, there are scores of monolingual English-speaking Métis who are profoundly immersed in their culture. It should also be recalled that the loss of the French language, like the loss of First Nations languages, was the product of the same process of cultural genocide. As central as language may be to culture, there is more to culture than just language.

In his "Speech on the Occasion of the Festival of St. John the Baptist," delivered in St. Boniface, Manitoba, on June 29, 1873, Riel recognized the existence of both a French-Canadian community and a Métis community that were interconnected. He spoke of,

> Your children, meeting under the flag of St. John the Baptist, which we adopt as our national holiday, come to greet you. It must be a great pleasure ... to see the founding of a new people celebrating their nationality here ... The French-Canadian Métis extending their hand to their brothers the French-Canadians, want to continue here the beautiful work which has long been pursued by the generous and noble province of Quebec.

Although the French-Canadian Métis were distinct in some ways from the French-Canadians who were devoid of Indigenous ancestry, they both belonged to the same overarching and overlapping culture. In other words, they were branches from the same tree. They were cousins, and cousins belong to the same family and share common ancestors and family customs. If some Western Anglo-Métis view French-Canadian Métis with suspicion, not to mention contempt, ridicule, and scorn, that was not the case with Louis Riel and his people. They viewed them as family. If they identified as Métis, and were connected genetically, culturally, and linguistically, then they were considered as kith and kin.

In his "Letter to C.-J. Coursel," penned on June 24, 1874, Louis Riel made a distinction between the Métis and the French-Canadians:

> I congratulate the French-Canadians for celebrating, as a people, our national holiday in such a dignified and grandiose way... I know that the noble heart of the French-Canadians loves the Métis Canadians of Manitoba and the Northwest. As one who works on behalf of the Métis, my dear compatriots, I am one of those who have the most reasons to congratulate the sympathies of the French-Canadians, and in the name of the Métis, I wish to assure you that I am united with you in both heart and spirit to celebrate this beautiful day...

In "The French-Canadian Métis People," a poem he wrote at St. Peter's Mission, Montana, in August of 1883, Riel spoke of French-Canadians, on the one hand, and the Métis, on the other, and asserted that the fusion of both would produce a single people. He praised the qualities of French-Canadians, their knowledge of power, politics, administration, and diplomacy. He expressed his love for the French language and his devotion to the Roman Catholic Church. Rather than reject French-Canadians, and the French-Canadian Métis, viewing them as an existential threat to a Métis Nation reduced to the Red River, Louis Riel called for the amalgamation of both communities for their collective benefit. It was not a matter of Métis people becoming French-Canadians but of French-Canadians becoming French-Canadian Métis. "While bringing [French] Canadian 'civilization' to the Métis," notes M. Max Hamon, Riel "also sought to bring Métis 'civilization' to the Canadians."

2.9 *Bois-Brûlés* / Burnt Wood

In *We are Métis: A Métis View of the Development of Native Canadian People*, Duke Redbird (b. 1939), the Indigenous poet, journalist, and activist, explains that "the Algonquin tribes, especially the Ojibway," referred to the Métis as "*wissakodewinmi*, meaning burnt-sticks and later Frenchified into *Bois-Brulés* by French colonists." The term *Bois-Brulé*s, appears in Johann Georg Kohl's (1808-1878) *Kitchi-Gami: Wanderings Round Lake Superior*, in the reports of George Bryce (1844–1931), Richard Henry Bonnycastle's (1791-1847) *Canada and the Canadians*, Joseph-Charles Taché's (1820-1894) *Forestiers et voyageurs*, as well as the works of Andrew (1785-1840) and David Stuart (1765-1853), and Alexis de Tocqueville (1805-1859). The term was also used in 1899 to describe the Métis people of Acadian and Mi'kmaq ancestry.

In his poem, "The Early Days," written in 1870 while he was in the Red River in Manitoba, Louis Riel invoked the "Métis Nation" and the "Burnt Wood of the North." In another poem, "While the Métis Planted," composed in Beauport, Quebec, on May 13, 1877, Louis Riel invoked "the zealous chiefs / of all the Burnt Wood." Riel appears to echo the famous "Chanson de la Grenouillère," composed by Pierre Falcon (1793-1876), the Métis composer and singer famous for his violent lyrics regarding the Battle of Seven Oaks which took place in 1816. Part of the Pemmican War, that war pitted the Hudson's Bay Company and the Northwest Company in a violent confrontation for control of the fur trade. In this Métis national anthem, the bard of the Prairies sings:

> Would you like to hear sung
> A song of truth?
> Would you like to hear sung
> A song of truth?
> On the nineteenth of June, the band of *Bois-Brûlés*
> Arrived as brave warriors
> Arriving at the frog pond [*grenouillère*]
> We took three prisoners:
> Three prisoners from the Orkneys
> Who are here to pillage our country.
> Getting ready to dismount,

> Two of our people cried out,
> Two of our people cried out:
> Here is the Englishman who comes to attack us.

As Michel Bouchard, Sébastien Malette, and Guillaume Marcotte note in *Bois-Brûlés: The Untold Story of the Métis of Western Quebec*, "the term *Bois-Brûlés* seems to have been adopted by French-speaking Métis to designate themselves... during the conflict." As they further explain,

> Evidence... suggests that *Bois-Brûlés* formed a distinct group. For instance, in an 1818 statement... William McGillivray wrote, "the half-breeds under the denomination of *Bois-Brûlés* and *Métifs* have formed a separate and distinct tribe of Indians for a considerable time back" ... It seems clear that this "tribe" was diasporic, their presence being noted in different areas of North America along the fur trade routes...
>
> The *Bois-Brûlés* were distinguished from English and Scottish half-breeds as Canadian Métis, which reveals the importance of the French language, Catholicism, and other cultural markers shared with French-Canadian culture. The equivalence of *Métis Canadiens*, or (French) Canadian Métis, and *Bois-Brûlés* is evident... Likewise, the term *Bois-Brûlés* was used in both Upper and Lower Canada...

The term *Bois-Brûlés* or simply *Brûlés*, was frequently used to refer to the French Métis from the Red River and was used by Cuthbert Grant (1793-1854) and Pierre Falcon (1793-1876). The term eventually waned in popularity after the merger of the Hudson's Bay Company and the North-West Company in 1821. That being said, it is clear that the term, which was used by Métis throughout North America, refers to one and the same people.

2.10 *Métis Canadien* / Canadian Métis

In "Letter to the Editor," co-authored in St. Vital, Manitoba, on October 6, 1869, Louis Riel and company spoke on behalf of the "the Métis Canadian population of the Red River." And they signed the letter to the editor as "two Métis Canadian residents of the Red River." By Canadian, they meant French-Canadian.

2.11 Half-Breeds

In his "Open Letter to Martin Maginnis [1841-1919]," written in Fort Benton, Montana, on October 16, 1882, and addressed to the politician and soldier, Louis Riel spoke of the "American Half-Breed citizens." He referred explicitly to the "Half-Breed American citizens of Meagher, Dawson and Choteau counties." In his "Letter to Thomas O'Hanlon," written in St. Peter's Mission, Montana, on September 4, 1883, Riel described himself as an "Assiniboine Half-Breed." And in his "Note about the Half-Breed Vote," written in Montana in 1883, he described his people as "Half-Breeds." In "I Can Sing in My Poetry," written in Helena, Montana, between June and September of 1883, Riel remarked that:

> [N]umerous Half-Breed families
> Born, rais'd and known as Montanians
> Have given me their sympathies
> As one amongst politicians
> They are satisfied that I like them
> While married to Indian women
> Understand that it's my system
> To do something for their children.

In his "Speech at Prince Albert," delivered on July 19, 1884, Louis Riel spoke of his people as "Half-Breeds." In his "Petition 'To His Excellency the Governor-General-in-Council, etc.,'" written at St. Louis de Langevin on October 1, 1884, he also described them as "Half-Breeds." In his "Statement to G.H. Young's Diary," produced in Batoche, Saskatchewan, between May 15 and 16 of 1885, Louis Riel described the population to which he pertained as "1/2 Breeds." He equally spoke of them as "Half-Breeds" in his "Interview with C.B. Pitblado," granted near Saskatoon, Saskatchewan, on May 19 and 20 of 1885. He repeatedly referred to his people as "Half-Breeds" in his July 31, 1885, "Address to the Jury." When he wrote to J.W. Taylor, the US Consul in Winnipeg, on October 15, 1884, Riel described his people as "Half-Breeds." He did the same in his "Interview with a Correspondent of the *Toronto Globe*," which dates from November 15, 1885.

2.12 English Half-Breeds

In his "Agreement of Surrender," written in Fort Garry, Manitoba, on December 7, 1869, Louis Riel spoke of the "English Half-Breeds." He wrote letters "To the English Half-Breeds of Red Deer Hill, St. Catharine & St. Paul," on March 21, 1886. He also wrote "To the English Half Breeds of St. Andrew's and St. Catharine" on March 23, 1885."

2.13 *Métis Anglais* / English Métis

Louis Riel wrote a letter, "To our Brothers, the English and French Métis from Lac Qu'Apelle and Surrounding Areas," around March 23 of 1885, addressing them as "dear relatives and friends." Between March 23 and 24 of 1885, he wrote another "Letter to 'Our Relatives'" to the English Métis of St. Anthony, Manitoba. Another "Letter to 'Dear Relatives'" was issued at the same time in English, imploring "our Father in heaven, to protect, to defend, to sustain, to save us all, with all our families, with all our tribes, with all our nation, with all our clergymen."

On roughly March 25, 1885, Riel wrote another "Letter to the English and French Métis of Rivière Bataille of Fort Pitt and Surrounding Areas" addressed to "dear relatives and friends." As Thomas Flanagan (b. 1944) notes, "the Métis whom Louis Riel championed were... the English-speaking, Protestant Half-Breeds and the French-speaking, Catholic Métis." For the Métis people, the English Métis and French Métis were siblings or cousins. Whether they were settled Métis, the free Métis of the Plains, or semi-nomadic hunters, traders, and *voyageurs*, they belonged to the same people.

2.14 *Métis Français* / French Métis

In his "Essay Dealing with the Problems of the Red River," from 1872, Louis Riel described his immediate people as "the French Métis." In his "National Program of the French-Canadian Métis," produced in 1873, Louis Riel spoke of "we French Métis" and "our

Indian right to the lands of the country." In "Letter to our Relatives," written in St. Anthony, Manitoba, between March 23 and 24, 1885, Riel wrote: "The Métis have taken up arms in mass. None of our people are against it. Tell our relatives, the Indians, to be ready to come and help us if need be."

2.15 *Métis-Celte* / Celtic Métis

Speaking of his blood, Louis Riel claimed that "I have some from Ireland" in his "Revelations against Beauport," written on May 22, 1876. In his "Ode to My Sister," written in August of 1879, he wrote: "I love that Métis-Celtic spirit." However, as John P. DuLong has shown, Riel's Irish lineage poses some problems.

The ancestor of Louis, Jean-Baptiste Riel dit L'Irlande, was reportedly born in Limerick, Ireland, and his parents are said to have been Jean-Baptiste Riel and Louise Lafontaine. He claimed this on his marriage certificate to Louise Cottu, which was issued on January 21, 1704, at Sorel, in Quebec. He was also listed as Irish when he was naturalized in May 1710. Neither his name nor the names of his parents were Irish or English. They were French. In fact, the earliest document that mentions him simply lists him as Jean. Did he adopt a French name and retroactively apply it to his father? Or was his original name Gallicized by French-Canadian clerks? While he might have been Irish, DeLong could have been born in Ireland to parents who came from the region of Bretagne in France. Either way, Louis Riel never described himself as Irish in his extant writings. He did, however, praise his sister's Métis-Celtic spirit. So, there was some pride in his Irish heritage. The same goes for many other Métis who included the shamrock on one of their flags to honour their ancestry and to extend a hand of solidarity to Irish Catholic anti-imperialists.

2.16 Métis

The term *Métis,* which means mixed, and its variant *Métif,* appear in French colonial records to describe people of mixed French and

First Nations origins. It should be noted that the old French script made the "s" look like an "f." In any event, *Métis* was one of many ethnonyms that these people used to describe themselves, and it appears in the literary record well into modern times. It is not a term that suddenly sprung into use in the twenty-first century after the Powley Ruling in 2003. It was used by Métis people in both Canada and the United States.

Although Louis Riel tended to qualify the term *Métis*, distinguishing between the French Métis and the English Métis, he was also in the habit of using the term Métis without qualifiers. In his "Letter to William Dease," written in Fort Garry, Manitoba, on February 15, 1870, Riel asserted: "I ask nothing in reward; nothing but the support of all the Métis." He insisted that "the Métis are but one." In his "Letter to 'Dear Friends'" from July 1870, he spoke simply of "the Métis." In an undated "Letter to A.-A. Taché" (1823-1894), the first Archbishop of Saint Boniface in Manitoba, Riel spoke of "the weak Métis people." In another, dated from September 30, 1870, he referred to his people as the "Métis." In his "Petition on Behalf of the Métis and other Residents of Manitoba to Lieutenant Governor A.G. Archibald [1814-1892]," written in St. Vital, Manitoba, in September of 1871, and directed to the Lieutenant Governor, Riel spoke about the "Métis."

In his "Address to the Residents of St. Vital to Robert Cunningham," written in St. Vital on July 24, 1873, Riel described his people as the "Métis" and stated that "We are the foundators [sic] of Manitoba." The man addressed, Robert Cunningham (1836-1874), was a Canadian journalist and member of Parliament who was a strong supporter of the Métis community. He called for land reform on behalf of the Métis and supported a general amnesty for those involved in the Red River Rebellion.

Finally, when writing to John McDougall in 1873, Riel spoke of the "Métis." Likewise, in his "Letter to 'My Dear Friends'" from 1873, he also addressed his friends as "Métis." There is no evidence, however, of Louis Riel employing the terms *Métif, Mitif*, or *Michif*, which are dialectical variations of the French word, Métis. These terms were not exclusive to the Métis of the Plains. They were used throughout North America and have survived in parts of Quebec into contemporary times.

2.17 *Métis Canadiens Français* / French-Canadian Métis

Louis Riel overwhelmingly referred to himself as a "French-Canadian Métis." He developed a "National Program of the French-Canadian Métis" in 1873. In his "Letter to C.-J. Coursel," penned on June 24, 1874, Louis Riel insisted that the Métis were French-Canadians. In his words, "The French-Canadian Métis of the North are a branch of the French-Canadian tree. They want to grow like that tree and with that tree. They do not want to detach themselves from it. They want to suffer and rejoice with it."

In "Revelations that Jesus Christ made to His Poor and Useless Servant, Louis 'David' Riel," written in Beauport, Quebec, between May 20, 1876, and January 23, 1878, Riel spoke of the "French-Canadian Métis" over a dozen times. Riel's most detailed exposition of French-Canadian Métis identity is found in his "Letter to Paul Proulx," written in Beauport, Quebec, on May 10, 1877. In this magisterial piece of central importance, Riel expressed the following:

> I would like, with the help of God, to work to make the French-Canadian Métis people great enough to be the heirs of Lower Canada [i.e. Quebec], in the same way that a good son receives and benefits from the goods that are bequeathed to him by his parents...
>
> And if you ask me why I do not want our people to be called French-Canadian, quite simply, I will answer you that this name being already his family name, it is advisable to give him another one which designates him particularly and which is in a way his baptismal name as a people. And I want that distinctive name to be the Métis name that we have always carried.
>
> I believe that the name Métis is likely to favour the founding of a powerful nationality in Manitoba and the Northwest. It's a name that means mixture. Until now it has been used to designate the race produced by the mixture of European and Indian blood. However, it is also suitable to name a race of human beings, created by the mixture between all

> bloods but which, while passing through the French-Canadian mold, would retain the memory of its origin, by calling itself Métis.
>
> The name Métis would be agreeable to everyone because it is not exclusive and has the advantage of properly referring to the contingent from which each nation would help found the new people. And from that point of view, I think it would be difficult to base our nationality in Manitoba and the Northwest as a broader and stronger idea than the Métis idea.
>
> To better complete the exposition of my thought, I will compare the founding of the French-Canadian Métis people to a piece of material that we would have to make ... And when the material is finished, it will be French material, because the workers of the beautiful profession of France will have worked there. It will be a truly [French] Canadian fabric because our weavers were true [French] Canadians at heart. It will be a French-Canadian Métis fabric...
>
> So let's have no worries. French, Canadians, and Métis, let us work together not only without suspicion but also with a lot of friendship, as God wants to use us all to found the Métis-French-Canadian people.

While he was in Montana, Riel wrote a letter to his mother in August or September 1882, informing her that "I have been married for more than one year [1881]. I took a girl from Prairie-du-Cheval-Blanc, a French-Canadian Métis, [as a wife]. Her name is Marguerite."

In his "Notes on the Intermarriage of People," written in Montana between 1881 and 1884, Louis Riel predicted that "All the Indian race of North America will give way to a new race, the Métis race, which will vary by country [of origin]; in Manitoba, it will be French-Canadian Métis." Riel, like many Métis, was concerned that the First Nations would be wiped off the face of the earth. At the time, such fears were well founded. While there had been a balance between First Nations, Métis, and French Canadians in the past, a time came when the influx of French Canadians, some with beliefs in racial hierarchies, consisting of superior and inferior races, made some Métis concerned that they would be diluted in a flood of French Canadians. However, when waves of Anglo-Protestant colonizers came crashing down upon the First Nations, Métis, and French Canadians, Riel concluded that they had to fuse as one for the sake of their own survival.

The most extraordinary poetic exposition of Métis identity composed by Riel consists of "The French-Canadian Métis," written at St. Peter's Mission, Montana, in August 1883. It reads, in part:

> I love beyond measure, and I admire
> The French-Canadian Métis
> This new people
> that has already made great accomplishments.
> It makes its glory known
> To the Indians of Minnesota.
> It was always victorious
> Over the tribes of Dakota...
>
> Although it is young
> Manitoba is great because it was founded
> Under the beautiful guidance of the Priesthood
> Which has always guided it so well.

The mixed origins of the Métis, and the hyphenation of Métis and French-Canadian, are not negatives in the eyes of Riel: they are a positive:

> If a hyphen is placed
> Between Métis and [French] Canadian.
> Both races assure
> that it will be all for the better.
> Métis, our varying
> Degree of Indian blood
> Which can reach extremes
> Is [French] Canadian all the same...
>
> Let us endow our French language
> With beautiful foreign words
> So that it may be even richer
> In these new parts.
>
> Let us borrow choice expression
> From the Indian languages

Some of their images
Some of their beautiful phrases.

These novelties will strengthen
The language of our dear ancestors.
Let's embellish it that way
According to our best taste.

Métis, Canadians, and French
Together, if our three elements
Fuse together well, it seems to me
That we will be greater one day.

The three leaves of the clover can
Exist on the same footing.
All three, pretty, move

In unison, as they see fit.
The clergy who build us up
Will unite us, of course,
As the clover showcases

Its three flowers admirably.
Its big heart endures a lot of pain
To consolidate, I know,
The Nation of Manitoba
of the French-Canadian Métis.

In his "Letter to J.-V. Grandin," written in St. Laurent, Manitoba, on September 5, 1884, Louis Riel asked the Monseigneur to bless his people: "Bless us, especially the French-Canadian Métis. Bless us along with the Métis of all other origins." On February 17, 1885, while in St. Laurent, Louis Riel consecrated the Métis to the Sacred-Heart of Jesus, praying: "Choose us, all the French-Canadian Métis, in a special way, and make us your Chosen People."

As Louis Riel expressed in his "Letter to Valentin Vegreville," written in Batoche, Saskatchewan, on April 10, 1885, he was committed to defending "the interests of the French-Canadian Métis." In fact, the "Version No. 1. Oath for the Guards," produced in Batoche between March and April of 1885, proclaims: "Swear before God that you will be faithful to the French-Canadian Métis movement and their Provisional Government." This is a veritable pledge of allegiance to the French-Canadian Métis Nation.

In his "Journal," written in Batoche between September and May of 1885, Louis Riel spoke of "our French-Canadian Métis hearts." And when signing political statements, declarations of war and independence, Louis Riel did so on behalf of "The Members of the French-Canadian Métis Exovidat of Saskatchewan." In his "Letter to A.-A. Taché," from July 24, 1885, Riel wrote of "You the Métis, especially all the French-Canadian Métis." In fact, he repeatedly wrote about the French-Canadian Métis.

In his "Address to the Jury," delivered in Regina, Saskatchewan, on July 31, 1885, Riel stated that he wanted "French-Canadians to come and help us there today, tomorrow." He recognized that they were a distinct people. As much as he was French-Canadian, Riel's identity was incomplete unless he acknowledged his indigeneity: hence, his insistence on being triple hyphenated as Métis-French-Canadian. In fact, Riel predicted that "Manitoba will become entirely French-Canadian Métis. Within five hundred years from now, the French-Canadian Métis population will consist of forty million souls." As Sébastien Malette and Guillaume Marcotte note in *Eastern Métis: Chronicling and Reclaiming a Denied Past*,

> The idea of a French-Canadian Métis Nation will nevertheless persist in different Métis organizations in Western Canada, most noticeably in the oldest French Métis organization created in 1887 by Riel's relatives and followers, *l'Union nationale métisse Saint-Joseph du Manitoba*.

Although some French-speaking Métis survive outside of Quebec and Acadia, a large part of them became assimilated due to "a series of legislative acts that limited the use of French in public institutions in Manitoba, the Northwest Territories, Alberta, Saskatchewan, and Ontario."

2.18 Conclusions

Although Louis Riel described Indigenous people as *sauvages* or Indians, and was proud of having some *sang sauvage*, or Indian blood, he never described himself or his people, the Métis, as *sauvages* or First Nations. What is more, Louis Riel never described himself as an Indian or an Indigenous Person. The closest he came to assert such a thing was affirming that he was a native of the Northwest who had Indian ancestry. Louis Riel only described himself as an Aboriginal on one occasion. Likewise, he only once referred to his people as Original Half-Breeds or Aboriginal Half-Breeds in his writings.

Although others perceived him as a savage Half-Breed, a French-Canadian or a white man, Louis Riel never identified as white while in Canada. He did, however, do so while seeking citizenship in the United States, as was the case with the other Métis of Montana and many other states. "When the Métis settled as homesteaders," notes Flanagan, "as around Lewiston, they were treated the same as white settlers." "When they were accepted onto Indian reservations," however, "it was under the legal fiction of being Indians." While Indigenous by identity, Riel recognized that most of his blood was white and that he was concerned about helping whites as well as Indians and Half-Breeds. Consequently, one cannot condemn Métis people for identifying as white, French, or Indian without condemning Louis Riel himself. This is part and parcel of the complexity of the Métis condition.

Of all the ethnonyms he employed Riel overwhelmingly preferred to identify as a French-Canadian Métis. While he described his people as "Half-Breeds," he did not use the term to describe himself. He also distinguished between the French-speaking Catholic Métis and the English-speaking Protestant Métis, although both of these communities would eventually merge together, with most of the former becoming assimilated into the latter, thereby losing an essential conductor of culture: language.

While he used numerous ethnonyms to describe himself and his people, including the terms French, Métis Canadian, Celtic Métis,

Bois-Brûlés, and Half-Breed, there is no evidence that he used terms such as *Métif*, *Michif*, *Chicot*, *Créoles*, *Gens Libres*, *Hommes Libres*, Freemen, Country-Born, Mixed-Blood or *Otipemisiwak*. Louis Riel recognized that there were Métis of many other origins and that they were found throughout the continent. Riel viewed the Métis as a multiracial race, a people, a flock, a tribe, a country, and a nation. He recognized that the Métis of the Red River and the Northwest had a particular history; however, this history did not deny other Métis histories. When it came to the Métis, Louis Riel was a proponent of diversity, plurality, tolerance, inclusivity, fraternity, and sorority. He opposed imperial efforts to divide his people and nation in the same way he was against internal division.

Chapter 3

LOUIS RIEL AND THE MÉTIS NATION

3.1 Introduction

When it came to identifying himself and his people, Louis Riel used the terms Aboriginal, Original Half-Breed, Aboriginal Half-Breed, French, French-Canadian, *Bois-Brulé*, Métis Canadian, French Métis, Celtic Métis, Métis, and French-Canadian Métis. None of these ethnonyms were mutually exclusive. There is no evidence, however, of Louis Riel using the French terms *Métif, Michif, Chicot, Bois-Grillés, Créoles, Gens Libres* or *Hommes Libres* to refer to his people The same applies to English terms such as Freemen, Country-Born or Mixed-Blood and the Cree term *Otipemisiwak*. However, this does not mean that these terms did not refer to the same ethnic group. When it came to his people, the Métis, Riel described them as a race, a people, a flock, a tribe, and a nation. Once again, these terms were not mutually exclusive. They applied at different times and places.

3.2 Métis Diversity

Although he identified himself as a French-Canadian Métis, Riel asked for blessings for "the Métis of all other origins." He did not deny that the Métis who belonged to other communities and geographic locations were also Métis. They may not have been Red River Métis; however, they were Métis nonetheless; namely, the "Other Métis." Those who were not French Métis, and who refused to fight the English, were not denied their indigeneity. He accepted that there were Métis who were of First Nations and Scottish origin, among many other ethnic admixtures. Riel understood that the Red River Métis were neither the first Métis nor the only Métis. As Joseph Kinsey Howard recognizes,

> There were *Bois-Brulés* long before ... [the appearance of the Red River] ... they visited Sault Ste. Marie as early as 1654 and "made a *rendez-vous*" at Mackinac before 1670. These first "Half-Breeds" were literally that, probably the offspring of Frenchmen from Champlain's company, which established Quebec in 1608, and of Indian women among the Huron and Algonquin tribes.

As Devrim Karahasan has shown in his 2006 doctoral dissertation titled *Métissage in New France: Frenchification, Mixed Marriages, and Métis as Shaped by Social and Political Agents and Institutions, 1508-1886*, there was a Métis identity in the Great Lakes Region by 1757. In fact, "by the late 1820s," writes Jacqueline Peterson in "Prelude to Red River: A Social Portrait of the Great Lakes Métis," "a sizeable portion of Métis, inhabiting a growing network of towns and villages" were established in the region.

As Bouchard, Malette, and Pulla argue, the ethnogenesis of the Métis of Ontario and Quebec "is contemporaneous with that of the western Métis, as these identities emerged within the context of the same continental fur trade." The same applied to the Old Northwest of the United States, which consisted of the current states of Ohio, Indiana, Illinois, Michigan, Wisconsin, and Minnesota, where a network of Métis settlements and trading posts were established. "When the Old Northwest became Americanized," notes Flanagan, there was "a population of ten thousand to fifteen thousand residents of Métis communities south and west of Lakes Superior and Huron."

As Étienne Rivard explains, Quebec "is one of the regions of North America where the *métissage* of the French and Aboriginal populations goes back the furthest." In fact, "it is well established that the history of the Métis began in the seventeenth-century *Nouvelle-France*, after which the fur trade pushed into distant reaches of the continent." As Foxcurran, Bouchard, and Malette have established in *Songs Upon the Rivers*, "a shared ethnicity ... emerged from the St. Lawrence Valley through the Great Lakes region, the American Midwest, the Pacific Northwest, and even to the far north." In the words of Denis Gagnon,

> Historical evidence points toward the fact that the Métis lived all across North America, from Nova Scotia to Oregon, from the Mackenzie to the Mississippi Delta, where some of their descendants still consider themselves Métis.

The Métis of Nova Scotia survive, as do the Métis of the Pacific Northwest. In fact, "three Métis arrived in the Pacific Northwest with the Lewis and Clark Party in 1805." One of them was George Drouillard, who "descended from a significant Detroit *coureur-de-bois family* and a Delaware-Shawnee mother." Drouillard "symbolized the retreating mixed bloods of the Ohio Valley," while the two others, Pierre Crouzette and Francois La Biche, "represented the early Missouri River Indian trade" out of St. Charles or St. Louis.

The Pacific Fur Company had recruited many of the Métis who settled in the Pacific Northwest in Montreal, Michilimackinac, St. Louis, and along the Missouri. As John C. Jackson puts it, "the roll call of the Astorians was a sampling of Métis origins whose degree of Indianness is unclear." When they arrived at their destination, these Eastern Métis bachelors took Native American wives, thereby producing the first generation of Pacific Northwest Métis.

Many of the Métis who set off to settle the Columbia District in Oregon in 1841 were recruited by the HBC from the Red River community. In fact, "several of them were related to kinsmen who remained and were active in later disputes with the Company." These 115 trail-worn Red River Métis reached Fort Vancouver on 12 October 1841 after completing an overland trip of 1,700 miles in 130 days. In the Pacific Northwest, as they had done in the Prairies and their forefathers had done in Eastern Canada, they engaged in hunting and trade. As John C. Jackson explains in *Children of the Fur Trade*,

> The Pacific Northwest mixed bloods were the children of European or Canadian fathers and native American mothers. In almost half of the nineteenth century, the Métis enjoyed a unique subculture built around hunting and mobility... Some Métis congregated around the trading post, where they were employed as laborers, packers, or boatmen. Most traveled with the trapping brigades in a loose business environment that took authority lightly and fostered a sense of independence...
>
> When the mountain hunt declined, a few French-speaking Catholics settled in western Oregon or the lower Puget Sound area. The three main areas of Métis concentration were the French Prairie of the lower Willamette Valley, the north Tualatin plains, and the open prairies along the Cowlitz River. Lesser communities grew in the Walla Walla Valley, in the Flathead country of western Montana, and around the old fur trade depot of Fort Colville. By mid-century, many Métis were already in retreat to less developed places or to the recently established Indian reservations.

The Métis of the Pacific Northwest maintained a distinct culture that included "eastern Métis decorative arts." The patterns and symbols of their clothing were borrowed from coastal, plateau, and plains cultures. The Bannock biscuits they cooked came from an old Métis recipe. Historical sources describe these people as "French Half-Breed Oregonians." One of the earliest studies on the Métis, completed by Dr. M. V. Havard in 1878, estimated that there were roughly three hundred Métis in the French Prairie and the Willamette and Kaoulis Rivers along with another two-hundred and fifty in Washington Territory. For Havard, the Métis of the United States, including those from the Pacific Northwest, belonged to the same race as those from the Red River and the Winnipeg Basin.

As in the prairies, the Métis of the Pacific Northwest were overwhelmed by Anglo-Protestant settlers. In response to racism and discrimination, many Métis opted to identify publicly as French-Canadians, while others retreated to Indian reservations. As Jackson notes,

> The children of the trade gave up the struggle to adapt to new social, racial, or religious attitudes, and retreated to new homes on less critical frontiers. During the last quarter of the century, many refugees found

> niches in the marginal hill country of southern Oregon or on the sagebrush uplands of middle Oregon. Some went to the Grande Ronde Indian Reservation, others to the Umatilla or Nez Perce reserves. A little knot of Canadians retreated up the Walla Walla Valley, eventually ending up in Flathead country.

Consequently, Métis names are found on most tribal rolls. These choices were imposed upon them by social and political circumstances. As John C Jackson notes, "Assimilation is a hard nut of concession and surrender. Accepting the dominant culture, or running away from it, was a dilemma that split the Métis soul."

The loss of cultural and historical consciousness is so significant that certain Red River Métis claim that their origins are in the West and that their people do not tell stories about their emigration from Quebec and the Maritimes. Nobody familiar with French-language Métis songs can make such a claim. They convey nostalgia and longing for Acadia and Quebec. They relate the adventures of the voyageurs, runners of the woods, and fur traders, the wars against the English and their Indian allies, the lifestyle of loggers along the Gatineau River. They are simply steeped in Eastern Métis history and culture. To claim that the Western Métis never evoked their origins in the East is an admission of cultural and historical amnesia. This is what happens when people lose their language and become assimilated into another culture. They lose knowledge of self.

The early Red River Métis knew that the Métis originated in Eastern Canada. In fact, they shared "many tales dealing with the old fur trade, and some specifically derived from the voyageur tradition." J.M. Bumsted also attests to the presence of Métis throughout North America. As he explained in *Louis Riel v. Canada: The Making of a Rebel*:

> The Red River Métis were descendants of the relationships between aboriginal or mixed-blood women and francophone voyageurs employed by the Northwest Company. Such descendants were to be found everywhere in the western fur trade country, from Detroit through the Ohio Valley to the Mississippi south of the Great Lakes and from the Sault to the Athabasca. Red River was probably the largest single concentration of Métis in the West.

The Métis resistance of the Red River Valley was not the beginning of the Métis Nation, it was a crest, a wave, in the Métis Ocean of North America; it was one of the moments that the Métis movement rose to the surface. It was a political peak that culminated after centuries of Métis history. It did not, however, lead to the creation of an ethnostate as some Métis historians have claimed. As Robert DesJarlait explains,

> Although the acts are often cited as clear evidence of the establishment of a Métis "Nation," nowhere in the documents does the name Métis appear. If it had been the intention of Riel to establish a separate, sovereign Métis nation, as Métis historians contend, then why wasn't the *Bill of Rights* titled the *Métis Bill of Rights*? or why wasn't the *Declaration of People Act* titled the *Declaration of the Métis of Rupert's Land and the Northwest*?
>
> The answer is that Assiniboia was not exclusively populated by Métis people. Certainly, the provisional government council would be tabled by a strong representation of Métis people, and the president would be Métis. Yet, Riel knew that all privileges, customs, and usage within the territory had to be respected. This included not only the Métis but the other Euro-Canadians who represented just under half of the population of Assiniboia. To guarantee their support, the *Bill of Rights* provided for a free homestead pre-emption law...
>
> There are those advocates of a Métis nation who cite Riel's establishment of a provisional government as marking the point in time when the Métis nation was created. However, Riel's *Declaration of the People of Rupert's Land* and the *Bill of Rights* made no mention of a Métis nation. Indeed, the word Métis or Half-Breed did not appear in the documents. That Riel sought to establish a nation is clear; however, the nation that Riel sought to establish was composed of other Euro-Canadians in addition to the Métis.

3.3 The Métis Race

In his "Letter to Paul Proulx," written in Beauport, Quebec, on May 10, 1877, Louis Riel described the Métis as a race. Speaking of the term "Métis," he noted that "Until now, it served to designate the race derived from the mixed blood of Europeans and Indians." In

Riel's view, the term Métis, until the Red River Rebellion, had a biological and genetic sense. It signified a person of mixed European and First Nations in the Canadian context.

In his "Petition to Grover Cleveland," written in Regina between August 23 and September 10, 1885, Riel recognized that he belonged, in part, to "the Indian race." At the same time, however, Riel recognized in his "Address to the Jury," delivered in Regina on July 31, 1885, that "the greater part of my... blood was white." So, racially, biologically, and genetically, the Métis were a mixed race of European and Indigenous ancestry. However, they were neither white nor Indian. As he stressed in "Notes on the Intermarriage of People," "the Métis race" was a "new race."

As far as Louis Riel was concerned, the Métis were a "three-blooded race," as he explained in "Some good French People from Overseas are our Hosts," which he wrote at St. Peter's Mission, Montana, around 1883. He viewed the European French as a race, French-Canadians as a race, and the Indians as a race. The French Métis, in his mind, were a combination of all three. The Métis, of course, were not a race merely because they were mixed. As Richard Slobodin (1915-2005), the premier ethnologist of the Dene, has pointed out, "It is a truism that all human populations are 'mixed' in heredity—or, more properly, that they are genetically heterogeneous—and that all cultures have more or less diverse origins."

In using the term race, Riel was referring to a grouping of humans that shared a similar ancestry, language, and culture that was viewed as distinct. Rather than speak of race, it would have been better to speak of culture and ethnicity and the Métis as mixed-heritage individuals. However, it is important to note that "the Métis are distinctly not the hybrids of two or more homogeneous races each with a monolithic cultural tradition." The fact is that "the Métis of Canada are 'mixed' genotypically and in cultural traditions." The Métis are not all of French stock, nor do they all descend from the Indian tribes that historically inhabited the regions in and around the Red River.

"The risk of cultural essentialism, metaphysical substantivism, and historical reductionism is huge," warns Malette, "if we rationalize

Red River neo-nationalism in terms of a single Métis/Half-Breed ethnogenesis." As Elizabeth Sperry asserts,

> The genesis of the Plains Métis... cannot be bound to one geographical area based upon a timeline of residence delineated by the first and later settlements. Neither should the history of a multi-ethnic people be confined to a single historical event, such as the 1885 Métis Resistance in Canada.

"To move beyond the current understanding of Métis peoplehood reduced to a single Métis nationalistic narrative," writes Denis Gagnon, "we need to capture all the nuances of Métis ethnogenesis and its various components (microgenesis, macrogenesis, intra- and extra-Indigenous ethnogenesis, and natiogenesis)." As Joyce Green points out, "Not all of us fit a formula, and not many of us fit only one formula." "The very polyvalent nature of Métis-ness," she notes, "will impel more inclusive, less absolute frameworks for identity." "Choosing a sense of 'Metiness,'" writes Tara J. Turner, "is a deliberate and spirit-driven process and the rights and abilities of people to make that choice should not be discounted."

The claim that the only Métis people are those who descend from ancestors who resided in the so-called "Historic Métis Nation Homeland" in west central North America on or before December 8, 1869, has no basis in history. The Métis, as a people and a distinct ethnic group, did not originate in Western Canada in the nineteenth century. They originated in Eastern Canada in the seventeenth century. The works of Russel Bouchard, Etienne Rivard, Pascal Huot, Laura M. Schaefli, and Jacqueline Peterson provide ample evidence in this regard. As Slobodin establishes,

> The Métis nationality or ethnic group as described in such works as those of de Trémaudan (1935), Giraud (1945) and Howard (1952), evolved in Quebec and Ontario during a period from the late seventeenth to the early nineteenth centuries, through the activities of the *coureurs de bois* and other fur-trade functionaries who, with their offspring by Indian women, developed a way of life partly Indian, partially marginal European, but in time distinct from both. Métis institutions were particularly those of the early North American fur-trade frontier

> (MacLeod 1928). On the prairies and the high plains, the Métis way of life underwent a further ecological adaptation. It was here, among the Métis centering on the Red and Saskatchewan River valleys, that consciousness was heightened to the level of incipient nationality, a tendency culminating in the declaration of Métis nationhood and the consequent insurrections of 1870 and 1855.

As Donna Sutherland acknowledges, many early Red River Métis descended from Eastern Métis:

> Many men formed marital unions with Cree women based on Cree marriage custom and ceremony... The children born to Cree mothers and European fathers shared a rich ancestry of two different continents....
>
> The true Métis people hold a much different heritage than those of Cree/Scottish or English heritage. The Métis descend from Saulteaux (Ojibway) mothers and French fathers.
>
> Over time, numerous fur traders and their Cree families moved south toward the Red River Settlement where they met with other First Nation groups and European traders. Some of those traders were French from Quebec. They had travelled to the region of Red River in search of furs and riches too.
>
> Along the way, they met a group of First Nations people near the Great Lakes. The French called them Saulteaux (pronounced Soto), meaning people who jump or shoot the rapids. They called them this because the people leaped and jumped across the rapids as they speared fish on the St. Mary's River near modern-day Sault Ste. Marie (Ontario).
>
> Today, Saulteaux descendants call themselves Saulteaux, Ojibway, and/or Anishinabe. Many French men formed marital unions with Saulteaux women based on Saulteaux marriage ceremony. Their children are the Métis. Most Métis people worked for The Northwest Company.

The claim that David Bouchard's Indigenous ancestors are too remote to make him a Métis person and that the *métissage* took place too long before the so-called "birth" of the Métis Nation in the Red River, is absurd. Louis Riel had only "one First Nations great grandparent on his father's side and none on his mother's side." Opponents of the Eastern Métis often claim that their root First Nations ancestors lived too long ago, making their descendants too diluted to truly be Indigenous. However, the same can be said of descendants of Louis Riel, and the other Red River Métis. As Bouchard, Malette, and Marcotte point out,

> Disqualifying the authenticity of ethnic identity by alluding to a dissimulated logic of blood quantum—that is to say, insinuating that ... Indigenous ancestors are too distant to qualify the descendant as authentically Métis—would make the emergence and transmission of a Métis cultural identity impossible. This simply does not fit the available evidence concerning the heritage of many Métis across the continent.

The Red River Métis did not become Métis in the Red River. Many of them were Métis before they got there. As Jacqueline Peterson demonstrated, Pembina, the earliest fur trade centre on the Red River, was settled by Métis from Ontario and the Great Lakes regions. As Sperry notes, the research of Ruth Swan illustrates that "many Métis settlers in Pembina" also came from the Saskatchewan River in northwest Canada." While new, first generation, Métis families were formed in the Red River, the community was composed of Métis who came from eastern and western Canada, and had been Métis for generations and centuries. They recognized that their roots came from various First Nations as well as Lower Canada and Acadia.

3.4 The Métis People

Louis Riel frequently referred to the Métis as a people. In his "Letter to A.-A. Taché," written around 1870, Riel spoke of the "the weak Métis people." In his "Speech on the Occasion of the Festival of Saint John the Baptist," delivered in St. Boniface, Manitoba, on June 29, 1873, Riel described the Métis as a "new people." In his poem, "Providence from the God in Heaven," written in Beauport or New England around 1875, Louis Riel invoked the "Métis People." He did so in "The French-Canadian Métis People," written in St. Peter's Mission, Montana, in August of 1883.

In his "Memoir to Ulysses S. Grant," which he wrote in Washington, DC, probably between December 10-15 of 1875, Riel described the Métis as a people. In his "Letter to Ignace Bourget," the Bishop of Montreal (1840-1876), written from the same city in April 1875, Riel spoke of the "little Métis people." In his letter to his sister, Julie Riel, he described the Métis as a people. He did so again in his "Letter to Ignace Bourget," written in the American capital between December 6 and 7, 1875. Louis Riel described the Métis as a people in his "Letter to Paul Proulx," written in Beauport, Quebec, on May 10, 1877. In "While the Métis Planted," written in Beauport on May 13, 1877, he described the Métis as a people.

In "Consecration of the Métis to the Sacred Heart of Jesus," written in St. Laurent on February 17, 1885, Riel asked God to make the French-Canadian Métis His Chosen People. In "Diverse Notes," written in Regina, Saskatchewan, on September 17, 1885, he prayed:

> My God! Take pity upon the scattered groups of my people; the people that you have given me, the people that are yours among all the people of the earth. My God, remember that you have never had such a good people like the Métis people.

Finally, in "Regina Prophecies," written between August and November of 1885, Louis Riel asserted that "the French-Canadian Métis people are the Chosen People, the People of the Holy Trinity."

3.5 The Métis Flock

In his "Letter to Paul Proulx," written in Beauport, Quebec, on May 10, 1877, Louis Riel spoke of "the small Métis flock." When Riel created the Provisional Government of Saskatchewan during the Northwest Resistance in Canada, he created the neologism, "Exovedate," meaning, "chosen from the flock," to name it. Its council members were called "Exovedes." And he adopted the title "Exoveed," which means "one of the flock." As Riel explained in his "Address to the Jury" in Regina on July 31, 1885, "I prefer to be called one of the flock; I am no more than you are, I am simply one of the flock, equal to the rest." This aligned with Riel's belief that he was the Moses, Messiah, and Prophet of the New World and that the Métis were God's Chosen People. In his words, "I say humbly, through the grace of God, I believe I am the Prophet of the New World."

3.6 The Métis Tribe

In his "Letter to 'Dear Relatives,'" written in St. Anthony, Saskatchewan, on March 23-24, 1885, Riel implored God "to protect, to defend, [and] to sustain... all our tribes." In most instances, however, Riel limited the term to the *tribus sauvages*, namely, the Indian tribes. This strongly suggests that Riel did not view the Métis as a mere tribe, namely, a "social division in a traditional society consisting of families or communities linked by social, economic, religious, or blood ties, with a common culture and dialect, typically having a recognized leader."

3.7 The Métis Country

In his "National Program of the French-Canadian Métis," produced in 1873, Louis Riel spoke of "the lands of the country" which belonged to them. In his poem, "The Métis Woman," written in the Red River in Manitoba between May and August 1870, the protagonist describes witnessing eight-hundred Métis defending their country. Moreover, in "While the Métis Planted," written in Beauport, Quebec, on May 13, 1877, Louis Riel laments that "every Métis" is "far from his dear country."

After he was imprisoned, Louis warned in his "Letter to R.B. Deane, Edgar Dewdney, and John A. MacDonald," written in Regina on July 6, 1885, that "Mr. Dumont will secretly prepare himself to suddenly declare that his country is free." Likewise, in his "Essay on the Question of the Northwest," written in Regina between August and November 1885, Riel proclaimed: "I declare my country free." Finally, in his "Essay on the Northwest," written in Regina during the same period, he asserted:

> As an American citizen, I believe that, without infringing in any way on international law, I am part of the republic with my people, the

> Métis, and with my Indian country, like so many other American Indian chiefs who are part of the United States with their tribes and lands, even before dealing with the government in Washington.

3.8 The Métis of the Northwest

While it is true that Louis Riel stated that "The Métis have for paternal ancestors the employees that the Hudson's Bay Company and the North-West Company had in their service, and for maternal ancestors, Indian women belonging to the various tribes," he was speaking specifically of the "Métis of the Northwest" and not the Métis people as a whole. In his words,

> The name Métis captures the idea of mixing [blood]. The French name, Métis, fits this race of men better than the English word Half-Breed. For as appropriate as that name was to the first mixed-blood generation, now that Indian and European blood are mixed to all degrees, the idea it conveys is not general enough.
>
> This *Métis* word, which seems to be a derivative of the Latin word *mixtus*, expresses this mixture as generally as possible and becomes a suitable name for a race...
>
> There are a lot of very polite and nice people who will often say to a Half-Breed, "but it does not look like you have much Indian blood; you look white. Oh, you hardly have any Indian blood." These people speak under the influence of their prejudices towards Indians, and their compliments seem to stem from the idea that a Half-Breed should be ashamed of his Indian ancestors, and it is probably to help him carry the weight of his shame that we hurry to say to him: "Oh! you hardly have any Indian blood."
>
> The Métis are Christians. Even though their Indian origin is humble, they want to honour their mothers as much as their fathers. The Métis is attached to the name of his race. He doesn't care about his degree of Indian [blood] and European blood. Regardless of how little he may have of either, he says, "I'm Métis," and his children will be so [forever].

In an alternate version, Riel captured the way the Métis viewed themselves:

> Our Indian origin is indeed humble. However, it is right that we honor our mothers as well as our fathers. Why would we care about our degree of European or Indian blood? Regardless of how little we have of one or the other, our acknowledgement, and our filial love make us affirm that "We are Métis."

As Thomas Flanagan notes, "This passage probably contains a personal element. Riel, who was only one-eighth of Indian blood and very Caucasian in appearance, must have often heard such remarks from well-meaning Quebec friends."

3.9 The Métis Nation

In his poem, "The Métis Woman," written in 1870, the main character proclaims, "I am a Métis woman, and I am proud / to belong to this nation." In 1873, Louis Riel developed a "National Program of the French-Canadian Métis" and spoke of "the Métis Nation." In a speech delivered during the same year, he described the French-Canadian Métis as a nationality. Moreover, in a letter from 1874, he described the festival of Saint John the Baptist as the national holiday of the Métis.

In a letter to Ignace Bourget, written in Washington between December 6 and 7, 1875, he prayed:

> Saint Peter, bless the Métis Nation. It is the youngest of all the nations of the world. It is so tiny. It loves the Blessed Virgin. Bless it as a Catholic nation. And in the midst of your family made up of all other peoples, the Métis Nation will be your joy.

In his "Memoir to Ulysses S. Grant" which he wrote in Washington, probably between December 10-15, 1875, Riel wrote: "Mr. President, if you please, help me get justice for my people, the new nation, the Métis." In a letter to his sister Julie Riel, written in July of 1875, the Métis leader prayed: "May the good Lord preserve and grow the small Métis Nation and may it be faithful to its mission. Because she has one and a beautiful one. The trials she is struggling with are proof of this." During the same year, while he was in Beauport or New England, Riel referred to the Métis as a "beleaguered nation."

Furthermore, while in New England, he wrote a poem in which he states that "The Métis Nation is new... / From its spirit, which is clear like a river / it will water all of the North."

In his "Letter to L.-A. Prud'homme," written in St. Vital, Manitoba, on June 23, 1885, Riel described the St. Jean-Baptiste festival as "the celebration of the French-Canadian Métis Nation" and insisted that it was the national celebration of the Métis. In March of 1885, Louis Riel spoke of "our nation." In his "Journal," written in Batoche, Saskatchewan, between September and May, 1885, Louis Riel spoke of "the Métis Nation" as well as "my nation." In his "Regina Prophecies," written between August and November, 1885, Louis Riel described "the French-Canadian Métis people" as a "fresh and new nationality."

While Riel recognized that there were Métis throughout North America, those from the Red River colony were the first to proclaim that they were a nation in the complete sense of the term, namely, "a large body of people united by common descent, history, culture, or language, inhabiting a particular country or territory." As Sealy and Lussier note,

> It was in Western Canada, however, where the intermixture took place in an area geographically and socially isolated from a dominant European society, that the Métis grew in numbers, flourished, and began to think of themselves as neither European nor Indian but as a distinct and separate people.

Louis Riel's vision of the Métis Nation was not limited to a part of the Prairie provinces. As Sébastien Malette and Guillaume Marcotte write,

> Louis Riel explicitly recognized the existence of the Métis across the territory under British jurisdiction, including the Métis in the eastern provinces and to the west of the Rocky Mountains... Louis Riel proposed a political vision whereby the French-Canadian Métis population would be integrated into a larger national project... Evidence thus suggests that the project of a "Métis Nation" that Riel was seeking to build was neither completed nor already determined by the sociological conditions of 1888.

3.10 Métis Self-Rule

The writings of Louis Riel shed light on Métis modes of governance. As he writes in "The Métis of the Northwest," written in Regina, Saskatchewan, between October and November of 1885,

> As a primitive people, simple, of good faith, and placed in a happy abundance of goods, and without much ambition, the Métis hardly needed a government. However, when they went buffalo hunting in caravans of several hundred families, there was naturally a pressure of interest among them. And both to maintain order in their ranks and to guard against horse theft and even enemy attacks, they organized themselves into a military force. (Every hunter was a soldier. The soldiers were grouped into tens. And each ten chose a captain.) A leader was elected; twelve councillors, a public crier, and guides were also elected. Every hunter was a soldier. The first started by choosing a captain. And when nine of those others who approved this choice came to line up freely under the captain who thus found himself at the head of a dozen men, they were all the more determined to follow him everywhere as their leader over them as a result of their choice. The hunting council had regulations. They were called the "Laws of the Prairie." The council was a provisional government; a tribunal that heard about legal violations and all disputes. The captains carried out the orders and judgments of the council. In ordinary affairs, the council acted according to its authority as entrusted to it.

3.11 Métis Nationhood

Louis Riel did not confine the Métis to a limited geographical area. He recognized that the Métis people were found throughout North America, in Quebec, the Maritime provinces, the Great Lakes, the Rocky Mountains, the Prairies, and the West. When asked where he lived, a Métis man encountered by Johann Georg Kohl (1801-1878) during his travels, and related in his book *Kitchi-Gami: Life Among the Lake Superior Ojibway*, which was published in 1860, responded:

> I can't tell you. I am a *Voyageur*—I am a *Chicot*, sir. I reside everywhere. My grandfather was a *Voyageur*: he died on a voyage. I will also die on a voyage and another *Chicot* will take my place. Such is our course of life.

The traditional homeland of the Métis was North America, namely, Canada and the United States. The Métis were present throughout the French and Spanish territory of Louisiana, which comprised the central third of the United States and a sliver of Canada. They were there before the arrival of any Englishmen or Americans. Some of them had even acquired Spanish citizenship in order to trap and trade there.

The Métis traveled and settled throughout the river systems of North America. Like other nomadic, semi-nomadic, and sedentary populations, they did not have their own state. Over time, however, this group of people started to perceive itself as a nation, namely, "a large body of people, associated with a particular territory, that is sufficiently conscious of its unity to seek or to possess a government peculiarly its own." They were an ethnic group that included some visionary leaders who wanted them to become a nationality and citizens of their own sovereign and independent state.

Obviously, this separatist, nationalistic view was not shared by all Métis. Many viewed themselves simply as a people, as opposed to a nation. They felt that all of North America belonged to them, not simply a segment of it. They did not want to be caged in. As the Free People, they wanted the liberty to roam. The same can be said of Quebeckers. Many of them, even nationalists, do not want to relinquish the rest of Canada, a landmass with which they have a deep historical connection, while abandoning the rest of the country's French Canadians. Those that are willing to do so view it as a last recourse to ensure the survival of the *Québécois*.

When Louis Riel was exiled to the United States, he joined the Métis of Montana. As he noted in his "Letter to Joseph Riel," written on December 28, 1879, "We are at the great detour of the Milk River. There are approximately one hundred and fifty Métis families there. I had the honor of being elected as the camp leader." In "I Can Sing in My Poetry," written in Helena, Montana, between June and September of 1883, Riel observed that

> numerous Half-Breed families
> Born, rais'd and known as Montanians

Have given me their sympathies
As one amongst politicians

They are satisfied that I like them
While married to Indian women
Understand that it's my system
To do something for their children.

Moreover, in "Montana," written between November and December, 1881, Riel noted that "I have been amongst the Half-Breeds for about two years and most part of the time in the neighbourhood of the Indian tribes mentioned." As Sperry notes, "the large seasonal hunting camps of Métis are recorded in documentary sources as early as the 1860s, but most likely existed prior to that time." Riel viewed them as his people. And not only did they recognize him as one of their own, but they even appointed him as their spokesperson. Furthermore, although they were Montana Métis, Louis Riel described them in "Joseph Parisien," a poem written between 1879 and 1883 as part of "the Métis Nation." The Métis in question had settled there in waves. Later, in a "Letter to James Isbister, Gabriel Dumont, Moïse Ouellette, and Michel Dumas, St. Peter's Mission" dated June 5, 1884, Riel noted that,

> There is in Montana a certain number of Half-Breeds who were residents of Manitoba, at the time of the Transfer. I found out last year that they have also been deprived of their share of the fourteen hundred thousand acres of land, ascribed to extinguish the Indian title to the lands of the province.

A certain number of the Montana Métis had previously lived in Manitoba and had been deprived of their land scripts. Although they were not Red River Métis, much less Manitoba Métis, they were, nonetheless, Métis. They were Métis before the Red River Rebellion. They were Métis before the Northwest Rebellion. They were Métis after the end of the Métis resistance in Canada. And they are Métis or Indians to this very day since some of their ancestors broke with Riel over the Half-Breed designation and tribal enrollment, wanting to reconnect with their Chippewa kin and their Dakota roots. Hence, "they supported negotiations for the Turtle Mountain Reservation."

The Montana Métis are not myopic in matters of history. While they realize that some of their ancestors passed through the Red River, they know full well that the Métis people did not originate there. As Martha Harroun Foster relates, "The Spring Creek band's Métis roots go far back into the fur trade history of what is today Canada, the Great Lakes, and the Upper Mississippi drainage."

Unlike certain Western Métis leaders, and a couple of non-Métis writers, who claim that there are no Métis in Eastern Canada, Louis Riel insisted that there were. Consequently, the views of the leader of the Métis people and the founder of the Métis Nation have more weight than those of revisionists who wish to rewrite history, inflicting violence upon a majority of Métis by denying their existence and rights. As Riel expressed in his "Letter to R.B. Deane, Edgar Dewdney, and John A. MacDonald," which he wrote on July 6, 1885:

> As for the eastern Canadian provinces, many Métis live there unrecognizable in their Indian costume. Their villages are villages of destitution. However, their Indian title to the land is as good as the Indian title of the Métis of Manitoba.
>
> To give them one day their seventh of the land, or an adequate income, the Germans of the United States will be invited to plan the invasion of the two Canadas and the Maritime provinces. If the venture were to be successful, the compensation for the Germans would be to occupy the entire Lake Superior and Lake Huron region from the American line to the sea on the north side; and thus found a Germany of their own in the New World.

So radical was Riel that he wanted to enlist German Americans to conquer Quebec and the Maritimes to create a homeland for the Métis on one-seventh of the lands. To claim, as Darren O'Toole has done, that the people described by Riel were merely mixed-blood First Nations, who identified as First Nations, and that Riel, by labelling them as Métis, was using the imperialist language of the early French settlers, is groundless. There were mixed bloods who identified as First Nations and others who identified as Métis. Many of the Métis who wished to live on reservations, and receive some legal recognition, were required to identify as First Nations, a common phenomenon in both Canada and the United States. As for the Métis who wanted more freedom and liberty, they generally lived in French-Canadian communities. Claiming that there are Métis in Quebec and the Maritimes is not imperialistic. Denying their existence most certainly is. It denies them their history, identity, and humanity. It seeks to erase their existence.

Speaking of Gabriel Dumont (1837-1906), the prominent Métis leader, Riel revealed that,

> He would like me to be recognized as the leader of the Métis throughout British North America. He himself would be the leader of the Métis of the Northwest on both sides of the Rocky Mountains, to the Sea. His saying is that the Métis of Manitoba had a seventh of the land in the province: that the Métis of British Columbia are also entitled to their seventh of the lands, since their title is absolutely the same.

Like Gabriel Dumont, Louis Riel recognized that there were Métis people throughout North America, namely, Canada and the United States, and that they were found from coast to coast. As Riel wrote in his "Prayer," written in Beauport on May 5, 1876: "Joseph have mercy on the great Métis family spread over the land and seas." Speaking of the Eastern Métis, Louis Riel had this to say:

> I will invite the Germans of the States, and I will say if you ever have an opportunity of crossing the line in the east, do it, and help the Indians and the Half-Breeds of the east to have a revenue equivalent of about one-seventh. The reward of the Germans would be, if they are successful, to take a part of the country and make a new German Indian world somewhere in British North America.

He insisted that, as a Métis, a person with Indigenous ancestry, he was a "co-proprietor of the soil with the Indians" and that he refused to relinquish his rights. As he stressed, "It is constitutionally acknowledged in the Manitoba Act by the 31st clause of that Act, and it does not say extinguish the Indian title." In the eyes of Riel, what applied to him applied to all the Métis of North America.

Louis Riel recognized that there were Métis with origins in Quebec, the Maritime provinces, the Great Lakes, the Rocky Mountains, the Prairies, and the West. As Stanley establishes,

> The Métis were the mixed-blood descendants of the French-Canadians who served the explorers and the fur traders and contracted marital alliances with the Indian women in the regions through which they travelled... As the years passed, the mixed-bloods began to develop a sense of community of their own, a sense of identity, a sense of nationality. They were a people apart. Neither Europeans nor Indians, they were an in-between people, one that possessed many of the ingredients of nationality—common origin, common language, and an organization distinctly its own.

The presence of Métis people in Eastern Canada was recognized by an early ethnologist, in 1886. As Sealy and Lussier note, Wilson

> observed that few people living in Sault Ste. Marie had not some Indian blood in their veins... He noted that in Eastern Canada he had recognized "the semi-Indian features" in people of all social levels. Not until the twentieth century did the process of assimilation cease. Only in this century have mixed blood people in Eastern Canada tended to be segregated from both Indian and White societies.

The fact that Métis people were found throughout Canada was recognized by Terry Lusty, the activist, historian, author, journalist, poet, artist, and survivor of Canada's residential school system, in his 1973 booklet on the *Métis Social Political Movement.* It indicated that there were five thousand Métis and Non-Status Indians in the Yukon, ten thousand in the Northwest Territories, sixty thousand in British Colombia, sixty thousand in Alberta, eighty thousand in Saskatchewan, eighty thousand in Manitoba, one hundred thousand in Ontario, seventy thousand in Quebec, one thousand in Newfoundland and Labrador, and five thousand in the Maritime provinces of New Brunswick and Nova Scotia, for a total of half a million in all of Canada.

These very same statistics appeared in *The Métis: Canada's Forgotten People*, by D. Bruce Sealy and Antoine S. Lussier, a work first published in 1975 by the Manitoba Métis Federation. The map shows the major population belts of Métis and Non-Status Indians throughout the country. While some of these populations expanded westward and northward out of the Red River settlement, they all emanated from the Great Lakes Region of Ontario, Quebec, the Maritimes, and south of the border. The nearly two hundred thousand Métis and Non-Status Indians in Ontario, Quebec, Labrador, and the Maritimes did not consist of Métis who had moved from western Canada at some point after the execution of Riel. They were Métis who were born and bred in those regions and had roots going back generations, if not centuries. There were not simply isolated Half-Breeds or non-status Indians.

As for Lusty's work, it includes a list of Métis associations based in Alberta, British Columbia, Manitoba, Newfoundland and Labrador, the Northwest Territories, Ontario, Saskatchewan, Quebec, Nova Scotia, and the Yukon, as well as friendship centers across the country. Both of these works argue that the traditional historic homeland of the Métis spans all of Canada. "If we could obtain the number of Métis in Canada [Ontario and Quebec], New Brunswick, Nova Scotia, Labrador, and in the northern part of New England, as well as that of the French-descended families tainted with Indian blood in the States of Illinois and Missouri," wrote V. Havard in 1880, "I doubt not that the total would reach at least 40,000 as the strength of the population of French-Canadian mixed-bloods in North America."

If the Eastern Métis were organized as families and communities for centuries, many have been politically organized for over half a century. As Emmanuel Michaux points out, "the political activism of the Métis in eastern Canada can be traced back to the 1960s." In his list of post-Riel Métis organizations, Duke Redbird lists the Ontario Métis and Non-Status Indian Association, which was founded in 1971, the Quebec Métis and Non-Status Indian Association, which was founded in 1972, the Union of Nova Scotia, established in 1972, and the Native Association of Newfoundland and Labrador.

The Eastern Métis are also recognized in *The Forgotten People: Métis and Non-Status Land Claims*, a work edited by Harry W. Daniels (1940-2004), the Métis leader, social activist, author, and actor. Daniels, for the record, was one of the founding members of the Métis Society of Saskatchewan. As the first president of the Métis National Council (1976-1981) and president of the Native Council of Canada, he was instrumental in ensuring that the Métis as Aboriginal People, along with the Indians and the Inuit, in the *Constitution Act* of 1982. Daniels, who served as president of the Congress of Aboriginal Peoples (1997-2000), also made another significant contribution to the rights of Indigenous people: In the *Daniels v. Canada* case, which was decided in January 2013, nearly a decade after its passing, the court ruled that Métis were "Indians" under the *Constitution Act* of 1867, namely, that the federal government had a fiduciary duty towards Métis and Non-Status Indians.

Harry W. Daniels' book, published in 1979, explores the rights of the Métis in the Maritimes, Ontario, and Quebec. At the time, it was estimated that there were upward of ten thousand non-status and Métis people in Nova Scotia, New Brunswick, and Prince Edward Island. According to Gary Gould, president of the New Brunswick Métis and Non-Status Indian Association, "The Acadians were the first white settlers in New Brunswick and Nova Scotia to come into contact with Indian people. Many Acadians intermarried with Micmac and Malecite people." This resulted in "the development of a mixed-blood population in New Brunswick." As Bouchard, Malette, and Pulla recognize, the ethnogenesis of the Acadian Métis predates that of the western Métis. As they explain,

> The forces that maintained their distinct and separate identity continued throughout the eighteenth and nineteenth centuries. In fact, it was the ongoing ostracization of the Acadian Métis, who were perceived by the "pure" Acadians as being *sangs-mêlés* or "mixed bloods" that resulted in endogamic marriages, some of which violated Catholic rules. As a consequence, this imposed otherness helped to maintain a Métis identity.

As far as Benjamin Sulte was concerned, the ancestors of the Acadians had intermixed so much with Indigenous Peoples that they represented a mixed race. This admixture was acknowledged by François-Edme Rameau de Saint-Père, Alfred Bailey,

Olive Dickason, Cornelius Jaenen, and others. Some, like Rameau de Saint-Père and Dickason, even asserted that "Métis communities had developed in the region." As Sean O'Connell has shown, "*Métissage* did occur in colonial Acadia," "Métis communities did develop," and they still exist. As he demonstrates, "the ethnogenesis of the Acadian Métis occurred well before the imposition of any form of effective European control in Acadia." This process took place during the seventeenth and eighteenth centuries.

The root ancestors of the Acadian Métis are duly documented. They lived in family clusters on the outskirts of Euro-Acadian settlements. Many of these families were "intimately linked to the fur trade, an interconnection that is also found in the emergence of the other North American Métis peoples." The Acadian Métis acted collectively against the British in the first half of the eighteenth century, leading to scalping proclamations and deportation. "Despite ... the discrimination and denigration of the Anglo-Canadian and Franco-Acadian societies," writes O'Connell, "the Métis have survived in scattered communities throughout eastern Canada to the present day."

If the Métis of the Maritimes were organized in the 1970s, so were those of Quebec, under the leadership of the Laurentian Alliance. In reality, the Métis of Quebec organized politically nearly a century before during the Paspébiac riots of 1886, an event that parallels the Northwest Resistance of 1885. As newspaper reports of the time make abundantly clear, the rioters were French Half-Breeds. As the February 19, 1886, issue of *Le Canadien* reported, "almost all of the rioters are Métis." The February 18 issue highlighted that "the rioters are Métis, from the union of first Acadians and Mi'kmaq Indians, and they can easily be recognized. Poor people, belonging to the English or French race, will very likely not take part in these troubles." The Métis of Quebec were distinguished from French-Canadians, Acadians, and English Canadians. They were organized. And they were militant. In fact, the *New York Times* did "not hesitate to compare these Acadian Métis to those of the Northwest."

"Nowhere in Canada," wrote Daniels, "are the historical claims of the Métis and non-registered Indians as diverse as in Ontario."

As Michel Bouchard and Tiana Mager have shown, the Métis were found throughout the Great Lakes Region on the Canadian and American sides of the border. As was common among the Métis, their French-Canadian and Indigenous Métis identities could overlap. In Ontario, early Métis communities were found "in and around Nipissing / North Bay, Mattawa, Temiskaming, and Fort Coulonge / Pembrooke."

While it is true that "the real effervescence in Indigenous social movements began in earnest in 2003, following the Supreme Court ruling in the Powley case," the fact that more Métis started to organize politically at the start of the second millennium does not suggest that they did not exist before. That is tantamount to saying that there were no African Americans in the United States before they organized to fight for civil rights in the 1960s. Some ethnic communities, like the Romani, only started organizing in the United States recently. For much of history, writes Michaux,

> The Métis populations of Canada have remained largely silent, perceived as having been integrated... On a few occasions, however, they have shaken these representations by asserting their identity and organizing themselves politically. This was the case with the Métis of the Red River starting as early as 1811, or yet again in the region of the Great Lakes when the Robinson Huron Treaty of 1850 was negotiated and signed. In 1886, in Paspébiac, social misery tied to the rise of modern capitalism compounded by colonial pressures endured for over three decades also contributed to a sudden and brief political awakening of the Métis.

People exist prior to political organization. The Powley Ruling did not create the Eastern Métis any more than the Red River rebellion created the Western Métis. They existed before. Moreover, they would still exist today had these events not taken place.

Although the Powley decision brought many Métis out into the open, it was not embraced uncritically by all. Tony Belcourt, the founding president of the Métis Nation of Ontario, disagrees with the ten-point test to determine Métis status established by the Powley ruling in 2003 as it places "the onus on an individual to prove they are Métis, that they meet the qualifications of the test...

That in itself is causing a lot of concern and upheaval within Métis communities." As Darlene St. George expresses,

> Since the Powley case, census numbers of people who self-identify as Métis have doubled, yet the overall Métis population in Quebec (69,369) accounts for a mere 0.85% of the total provincial population (Census Canada, 2016). What value is there in emphasizing the increase in self-identification as an imposition or as a watering down of authentic Métis-ness? Self-identification and a statistical increase in people identifying as Métis are viewed by the Métis National Council (2014) as a result of people coming forward because the Métis population has not previously been recorded. Isn't this emergence good? Doesn't it reflect a long overdue resolution toward truth and reconciliation? Others challenge these findings, by pointing fingers at people who courageously ticked the box on the census form as self-identified Métis, perhaps as a first step for many in reclaiming their identity publicly. Are they to be ashamed? What does this accomplish?

Maria Campbell (b. 1940), the author of the seminal book *Halfbreed*, which exposes the discrimination suffered by many Métis people, also denounces the "foolishness" of Métis associations from Ontario to British Colombia who engage in a "sick kind of politics." As Tony Belcourt (b. 1943), the Métis rights leader and activist, points out: if the existence of the Eastern Métis is denied, then "that leaves out the vast, vast majority of what we call the Métis Nation." In fact, "neither Belcourt nor Campbell have a connection to the Red River Métis." "For Belcourt," writes Shari Narine, "his homeland is Lac Ste. Anne in northwestern Alberta, and for Campbell, it's the tract from Fort Carlton in Saskatchewan to Fort Edmonton in Alberta." Nonetheless, "they do have their own rich Métis history."

Both Campbell and Belcourt recognize the historical, cultural, and linguistic diversity of the Métis Nation in North America. As Campbell expresses, "I don't want to take anything away from Red River people, but I don't want them to take anything away from me either." Regarding Métis rights in Quebec, Campbell had this to say: "As Métis people, we have our own cultures and dialects of language, and we have our own territorial homelands." They are found in "different parts of the country." They are "who we are," states Campbell, "and I don't know why it's necessary [that we] have to be this one big lump of something." "It's not up to us to determine for the people in Quebec what they want to do or how to go about doing it," asserts Belcourt. "It's not up to us. It's up to them." The direction that the current debate regarding Métis identity has taken in some circles is concerning to Campbell:

> It frightens me because if this is what's happening now, what's going to happen to my great grandchildren's generation? Is somebody going to tell them they're not Métis? They see themselves as Métis, but they're made up of a whole lot bigger tapestry than was there for me. What's going to happen for them?

Despite all of his defects, shortcomings, and even delusions, Louis Riel was right about one thing: defending the rights of Métis people from coast to coast. In fact, in order to ensure that the Métis of the West coast received their rights, Louis Riel had envisaged enlisting the help of other nationalities. In his words,

> The plan concerning British Columbia is to offer to share it with Belgian, Bavarian, Danish, Swedish, and Norwegian corporations, on the condition, when they can seize it, to leave the seventh of the lands, to the Métis.

Riel realized that it was impossible to stop the flood of immigrants from Europe. His goal was not to prevent it but to control it to ensure the rights of the First Nations and Métis.

If Riel requested land for the Métis in what is now British Columbia, it was because they were already there, and he did not want them to end up landless. In fact, he indicated that there were Métis "over and beyond the Rocky Mountains." He was willing to offer Vancouver Island to the Belgians and part of mainland British Columbia to the Jews so long as the Métis received one-seventh of the land. As he expressed in his "Address to the Court" on August 1, 1885: "on the other side of the mountains, there are Indians and as I have said Half-Breeds and there is there a beautiful island, Vancouver."

The Métis did not come to exist as a people in the Red River in the nineteenth century. They gradually developed from the seventeenth century on. To ensure the survival of the French in North America, Samuel de Champlain founded the city of Quebec in 1608 and strengthened the colony by sending young Frenchmen among Indian tribes to learn their languages, encourage trade, and acquire diplomatic skills. As Champlain told Indigenous leaders: "Our young men will marry your daughters, and we shall be one people." In fact, by 1666 "the civil government of New France had a policy of encouraging marriages between the French and Indians in an effort to strengthen the life of the new colony and render Indian populations more open to French trade and traditions." When did the Métis originate? "Nine months after the first White man set foot in Canada. It is a historically correct answer." As June Schreiber explains, the process of ethnogenesis was plain and simple:

> The Indian wife and the white husband began to mix together ways of thinking and doing things from both their cultures. Out of their two cultures, another culture was made. This became the culture of the Métis people. Over the years, the children of these mixed marriages married each other. Their children were also called Métis. Soon the Métis began to think of themselves as a special group of people. We call such a group, a nation. This is how two ways of life became one.

In the words of Jennifer Howse,

> More than 400 years ago, European men traveled to the Canadian territories to work in the fur trade.... they began families with First Nations women. The children of these European and First Nations unions are called Métis. These children grew up and married other Métis, and a unique culture began. Métis communities developed along fur-trade routes and near large fur-trade forts... the name Métis is used by people who identify themselves as having both First Nations and European ancestors.

The fur-trading routes in question included the Hudson Bay Trade Route, the St. Lawrence River Route, and beyond. Consequently, the Métis developed communities throughout Quebec, Ontario, Manitoba, and beyond. What is more, the territories of the two fur companies, the North West Company, and the Hudson's Bay Company, included what is now Manitoba, Saskatchewan,

Manitoba, over half of British Columbia, large swathes of the Yukon and Northwest Territories, much of Ontario, and half of Quebec. This was, therefore, part of the traditional territory of the Métis people, where they married, had children, and created communities.

As Paul Driben notes, "the Métis... were literally the offspring of the fur trade and were found wherever trading posts were located." These trading posts included St. Esprit, founded on Lake Superior in 1665, St. Marie, between Lake Superior and Lake Huron in 1668, Fort Michilimackinac, on the straits between Lake Huron and Lake Michigan in 1669, Fort Miami on Lake Michigan in 1679, Fort Crevecoeur founded in 1679, Fort St. Louis in 1682, Detroit in 1701, Lake Erie's Presque Isle in 1759, Kaskaskia in 1695, Cahokia in 1700, Vincennes and Ouiatenon in 1732, and Fort Duquesne (later Fort Pitt) in 1754, along with many others. As Georges-Hébert Germain (1944-2015) explains in *Adventurers in the New World: The Saga of the Coureurs des Bois*,

> Scattered clusters of Mixed Bloods... appeared very early on the wake of the expeditions by Radisson and Groseilliers to the Great Lakes and by the Chevalier de Troyes and Sieur d'Iberville to the coast of the Hudson Bay. But they were also to be found around the trading posts, forts, and missions—indeed, anywhere that white men came into contact with Indian society and women.

In the words of Gerhard John Ens:

> Throughout North America, intermarriage between Indians and Europeans accompanied the fur trade... [However], frequent intermarriage did not lead inevitably to separate, identifiable Métis communities. Some "mixed-blood" progeny were raised among their mother's people and assumed an Indian lifestyle, while others were taken to European and American metropolitan centers by their fathers to be educated and assimilated into European society. Instead, the emergence of identifiable Métis communities awaited specific political and economic conditions... The emergence of these distinct sociocultural entities occurred both among the fur trade communities of the Great Lakes and in the river valleys of the Red and Saskatchewan Rivers along the northeastern fringe of the Great Plains.

> The crystallization of a Métis identity in the various communities along the Great Lakes occurred after the British conquest of New France and the fall of Michilimackinac to the British in 1763. The British takeover encouraged a pronounced exodus of [French] Canadians and Métis from Michilimackinac and its environs to smaller communities along the shores of the Great Lakes. In these communities, the traders and their Métis families were left to follow their own social and economic customs. The establishment of permanent villages that were geographically separate from adjacent band villages was a hallmark of Métis development in the Great Lakes area.

In Western Canada, writes Ens, the Métis developed into two distinct groups, the French Catholic Métis, and the English Protestant Métis. In a similar fashion, distinct Métis communities developed throughout North America. As Travis R. Arnette notes,

> The Métis, descendants of white fathers and Indian mothers, lived in scattered groups throughout the Canadian West, but congregated primarily along the Red River. Mixed-bloods were found throughout the Great Lakes region since the advent of the French onto the continent.

The Métis timeline provided by Jennifer Howse is historically sound. The contact period between the Europeans and the First Nations took place up to the year 1600. The Early Fur Trade covered the period between 1600-1800. This was the period during which many Métis worked in the fur trade. She treats the years 1800-1850 as the period of Settlement, 1850-1900 as the period of Resistance, and 1900 onward as the period of Recognition.

The ethnogenesis of the Métis people was not the product of monogenesis but polygenesis or, to put this academic sentence into plain English, the birth of the Métis people did not take place in a single place at a single time among a single group but took place over a large geographic area over a broader period of time among various different groups. In other words, it did not take place in a single focal point in west-central North America. It took place throughout New France over centuries. In the Outaouais region in western Quebec, the first Métis emerged from the fur trade. As Sébastien Malette and Guillaume Marcotte relate,

> The Métis have plied the waters of the Outaouais, and its tributaries, for centuries... this region was home to "Indians," Métis, and the French in the eighteenth century... And the evidence of the existence of a Métis community in the region in the first half of the nineteenth century is also quite compelling.

"Even if the majority French-speaking population can make it challenging to discern the contours of a French-speaking population in the province," argue Bouchard, Malette, and Marcotte, "it does not mean that such a community did not or does not exist." In fact, their rigorously researched work, titled *Bois-Brulés: The Untold Story of the Métis of Western Quebec*, "conclusively demonstrates that a Métis community emerged in early-nineteenth-century Quebec and can be traced all the way to today."

Although there were unions of French-Canadians and other people of European stock with First Nations women in the Red River and Western North America, many of the explorers, traders, and settlers from Eastern Canada were already Métis when they arrived there. As Duke Redbird acknowledged, "the first Half-Breeds in the West were Eastern Métis who spearheaded the movement into the Red River country." Case in point, Paul Driben found that thirty-six percent of the ancestors of the East Prairie Métis population descended from "the union of a French trader and an Iroquois woman during the early period of French rule," while fourteen percent traced their origin back "to the union of a French trader from Trois-Rivières and a Cree woman." As Jesse Thistle (b. 1976), the Métis-Cree author and professor, wrote in "We are Children of the River,"

> The senior governing body of the Métis Nation of Canada, the Métis National Council (MNC), defines the eighteenth-and nineteenth-century historic homeland of the Métis as the area now encompassed by the three prairie provinces of Manitoba, Saskatchewan, and Alberta, portions of Ontario northeast of Sault St. Marie up along the Quebec border and westward to the Manitoba border, areas of British Columbia, the southern geographic strip of the Northwest Territories, and the north-central United States. The Toronto area has been left out of the MNC-designated historic homeland. The modern political

> border of the MNC's Métis homeland, however, is not representative of the historic Métis homeland, which was not a bounded territory but was rather a fluid system of overland and river transport and portage routes that stretched across North America...

The fact is that "the French river system fur trade emanating from Montreal... gave rise to a proto-Métis population between the years 1620 and 1821." As Auguste-Henri de Trémaudan (1874-1929) notes in *Histoire de la nation métisse dans l'Ouest Canadien*,

> The Métis nation emerged from the mixing of the red and white races. During the first century in which these alliances took place, that is to say, from 1650 until the cession of Canada to England, the Métis nation was naturally only in the process of formation... It was especially during the century that followed, that is to say from 1760 to 1860, and even in the first fifty years, that is from 1760 to 1810, that the various elements crystallized.

"By the beginning of the nineteenth century," write Ron Rivard and Catherine Littlejohn, "Métis families were increasing in number... and a Métis self-consciousness emerged." In their words: "We were very aware of our distinctiveness from both our mother's people and our father's people." However, what happened in the Red River during the mid-1800s, was not the birth of an ethnic group. It was the development of the political and national consciousness of a pre-existing ethnic group that had existed for centuries. They did not want to be subjects of the Hudson's Bay Company, the Crown, or Canadian Confederation. They wanted independence and political sovereignty. They "aspired to nationhood." The Métis or *Michif Otipemisiwak*, the People who Own Themselves, the *Gens Libre*, or Free People, always wanted freedom. Consequently, they were a people on the move.

While Auguste-Henri de Trémaudan is correct that the origins of the Métis people trace to seventeenth-century New France, and that the geographic position of the Métis in the West allowed them to maintain their national consciousness, he is incorrect when he claims that "their brethren from Acadia and Quebec fused with the dominant elements of the [French] Canadian people."

While it is true that some Métis identified as Indians, and others as Acadians and French-Canadians, many continued to identify themselves as a distinct population that was the product of racial and cultural synthesis. They formed communities throughout Canada and the United States. As Gerhard Ens and Joe Sawchuck emphasize, the birth of the Métis ethnic identity occurred in different regions of North America:

> It was in these residential enclaves, separate from both European trading posts and Indian groups, that a new identity was forged... Here successive generations of Métis children would marry among themselves (endogamy), and sons and daughters would follow the occupational and cultural patterns of their parents.

As Christine Elsey writes, "Métis families who are the descendants of fur trade employees... belong to a larger Métis continental community that shares many features with their fellow Métis in the East." These communities have "deep ancestral ties and kinship dating back to long before the emergence of Métis nationalism." As Elsey notes, the communities in question are not "contingent upon a larger national narrative tied to grand historical and political events." Rather, their identities are "lived and observed." They are living and observed Métis cultures.

Despite prior assumptions that the Métis outside of the Prairie provinces were entirely or mostly assimilated, their ancestors survive to this day in eastern, western, and northern Canada and are found in many northern American states. Whether they were called *Métis, Métif, Michif, Gens Libres, Hommes Libres, Bois-Brulés, Chicots,* Freemen, Half-Breeds, Country-Born, Mixed-Blood, *âpihtawikosisân, otipêyimisowak,* French Indians, or Creoles, they were one and the same and shared a single identity and culture that spanned the continent of North America. To claim that only the Red River Métis can be citizens of the Métis Nation is like claiming that only Palestinian Jews are entitled to be citizens of the State of Israel to the exclusion of Sephardic, Mizrahi, Ethiopian, and Ashkenazi Jews.

3.12 Métis Nation or Métis Reservation?

As *voyageurs* and *coureurs-des-bois* or runners-of-the-woods, who were occupied in the fur trade, the Métis spread from Acadia and Quebec into the Great Lakes Region. As Logan Esarey notes, the *coureurs-des-bois* "lived with the Indians in true Indian fashion." They "were no better, perhaps no worse, than the ordinary Indians with whom they lived and whose customs they adopted." In fact, "many of the early English visitors misunderstood the French and came to think of them as little more than White Indians." One Indian agent, George Croghan, viewed them as "a parcel of renegades, worse than the Indians."

From the Great Lakes, the Métis wood-runners spread to the Prairies and Mid-West. They established Métis communities along the lakes and rivers of Canada and the United States, in places like Michigan, Indiana, Illinois, Ohio, Minnesota, North Dakota, and Montana. By the end of the seventeen hundreds, "the Miami [Indians of Indiana] were incorporating the French ... into their society and beginning to create a mixed-blood or Métis society of Indianized Frenchmen who could act as intermediaries and further strengthen Miami interests." Even after the French lost control of the western Great Lakes, "the French element persisted in the Miami and other western tribes into the distant future." As Stewart Rafert explains,

> While new sovereignties – British, Spanish, and American – challenged Indian communities, nearly all had a Métis, or mixed-blood, population formed by the offspring of French-Indian marriages and sexual alliances. Often called "Canadians" in local communities, the Métis grew in numbers with later marriages among French traders and by intermarriage with other tribes. In some tribes, the mixed-blood people, who tended to be more acculturated, achieved wealth and higher social standing through their dealing with white officials. In other tribes, they pursued leadership within the confines of more traditional tribal leadership and did not differentiate themselves as a separate social class. In either case, the Métis frequently acted as intermediaries between tribespeople and white officials...

Jean Baptiste Richardville (Peshawa) (c. 1761-1841), a Métis, rose to be Chief of the Miamis. Another Métis, François Godfroy (Palonswah) (1788-1840), also became a prominent Miami leader. These children of the fur trade created Métis communities in the Pacific Northwest. Some settled as far south as New Mexico. In *Songs Upon the Rivers*, Foxcurran and his co-authors suggest that,

> Métis identities emerged not solely in isolated territorially based communities, but rhizomatically. These ... networks were made up of individuals connected by their continual and shared movement as part of the continental fur trade and united by various cultural markers and shared customs.

Louis Riel tried to create a Métis Nation in Manitoba and was defeated. He then moved to Montana, where he invited the Métis to join him. As he explained in his "Letter to Joseph Riel," which he wrote in Wolf Point in July of 1880,

> There is [game for] hunting around here. If the Métis can no longer live in our beloved Province, let them come straight to Montana with their plows, their animals, and their horned beasts. Maybe it will be more advantageous for them here than elsewhere. As for me, I have decided to become an American citizen. I have declared my intention to do so according to the law. And I received my papers on May seventeenth. I think I can help the Métis better this way than not.

While he was in Montana, Louis Riel petitioned the government to provide the Métis with a reservation of their own. As he wrote in his "Petition to N.A. Miles," written at the Musselshell River on August 6, 1880:

> We ask the government to set apart a portion of land as a special reservation in this territory for the Half-Breeds as, scattered among other settlers, it becomes a very difficult matter for us to make a living and owing to our present limited means and want of experience in economy, we cannot compete with the majority of our fellow countrymen.
>
> We ask the government to kindly consider that as Half-Breeds we stand between the civilized and uncivilized man and are closely related with the several tribes of the northwest, owing to which fact

> we indirectly exercise some influence and from the Indian blood in our veins, we are inclined to believe that Indians will listen to us more favorably than to the majority of those who are not connected by family ties with them.
>
> If the government would wish to use our influence, such as it is among the Indians, we freely offer it and will always be ready to do everything that lays in our power to fulfill [our] peaceful mission; and if it should be desired to have Half-Breed scouts a willing answer to the call would be given.

In the case a Métis reservation was not in the realm of possibility, Louis Riel offered a compromise: "two small Half-Breed counties in the Crow reservation, or in some other large Indian reservation, near the buffalo region between Musselshell and the Yellowstone," as he offered in his "Letter to N.A. Miles, Fort Keogh" dated August 20, 1880. Riel's efforts met with failure; however, he remained diplomatic, as noted in his "Letter to H.M. Black, Fort Assiniboine," date March 16, 1880:

> On behalf of the Métis hunters of the Big Bend of Milk River who were asked to leave the Indian reservation. They consider that the American authorities have conferred a great favor on their children, on their families, and on themselves, in allowing the Métis Hunters, to winter on Indian reservations at the Big Bend of Milk River. Having no other way to acknowledge efficiently such a favor, those Métis have exerted themselves during the whole winter to pacify the Sioux; Sitting Bull himself and all his band.

As far as Riel was concerned, the Métis played a crucial intermediary role between First Nations and European politicians and settlers. "A considerable number of half breeds," he notes, "have always played the most conciliatory role between their white parents and their Indian relatives, understand the views of the government, and are anxious to comply with them." As he expressed in "The Future of the French-Canadian Métis Chiefs in the United States," written in Big Bend between October 1879 and March 1880, "Louis is the only one who can bring the Blackfoot, the Crow, the Gros-Ventre, the Pend d'Oreille, and the Flathead, etc."

A.C. Botkin, a US Marshall, met Louis Riel in Benton in 1882 while he was campaigning for a seat in Congress. The two developed a working relationship. During one of their meetings, recalled Botkin, Riel had revealed his plans to create an Indigenous Métis Republic in the West and his desire to obtain the official support of the United States. As Thomas Flanagan notes,

> Over the winter of 1879-80, he embarked on a desperate scheme to organize a military confederation of Métis and Indians to invade western Canada. He tried to make an alliance with Poundmaker, Big Bear, Sitting Bull, and other chiefs in the region, but they would not let themselves be mobilized for Riel's purpose.

However, as Thomas Flanagan has added, "it appears that Riel could not make his radical view of aboriginal rights prevail among the English wing of the movement." He could not count on the Anglophone, primarily Protestant, Métis. It was the original Métis, the French Métis, who remained more closely connected to their First Nations cousins and culture that came to his support. The same phenomenon would take place during the 1885 rebellion. As Flanagan points out, "Only the French followed Riel on his radical path... the English Half-Breeds, with a handful of exceptions, were not willing to support an insurrection." "If a Métis reservation had been formed in Montana," speculates Flanagan, "and Riel had remained there to lend it the prestige of his name, it might have attracted many Métis from the Canadian Northwest. A cohesive society, openly acknowledged as Métis, might have resumed its existence there."

3.13 The Future of the First Nations, Colonization, and Mass Immigration

Louis Riel was very pessimistic about the plight of the First Nations. Their demographic decline from the fifteenth century to the nineteenth century was catastrophic. As he wrote in "Notes on the Intermarriage of People," written in Montana between 1881-1884, Riel believed that Indians were destined to disappear as such. They were destined to become mixed with various European populations, thereby becoming Métis.

Louis Riel's pessimistic outlook on the survival of the First Nations was shared by his secretary, Honoré Jaxon (1861-1952), who, despite not having a single gene of Indigenous ancestry, presented himself variously as an Indian, Half-Breed, and Métis. Following the predominant views of the time, he conceded that the First Nations were a vanishing people and referred to them as the "race that is going and has gone." Madman or visionary, "he devoted the remainder of his life to fighting for the working class and the Indigenous people of North America."

Louis Riel's plan for controlled colonization was designed to protect the racial, ethnic, cultural, linguistic, and religious makeup of nineteenth- century Métis North America. He was not opposed to immigration, per se, so long as the immigrants married and integrated into the Indigenous Métis culture. It was up to the immigrants to assimilate, not the other way around. It was a must that the Métis remain the majority and the dominant culture. Ironically, this was the attitude of the dominant European settlers in the Americas.

Even though Riel has been deployed in defence of liberalism, neo-liberalism, multiculturalism, and pluralism, it is ironic to note that the Métis leader was opposed to any mass immigration that upset the racial, ethnic, cultural, religious, and linguistic equilibrium. It was the flood of Anglo-Protestant settlers in Western Canada, a region populated by First Nations, Métis, and French-Canadians, that triggered the Red River Rebellion of 1869-1870, as well as the Northwest Rebellion of 1885. If Riel defended the Asian Exclusion Act of 1882 on the grounds that certain peoples did not share the same democratic values of the Cree, the Métis, the Founding Fathers, and Americans, it is inconceivable that he would have supported the mass migration of East Indians, Asians, North Africans, Middle-Easterners, and Africans to Canada. Likewise, he would have opposed any policy of multiculturalism. Most importantly, he would have insisted that people who come to North America have to integrate into one of three founding cultures: the

First Nations, Métis, and Inuit, that of the French, or that of the English. Such was his stance.

At the current rate of immigration, Eric Peter Kaufmann (b. 1970), the author of *Whiteshift: Populism, Immigration, and the Future of White Majorities*, calculates that eighty percent of the Canadian population will be non-European in less than a century. "Canada," he explains, "is undergoing the fastest rate of ethnic change of any country in the Western world." The First Nations, French-Canadians, and Métis have long gone from majorities to minorities. This form of social engineering, in which existing people are displaced, superseded, or supplanted by people from elsewhere, is now impacting English Canadians, leading to claims, rightly or wrongly, of population replacement and genocide.

Since Louis Riel was staunchly for the underdog at a time when racial purity and the rights of the conqueror and the rich were protected and promoted by the state, we cannot say how he, as a pragmatist, would have reacted today. Riel recognized that immigrants brought many positive qualities; however, they also brought negative ones. As Riel reasoned,

> With their good qualities, the nations have defects. Consequently, they live in certain immoral conditions which cannot be put in doubt. Their emigrants to this country carry those bad characteristics with them. And as the persons mingle together to make a same and one community of ours, their defects likewise blend up together and constitute an immense power of perversity which becomes greater and greater every day.

While it is true that Riel invited other ethnic groups, European and Jewish, to immigrate to the Métis Nation, it was with the understanding that they would become Métis through marriage with Aboriginal People. They would integrate into Native North American culture. He was fighting for the rights of First Nations, Métis, and French-Canadians to this land, not trying to turn it over to outsiders.

As for Riel, there is no doubt that, in his day and time, he opposed multiculturalism and defended integration, Francization, and Anglicization. If they were disseminated today, his ideas would find continued favour in Quebec among many of its politicians and the majority of its population. They would also find great appeal among conservative Americans on the right of the political spectrum. Liberals can be consoled in the fact that Riel was open to immigrants from all over Europe, including Jewish people, praising their qualities and contributions to North America, thereby showing that he had a good heart.

3.14 Confederation or Separation?

As any political leader, Louis Riel was pragmatic. Initially, he was concerned with Métis and First Nations rights within Canada. Consequently, he wanted to "bring the Government of Ottawa to deal with us and make it recognize and respect our rights, the rights of the Métis and the Indians." At times, he insisted that the Métis maintain Indigenous title to the land. At others, he was willing to negotiate it away in return for independence, land, recognition, and rights. As he expressed in his "Letter to A.-A. Taché," written in Regina on July 24, 1885, his colonization plan for North America involved the "extinction of the Indian (land) title of the Métis," in return for one-seventh of the lands. Speaking of Gabriel Dumont, Louis Riel was convinced that

> He will address the companies known for their hostility to Canada. He will tell them quite briefly that the Canadian government is committed, by faith of treaty, to grant to the Métis of the Northwest a good seventh of the lands, for the extinction of their Indian title to the land... Mr. Dumont will secretly prepare to declare, all of a sudden, his country free.

After failing to rally the Métis of Montana to launch an offensive to break Riel out of prison, he abandoned militancy and guerrilla warfare. Although some sources suggest that Dumont's revolutionary days were done and that, from 1886 to 1888, he preferred to wander around as part of Buffalo Bill's show, the fact of the matter is that after the defeat in Batoche, he spent several years, 1886-1889, travelling to Montana, North Dakota, New York, and Quebec, in order to raise awareness about the Métis cause.

Gabriel Dumont travelled, communicated with many important personalities, and gave public speeches. He was very much the roaming ambassador of the Métis. In Quebec, his homeland, he spoke in Montreal, Quebec City, Trois-Rivières, Lévis, Montmagny, Rivière-du-Loup and elsewhere, to popular acclaim. Denis Paul Combet and Ismène Toussaint ask a poignant question:

> Did he take advantage of his trip to visit his brothers, the Métis of Quebec, some of whom lived on reservations and others who lived as free men, and who had been previously described by Louis Riel as living there "despised in Indian costume"? It is quite possible as Riel had paternal family in the Outaouais region.

There is no doubt that Gabriel Dumont stressed the family ties between the French-Canadians of Quebec and the French-Canadian Métis of the West. In fact, during a large rally of some fifty thousand people, Honoré Mercier (1840-1894), referred to Louis Riel as *notre frère* or "our brother." While it is true that after campaigning for Mercier for Premier of Quebec from late 1887 to 1888, Dumont concluded that politics and public speaking were "ineffective in the cause of creating and legitimizing a Métis nation"—understanding, as Mao did, that "power comes from the barrel of a shotgun"—he did not simply retire to a life of hunting and fishing. Rather, he decided to publish his memoirs and autobiography in 1888, as well as 1902-1903, to present his version of the facts. The Métis had been defeated. There is no doubt about that. However, Gabriel Dumont was not a defeated man or a burned-out revolutionary. Unlike Cuthbert Grant, who left no paper trail, Gabriel Dumont left his own literary legacy for generations to come and his words and determination resonate to this day:

> It was not the first time, in 1885, that the French Métis made people tremble, and so long as we have a drop of French and Indian blood in our veins, we will stand up for the rights that we fought for and for which the late Louis Riel was legally assassinated.

3.15 The Birth of the Métis Nation

Although the Métis National Council treats the Red River Rebellion as the foundation of the Métis Nation as a political entity, this is not a view that was held by Louis Riel. In his "Letter to R.B. Deane, Edgar Dewdney, and John A. MacDonald," written in Regina on July 6, 1884, he indicated that

> Many years before Confederation, Mr. Gabriel Dumont was in the Northwest at the head of a Métis council. This council was called the Prairie Law Council.... All, even the smallest Indian chieftains, have been recognized in one way or another, with their small camps. But Monsieur Gabriel Dumont was completely ignored. He was always offended by that in his soul.

For Louis Riel, the Métis prior to confederation and prior to the Red River Rebellion and the Northwest Rebellion were not only a race, a people, a flock, and a tribe. They were, like the Indians, among the First Nations. In the case of the Métis, they were the First Métis Nation. And among the Métis of Montana, who were ruled by a council, Riel had been elected their leader. Wherever they were found in North America, the Métis were democratic before there was democracy in Canada and the United States, a system of governance they had inherited from the Cree. The Provisional Government they created in 1870 and 1885 was part of a process of political evolution. With land, and without land, the Métis were always a nation, in the First Nations sense of the term, namely, a sovereign people, whether they were in New France, British North America, the United States, or Canada. They remain nations within nations, much like the Jews, the Kurds, the Romani, and other historically stateless ethnicities.

3.16 Conclusions

Riel's concept of a Métis political nation was not that of an ethnostate. It was inclusive as opposed to exclusive. The Métis, the First Nations, the French-Canadians, and other ethnicities were welcome to join the Métis Union. It revolved around rights, not just race.

However, he expected such people to marry into the Métis community, thereby making their families Métis, as well. He insisted that the Métis had the right to self-rule and that they composed a nation; however, that nation was not limited geographically. He believed in defending the rights of the Métis wherever they were found, both inside and outside of the Red River and the Northwest. According to Louis Riel, Gabriel Dumont aspired to lead the Métis of the West, from the Rocky Mountains to the Pacific, while he would lead all of those to the east of the Rockies all the way to the Atlantic Ocean, including Quebec and the Maritime Provinces.

The claim of the Manitoba Métis Federation that "the Red River Métis is the origin, root, and core of the Métis Nation" and that "the Red River Métis is the Métis Nation" is disconnected from history and reality. Anyone who makes such claims lives in an alternate universe of their own creation and imagination. The Manitoba Métis Federation claims that:

> No one else can lay claim to our culture. Its genesis and evolution is here, at the Red River. Any attempts to claim our culture by those who are not us is indeed cultural misappropriation and identity theft: We are the people who created distinctive Métis fiddle music and dance that includes the Red River Jig; and the artistry of our flower beadwork - a beadwork so unique, beautiful, and prolific that we were called the "flower beadwork people." We also have our ancestral language called Michif, spoken only in our western prairie homes. It is not only the name of our language but also the name of our People. We are also the People of the Red River Cart—today a strong symbol of travel and trade.

The Red River Métis did not create Métis fiddle music. It came from Eastern Canada, from Quebec and Acadia. It was created by French-Canadian Métis, French-Canadians, and French people. The Red River Métis did not create flower beadwork. It is Indigenous and French in origin. Michif, whatever that means, since it can refer to French Michif, which is merely French with a few Cree words, Cree Michif, which is merely Cree with some French words, or Michif, a mixed language combining both Cree and French, is not nor ever was the dominant language of the Métis people. It was only spoken by a small number of buffalo hunters. At last count in 2011, fewer than seven hundred and thirty people could speak one of its variants in Canada, and they were all elderly. Most of them do not even speak Michif. They speak French Michif, a variant of French-Canadian French, readily comprehensible to any Francophones in Canada and Louisiana. That being said, a dead language cannot be at the core of a living culture. Finally, the Red River cart is merely a French-Canadian *charette* or wagon. None of these three elements are unique or distinctive to the Red River Métis. Consequently, critics contend, the Red River Métis could be accused of cultural appropriation and identity theft. And they most certainly have by Claude Aubin.

Although he aspired to create a political nation, with borders, Riel was willing, at some point, to accept reservations in an apparent act of desperation, resignation, or dire need. With all the land being engulfed and occupied by white settlers, Riel was anxious to ensure that the Métis people received, if not a piece of the pie, then some leftover crumbs. At one point, he would have contented himself with parcels cut out of existing Indian reservations. While Riel had grandiose aspirations at some points in his career, he was pessimistic when it came to the future of the First Nations. He believed that they were doomed and would be supplanted by the Métis and immigrants of European origins. Riel, however, was hoping these immigrants would mix with the Métis and become Métis. In other words, they would merge into the Métis melting pot. Riel was not adamant about the need to create a Métis political nation. He only espoused separation if the rights of the Métis were not assured through confederation with Canada. He was concerned about rights. So long as the rights of the Métis were secured, he was willing to give up their Indian title to the land in exchange for property rights or the interest accrued on the value of the lands that they had turned over to the government.

Finally, Louis Riel did not view the Red River and Northwest Rebellions as the birth of the Métis Nation. He insisted that the Métis were a nation, a self-governing people, before confederation. He points out that Gabriel Dumont was the head of a council that ruled the Métis according to the laws of the Prairies. While he does not mention it, this system of laws was of joint French-Canadian and First Nations origin. It was a fusion of two political traditions. The Métis had laws, and they had democratically elected leaders. They were, thus, in the eyes and mind of Louis Riel, more than a tribe, a flock, and a people: they were a nation in the full political sense of the term and with all the rights it implied. It would seem that Louis Riel was fully conscious of the fact that the Métis needed to negotiate with the Crown on a nation-to-nation basis.

For Rob Ferguson, the birth of the Red River Métis was motivated by politics and economics. They fused two identities, as British subjects, and Aboriginal descendants, into a single Métis one to further their rights. Riel was all the more wiser. He used the legal tools at his disposal to defend his people. The short-lived Métis Nation that he created was meant to empower and not dispossess the Métis outside of its territory. Although contemporary Métis nations and organizations exclude status and non-status Indians, Riel's national vision included them all. After the failure of the Red River Rebellion in 1869, in which an inclusive Métis Nation was created with its own Provisional Government, Louis Riel moved to Montana where he conceived of a political project that was far greater in scope: the creation of an Independent Indigenous Republic. As late as 1885, he was calling for the creation of a homeland for the Métis of Quebec and the Maritimes. From coast to coast and province to province, he demanded that the Métis be granted one-seventh of the land. Riel's vision was not local, it was national and international. He wanted to secure the rights of his people transnationally. Many Métis leaders, however, remain prisoners of the past, focusing on a specific stage and not the ultimate goal.

Chapter 4

LOUIS RIEL AND THE "INDIANS"

"Le peuple de la Rivière Rouge ne veut pas les laisser maltraiter par le Canada." Louis Riel

4.1 Introduction

Louis Riel was a proud French-Canadian Métis. As such, he honoured and respected both his European and First Nations ancestry as these informed his identity. Pride, however, is not tantamount to blindness, and Riel refused to be sidelined by the shortcomings of any racial, ethnic, or cultural group, be they French or First Nations. He was frank and forthcoming and no partisan of political correctness before that concept existed. Consequently, his assessment of Indians, or First Nations, combines positives and negatives, a standard he equally applied to his people, the Métis.

4.2 A Name is a Name is a Name

While it may be startling to some readers in our day and age, Louis Riel used to refer to the First Nations as *sauvages* which should not be confused with the English word "savages." This was simply the French Métis name for Indians and First Nations. There was no pejorative intent. In fact, he himself was proud of being part *sauvage*.

In French, the term *sauvage* does not have the universally pejorative sense that "savage" has in English. It is used to signify many different things, including being non-conformist. People often say, *C'est mon côté sauvage*, meaning, my non-conformist or rebellious side.

Also people still do *camping sauvage*, which means real camping, not the glamping (glamour camping) we have today. It refers to roughing it in the wild and great outdoors. In English, however, the term "savage" means "ferocious," "cruel," "vicious," "brutal," and "bloody." When applied to people, it can be a synonym for primitive barbarians. This, however, is not the sense of the word in French, Métis French, or Michif where it means wild and free in a positive sense. *Sauvage* is a synonym for Indian or First Nations; not for "savage."

As Riel's works manifest, "Indian" was the English translation of the French Métis *sauvage*. As such, he described the First Nations as "Indians." Even in French, he prayed to Jesus "for the Indian Tribes." When speaking about a specific Indigenous population, the Métis leader was more precise. For example, Riel spoke of "the Wood Indians" and the Cree. Since the Cree had mixed so much with the Métis, he described its tribe as his "little sister."

4.3 The People of the Red River Will Not Allow the Indian Nations to be Mistreated

In a declaration issued from Fort Garry, Manitoba, on March 23, 1870, Louis Riel reassured the First Nations that he had their interests at heart. He notified the Canadian government as follows:

> To prove to the Indian nations that the people of the Red River do not want them to be abused by Canada; we told the Canadian government that we would consent to enter with it:
>
> 1. If Rupert's Land and the Northwest enter Canadian Confederation with all the rights common to the other provinces.
>
> 2. If treaties are made between Canada and the various Indian tribes of Rupert's Land and the Northwest, by the advice and cooperation of the Legislature of the country.

4.4 Ban the Booze

While in Montana in 1882, Louis Riel waged a struggle against those who sold alcohol to Indians and Métis. After all, as Ohiyesa

(1858-1939) observed, "the two great 'civilizers' ... were whiskey and gunpowder, and from the hour we accepted these we have in reality sold our birthright, and all unconsciously consented to our own ruin." As much as he fought the whites who sold alcohol, he was also critical of Indigenous people for being the agents of their own destruction. Riel, after all, believed the nomadic mode of life of the Métis was a public embarrassment since they hunted, most of the time, on Indian reservations without permission. And like the Indians, when the hunters dealt with white traders, they were often met with intoxicating liquor and trickery, further demoralizing and impoverishing them. Ultimately, Riel was unsuccessful. As Gilles Martel notes, "Riel was trying to gain acceptance of his own interpretation of the law, which assimilated the Métis with reservation Indians as far as the sale and consumption of alcohol were concerned." However, since the Métis were not recognized as Indians under American law, a convenient loophole to deny them their rights to the land they had occupied for generations and centuries prior to the arrival of Anglo settlers, the sale of liquor to them was considered legal.

4.5 Organize the Indian Movement

As early as 1878, Louis Riel wanted to conscript the Indian nations, namely, the First Nations of the Missouri Territory, which included the entire Missouri River basin, to reconquer Manitoba. As Glen Campbell notes, "Riel dreamed of a large confederation of Métis and Indian tribes from western Canada who would establish an independent Indigenous republic there."

While in Montana between 1879 and 1884, Louis Riel immersed himself in Métis and Indian life. As Gilles Martel explains:

> These four and a half years of Métis life and struggle in Montana are of tremendous importance to our knowledge of Riel. For the first time in his life, Riel knows the life of the Métis of the Plains, from within and shares it as a buffalo hunter.

According to a letter by Evelina Barnabé, Louis Riel had set off to the West to organize an "Indian movement," one that she hoped would lead to the extermination of the vile race of Orangemen, namely, the Freemasons and fanatical Protestants. This was confirmed by Jean L'Heureux who reported that while head of a hunting expedition during the winter of 1879-1880, Riel tried to incite Indians and Métis in an alliance against Canada. As Gilles Martel writes,

> Riel... tried to convince the Indians to unite with the Métis and seize the Northwest territories by force and then to set up a provisional government and renegotiate better treatment for Indians and Métis. A great Indian-Métis council was to be held in May 1880 at Tiger Hills on the Milk River, and the order to march would be given at the beginning of June. Sitting Bull and all American hostile Indians were to be invited to join with promises of plunder and horses.

4.6 Feed the Indians

Louis Riel cared deeply about the First Nations. However, the tone he would adopt could be sometimes harsh. In a "Memorandum Prepared by Riel and Shown to Monseigneur Grandin," written in St. Laurent on September 5, 1884, he wrote:

> May the Canadian government feed the Indians. Do not give Christendom the heartbreaking spectacle of starving them to death. If the civilization of our century allowed it, and if the Power wills it; that the government makes the Indians work as much as Pharaoh made the Jews work, but at all costs, that it does not leave them in the grip of hallucinations, and the delirium of hunger.
>
> We don't want people to speak for these Indians; but the Indians overwhelmed the Métis settlements. The Métis and other settlers spent more on the Indians than the government. And we want to forbid the people to mention this state of affairs. This is not the way the Federal government should run Indian affairs.

Likewise, in his "Petition 'To His Excellency the Governor-General-in-Council, etc.,'" written at St-Louis-Langevin on October 1, 1884, he complained that "the Indians are so reduced that the settlers in many localities are compelled to furnish them with food, partly to prevent them from dying at their door, partly to preserve the peace of the Territories." In his "Petition to 'Your Excellence in Council,'" which was perhaps written in St-Louis-Langevin in September of 1884, he insisted that "The way to please the Indians is to give them what is theirs, by paying them the value of their land."

For Riel, starving Indians into submission was immoral and unethical. However, giving them handouts, without expecting work in return, was also objectionable as, in his mind, it would lead to dependency and degeneracy. He insisted that they should be given the value of their land. However, experience would show that most First Nations who received cash payments for their lands were exploited to the extreme and that they soon squandered the pithy sums they were paid, incurring debilitating debts. With yearly annuities in cash or goods, the First Nations saw no motivation to hunt, fish, or engage in agriculture or trade. Many First Nations also ceased producing traditional goods, arts, and crafts. Economic dependency resulted in despondency. With alcohol added to the equation, many demoralized First Nations became indolent.

4.7 Métis-First Nations Relations

Louis Riel lived most of his life among sedentary or semi-sedentary French Métis and French-Canadians. It was only when he was elected "chief of camp" at Big Bend on the Milk River during the winter of 1879-1880 that he was fully immersed in Indigenous culture, that of various First Nations, as well as the nomadic Métis bison hunters of the prairies.

In "The Future of the French-Canadian Métis Chiefs in the United States," written at Big Bend, Montana, during the winter of 1879-1880, Riel played word games with the names of certain First Nations as a means of describing them honestly and frankly as well as to describe people, in general, from an ethical standpoint.

Louis Riel described the Crow Indians as being poor, dull of skin, poorly dressed, messy of hair, and ugly in physical appearance. He described the Gros Ventre Indians as frugal in matters of good and praised the fact that the Pend d'Oreille Indians were "profoundly humble." Although Riel viewed the Flathead Indians as ignorant, he praised their spirituality:

> [T]hese people... recognize the absolute domain of God over all things. They openly speak to Him in their trials here on earth; and their natural recourse to the Master of Life gives their conduct a measure of charity and good sense, much more moral than one might imagine. They break their bite of bread in half, to share it with the needy. They have great regard for family ties. They are not attached to riches. They are fond of good. They themselves make known what is the character of this affection when they say that "they love nothing:" expressing that their esteem for material goods does not go so far as to make them put these goods before love for others.

As he noted in "Montana," written in November or December 1881, "I have been amongst the Half-Breeds for about two years and most part of the time in the neighbourhood of the Indian tribes." On the basis of this limited experience and observation, he felt that he was able to judge them. He felt that,

> The Cree have a very good chief in Big Bear. He is a man of good sense. Whenever the young men of his camp bring any horses branded and showing signs that they are stolen from white people, he invariably will go to a responsible man: put the stolen property into his hands asking him to advertise and find the owners if possible, and his first soldiers are helping him as much as they can in that pursuit.
>
> Big Bear has not yet made any treaty with the Canadian government. He thinks that the Indians of the whole Northwest are too badly treated. And his expectation has been up to this day that perhaps he could become an American Indian with his camp... The Cree are the most civilized Indians of the Canadian Northwest, because they have been for a good many years in constant communications with the Half-Breeds.
>
> The Blackfeet and the Bloods are Indians who are wild, free, and fierce. They are Indians in the true sense of the world. Last winter, I was on the flat willow in the month of January, no less than five different war parties passed by my place, all together they numbered about [one]

> hundred and fifty men. The first war party came back with eighty-five horses stolen from the ranch men along the Yellowhead and the Musselshell. And, at the end of April, there were in those two camps not [less] than four hundred horses belonging to citizens and American Half-Breeds.

Louis Riel often adopted a paternalistic tone when dealing with the First Nations. In his "Letter to the Editor of the Helena *Daily Herald*," written in St. Peter's Mission, Montana, on April 12, 1883, Riel argued that the Métis were "too civilized for the Indians." Consequently, "they cannot stay nor live with them." At the same time, he felt that,

> As regards the whites, they are not civilized enough to compete with them. This is why each of their efforts to settle becomes a failure as soon as their weak settlements fall under the reach of a civilized community and begin to enter into competition with them. So the Half-Breeds, generally speaking, cannot remain long at the same time, side by side with the whites, without being ruined. Thus, they are reduced to float between a semi-nomadic state and the civic mode of life.

As he manifests in "The Métis of the Northwest," written in Regina, Saskatchewan, between October and November of 1885:

> The Métis dominated them by their superiority in everything over the Indian tribes, but without any abuse of force. The human and gentle relationship they had with them civilized them more or less. (Sometimes they refused the Métis the right to hunt and sought to [push] them back by war). They were charitable to them. Sometimes when hunting, the Indians declared war on the Half-Breeds or stole horses from them. Satisfaction was demanded. In case of refusal, never in aggression; but always in its own defence, or in defence of its rights, the Métis nation entered into wars with the malicious ones. But let it be noted; it never waged aggressive wars, its wars were always in defence or protection of the law. There was no circumstance where it was defeated. Thank God, the Métis Nation has always had the honour of defeating its Indian enemies. The benefits it claimed from its victories were peace first and [its] freedom of communication and trade with the vanquished tribe.

As Robert DesJarlait notes, "Riel's statements contain all the terminology of the dominator. The Métis dominated them; the Métis tamed them; the Métis pacified them." While he was proud of his Indigenous ancestry, Riel was nonetheless influenced by European concepts of race. In so doing, he seems to have forgotten the first of the Seven Grandfather Teachings, namely, humility, the belief that no group is superior to another, as well as the sixth teaching, that of respect, namely, to honour others and not to hurt them, not to mention, the seventh, the call to love others. Perhaps Riel was focused on the fifth, telling the truth.

Riel's apparent sense of superiority over the First Nations is also shared by some Métis. Bruce. D. Sealy, for example, went so far as to claim that "Métis people are the true Natives of Canada, Indians and Europeans were immigrants." Such a statement is truly outrageous. While some Métis seek to supplant the First Nations, Sealy denies their very indigeneity, placing them in the same category as European settlers and immigrants. For his part, Duke Redbird (b. 1939) asserted in bold type that "the Métis are the only ethnic group indigenous to the continent." While it is true that some of the ancestors of the First Nations immigrated to the Americas, their progeny was born here, and are thus as Indigenous to the Americas as the Métis, and even more so, having lived on the continent for tens of thousands of years as opposed to a matter of centuries. Even Maria Campbell (b. 1940), it could be argued, was not immune to sentiments of superiority. Contrasting the First Nations to the Métis, she observed that "Indians were very passive—they would get angry at things done to them but would never fight back, whereas Half-Breeds were quick-tempered—quick to fight, but quick to forgive and forget."

The fact that the First Nations did not fight against the white invaders and occupiers more often does not mean they were meeker or weaker. It does not mean that they lacked courage. On the contrary, it could mean that they had more wisdom. They saw the futility of the situation and viewed resistance as suicidal. They wanted to survive first and foremost and gradually built their strength over the centuries. In this sense, it could be argued that they were farsighted instead of shortsighted.

As critical as he may have been of the First Nations, Riel was equally critical of the Métis. As he wrote in "Essay on the Métis: The Three Main Flaws of the Métis of Montana," written between 1881 and 1884, "1) The Métis are not economical. 2) They are carefree about the next day. 3) They are indolent." Riel, however, was imposing capitalist notions upon the Métis, judging them from a white perspective. For Riel, the Métis were not good with money. The truth of the matter is that they were not materialistic. For Riel, the Métis were careless as they lived day by day. In reality, they rejected the capitalist rat race. They sought to live to the tune of the seasons and in harmony with natural cycles. They were interested in the necessities of life: not in hoarding wealth. For Riel, the Métis were indolent. In fact, they were very hard workers, famous for their fortitude and physical fitness. They did not like senseless, repetitive tasks. They tended to farm the minimum required for their sustenance. They preferred hunting, fishing, and trading, to plowing fields or working in factories. They were hard workers who happened to love freedom and the great outdoors.

As proud as he may have been of being Métis, Louis Riel was still very Western in his mindset and stood in stark contrast to those Métis people who had a more Indigenous worldview. If Gabriel Dumont was very Indian, and spoke six Indigenous languages, Louis Riel was very French-Canadian. At times, Riel does not sound very Métis at all. He does not even sound like a French-Canadian. He sounds like a white, Anglo-American, capitalist, and industrialist, filled with faith in progress.

Louis Riel went into even greater details in "The French-Canadian Métis," written in St. Vital, Manitoba, probably between June and August 1883. Comparing the Métis to the whites, he had this to say:

The French-Canadian Métis have several advantages over the whites:

1. They believe more simply and more truly in God.
2. Their hopes as Christians are firmer.
3. They are much more charitable.

4. They are more modest in their clothes.
5. They are franker in their social relations.
6. Their politeness is more natural and more cordial.
7. They curse less, swear less, and are less blasphemous.
8. They are peaceful and gentler in their dealings with everyone.
9. They are more patient in misery and in difficulties of all kinds.
10. Their ways of thinking and judging are more upright and more just.
11. Their life is more in accordance with nature; it is more regulated.
12. They forgive insults more easily; they more readily excuse their neighbour.
13. They are more submissive.
14. They know how to be satisfied with little.
15. They are more respectful.
16. They talk less.
17. They are better judges of men.
18. They have more knowledge of men.

While he stereotypes First Nations and Métis people, both positively and negatively, as there is no one-size-fits-all for any ethnicity, Louis Riel does the very same with white people, a category that denies European people their plurality and diversity and lumps them in with North Africans and people of Middle Eastern origin. Riel's prejudice against Protestants is patent. How could he measure faith and religiosity? What proof could he have that Métis people were more generous? They indeed helped each other out; however, many European settlers, pioneers, and immigrants did the very same.

Politeness is a matter of class and education. It varies in each society. The claim that the Métis swore less than whites is questionable. Profanity was prevalent among many French-Canadian and Métis men, particularly blasphemy directed toward the church. French-Canadian and Métis folksongs refer to this reality. For example, "The Log Drivers of Gatineau," (*Les draveurs de la Gatineau*) mentions the prolific cursing of the *hivernant*, namely, the Métis who spent their winters hunting, trapping, and working in the woods: "You curse our rivers / our paddles, our oars / You even curse the air that we will breathe." After describing the character of the Métis, Louis Riel lists their physical attributes as compared to those of whites, namely, of Anglo-Canadians and Americans.

Physically

1. They are more vigorous.
2. They are more resistant to various ailments and deprivations.
3. They have a healthier body.
4. They have better, clearer, and stronger eyesight.
5. They are generally better made.
6. They are more sure of foot.
7. Their face expresses more kindness.
8. They have better health.

While it is true that the Métis were known for their strength and resilience, to claim that they were fitter than Europeans, in general, is problematic. Farmers and factory workers of various European ethnicities were a robust lot. The Métis, French-Canadians, and Europeans had an advantage over the First Nations regarding herd immunity against diseases from the Old World. The First Nations, Métis, and French-Canadians were accustomed to the cold; however, the same could be said of many Europeans. Claiming that one people have superior vision to others, that they are of better physical disposition, kinder of face, and healthier, is subjective and stereotypical. In terms of their spirit, Riel considered that white people had the following advantages over French-Canadian Métis;

As for the good of the spirit, the whites have the advantage over the French-Canadian Métis,

1. more learned.
2. more artistic.
3. more experienced.
4. more hardworking.
5. more constant.
6. more temperate.
7. more economical.
8. more disciplined.
9. more careful.

They no longer have the knowledge of things.
In terms of the physical, whites are:

1. Of lighter complexion.
2. They are better dressed.
3. They are better off.
4. They are better fed.
5. They are richer.

While it is true that in some cases whites were more educated than the Métis, that was not universally so. That may have applied to the nomadic Métis and those living in isolated communities; however, those who lived in villages, with churches and schools, were just as educated as whites. This was certainly the case for the Métis in parts of Canada and the United States. Riel's claim that whites were more artistic than the Métis is also a white stereotype, namely, the belief that whites produce art while Indigenous people produce arts and crafts, and that whites produce music while natives play folk music. Riel's claim that the Métis were not as hardworking and constant as the whites would have offended many.

While alcohol abuse became rampant among certain First Nations and Métis people, to claim that white people are more "temperate" than Indigenous Peoples is a negative stereotype. That was not the case prior to the white conquest. Much of it was the result of trauma. Statistically speaking, more Indigenous people abstain from alcohol than whites. It is true, however, that those aboriginal people who abuse alcohol, do so to a greater extreme. Much of this, however, is genetic, as whites have consumed alcohol for millennia while, in most cases, it was only introduced to Native peoples through their contact with whites. Sometimes, it is a harmful form of self-medication to cope with poverty, misery, family problems, trauma, and mental illness. For others, it is an escape that takes them on a downward spiral.

It may be true that the Métis were less disciplined than the whites, at least in military terms. However, this was strategic. The whites fought in formation while openly exposed, resulting in high casualty counts. The Métis fought the Indian way, comparable to guerrilla warfare, using cover and ambush. Killing was the objective of white war. For the First Nations and the Métis, the purpose of war was to prove one's bravery.

Stealing a horse from behind enemy lines was more courageous than killing a man from a mile away. "In our natural state," writes Ohiyesa, "it was the degree of risk that brought honour, rather than the number slain." Likewise, as Gabriel Dumont noted, the goal of Métis and First Nations warfare was "to score a direct hit, and temporarily disable and man, but not necessarily kill, the enemy soldiers." As he noted, "a simple bullet wound would disable a man and his wound would get better." The Anglo-Canadians, however, deployed machine guns to massacre Métis and First Nations fighters. In the words of Dumont, by using exploding ammunition that caused shattered bones and internal damage, "the government troops committed a huge crime against humanity and against the rights of the men of the Métis nation."

As for Riel, his comparative analysis of First Nations, Métis, and whites, suggests that he was more French-Canadian than First Nations to a certain degree, and in certain aspects. It could even be claimed that, in some ways, he was more white than Métis. He may have fought the colonizer; however, he was, to a certain extent, mentally colonized, a challenge with which most colonized people, even revolutionaries, have to contend. The colonizer may leave the land yet remains in the mind and manners of the formally colonized.

4.8 Joint Ownership of the Land

Since the Métis were of Indigenous ancestry, Louis Riel believed that they had blood rights to the land. Speaking of the Métis, he stated that "the Indian blood in their veins established their right or title to the land. They owned the land jointly with the Indians." However, the concept of "land ownership" was alien to Indigenous Peoples.

As Kanekuk (c. 1790-1852), the Kickapoo prophet, stated, "Some of our chiefs ... claim that the land belongs to us. It is not what the Great Spirit told me. He told me that the lands belong to Him, that no people owns the lands." In the words of Tecumseh (1768-1813), the Shawnee prophet, "No tribe has the right to sell, even to each other, much less to strangers... Sell a country! Why not sell the air, the great sea, as well as the earth? Didn't the Great Spirit make them all for the use of his children?" Or, as Black Hawk (1767-1838), the Sauk leader, said:

> My reason teaches me that land cannot be sold. The Great Spirit gave it to his children to live upon and cultivate as far as necessary for their subsistence, and so long as they occupy it and cultivate it, they have the right to the soil, but if they voluntarily leave it then any other people have the right to settle on it. Nothing can be sold, except things that can be carried away.

The Métis may have owned their cabins, along with small family gardens, however, they shared the pasturelands, forests, rivers, and lakes. They could not conceive how anybody could stake a claim of ownership to the vast prairies. As Joseph Kinsey Howard (1906-1951), the American historian, remarked,

> The Métis had never before concerned themselves about "ownership" of the country, for this was a concept foreign to the Indian or Métis mind. With the urging of the whites, however, the mixed bloods were quick to catch on. Some of their Indian relatives rather indifferently accepted the new idea, but they never did make as preemptory a claim to the country as the Métis made for them.

Riel, adopting European notions of land ownership, convinced the Métis and First Nations that they owned the land and should be compensated for it through allocation of land tracts or monetary payments. He was even willing to negotiate away their "Indian title" to the rest of the land that they had held in trust since time immemorial. Riel, it would seem, was being pragmatic and adjusting to the new reality. He realized that all the land would soon be divided among settlers. Rather than be left with nothing, he wanted to ensure that the First Nations and the Métis were left with something, however scarce.

4.9 The Indians are Sell-Outs

As much as he advocated for the First Nations, Riel was critical of the fact that they surrendered to Canada:

> The Power took care to make the treaties with the Indians of the Northwest, it recognized all the little Indian camps with their leaders. It is true that by recognizing these poor Indians, she had the finesse, not to recognize their right or to value their land or to price it.... It is true that she calumniated Big Bear and his tribe of all civilization because Big Bear and his Cree were not sufficiently enlightened to demand the value of their lands; they had, nevertheless, enough common sense and knowledge of things to claim real compensation.

As far as Riel expressed in May of 1885, "The Indians who took treaty sold what interest they have in the country." That was not the case of the Métis.

> No treaty has been made with us. We never transferred our rights... We simply defend ourselves... The Half-Breeds of the Territories are the owners of the land they occupy... They have an interest in the country with which they have never parted... They stand on the rights they enjoyed before the transfer.... The Half-Breeds never sold their rights, or agreed to give up their government, or in any way to recognize the Dominion Government, but they are ready to enter into a treaty, by which they will become loyal and contented citizens of the confederation. We did not rebel, we defended and maintained rights which we enjoyed and had neither forfeited nor sold.

Riel's condemnation of the First Nations appears unduly harsh. The federal government was imposing treaties on Indigenous people by force of arms, famine, and outright theft, expulsion, and occupation. The First Nations had guns to their heads. It was real dispossession. The fact that they were not devoted entirely to agriculture and the raising of livestock did not diminish their right to the land. It is not that they did not use the land properly. It is that they used it differently. They took what they needed, and nothing more. They were careful not to overhunt and to manage natural resources properly. They viewed nature as a friend, not as an enemy to be conquered, controlled, and exploited. They considered themselves part of the same natural system.

In Riel's assessment, which was not influenced by Indigenous thought, the Métis used the land in a more civilized and advantageous view. While many First Nations tended to be nomadic or semi-nomadic, and lived primarily from hunting, gathering, and fishing, with limited agriculture compared to European settlers, many of the Métis were sedentary, engaging in subsistence agriculture and other trades, reverting to a semi-nomadic lifestyle only during the yearly bison hunt. Riel recognized, in a fatalistic fashion, that the First Nations way of life was doomed, and that survival depended on citizenship, land ownership, agriculture, and trade. As he assessed in his "Memoir on the Indian Question: The Indian Question is Ripe," written in Montana in 1883:

> 1. The destruction of game of all sorts, principally of buffalo, is almost complete.
> 2. All the territories are opening and settling fast.
> 3. The wildest solitudes where the Indians used to hide and trade to preserve their fierce independence are now being invaded by civilized people.

4.10 And the First Nations Shall Become Métis

While Louis Riel had high hopes for the Métis people, if they succeeded in creating a sovereign nation-state of their own, he had little hope for his First Nations cousins. In "Notes on the Intermarriage of People," written in Montana between 1881 to 1884, he expressed the following pessimistic perspective:

> I believe that in a relatively short space of time, this way of proceeding vis-à-vis the Indians would have the effect of causing them to gradually disappear without commotion. The tribes located in Manitoba would amalgamate with the Métis and French-Canadians of that province. And the tribes located in the Northwest would mingle with the Italians, the Irish, the Bavarians, and the Poles.
>
> Thus, the whole Indian race of North America would give way to a new race, the Métis race, which would vary from country to country; in Manitoba, she would be French-Canadian Métis. In the new Italy, she would be Italian Métis. In the new Ireland, she would be Irish Métis; in the new Bavaria, she would be Bavarian Métis; in the new Poland, she would be Polish Métis.

> And all these nations would learn from Washington the art of government as the European nations once learned from the Roman Empire obedience and leadership.

4.11 Indian Rights

During his final days, Louis Riel reasserted the centrality of Indigenous rights. As he noted in his *Journal*,

> The Spirit of God has allowed me to see that the Indian possesses great rights to the soil of the Northwest. Yes, the depth of Indian rights; the greatness of the Indian cause are well-above all other interests. As they say, the Indian is at the edge of an abyss. He is not the one who is at the edge of an abyss: his claims are not false. They are just... Every course of action taken by the Indian is profoundly right.

4.12 Conclusions

Louis Riel was convinced that the First Nations had no future and that those who survived would become Métis. While the situation appeared as such at the time, fortunately, he was proven wrong. The First Nations did not disappear, nor were they assimilated into the broader Métis community. Their resilience and ability to rebound, increase their numbers, preserve their languages, and transmit their teachings and culture, were remarkable. Both communities followed diverging paths. While it is true that many First Nations underwent a process of admixture, some with whites of various origins, while others with blacks, they never identified as members of the Métis Nation, which they viewed as distinct people.

As Europeanized as some of them became, to the extent that some look Scandinavian with their blue eyes, blond hair, and porcelain skin, they consistently identified variously as Indians, Natives, and First Nations. While the French Métis maintained a distinct identity, in the same fashion as the Scottish Métis and the Bungee, no new hyphenated Métis groups were formed. There are no communities that identify as Italian Métis, Irish Métis, Bavarian Métis, Polish Métis, or even German Métis. Many of those ethnic groups preferred to mix with their own people and identify on the basis of their European nation of origin. As for Riel's conviction that the First Nations turned hyphenated Métis would adopt the American model of governance, it was erroneous. If anything, First Nations have strived to maintain their ancestral cultures and customs.

Chapter 5

LOUIS RIEL AND THE JEWS

"I have good friends amongst the Jews / How I love them, they'll know one day." Louis Riel

5.1 Introduction

Louis Riel, the Métis revolutionary who shook Canada to its core by confronting Anglo-Protestant colonialism in the Red River (1869-1870) and Northwest Rebellions (1885), was a staunch supporter of those he perceived as the oppressed of his age, the First Nations, the Métis, and the French-Canadians. Moreover, while it may come as a surprise to some, Louis Riel also defended the Jewish people. At one point, he even identified as Jewish, claimed that Native North Americans were of Jewish origin; professed to be a Hebrew prophet like Moses; claimed to be the Messiah; and, most extraordinarily, called for the creation of a Jewish State in North America in the late nineteenth century.

5.2 Louis Riel, the Jew

Although Louis Riel was a Métis person—in his case, an individual with one Métis grandmother, all the rest of his grandparents being French Canadians—he identified, for a time, as a Jew by the name of David Mordecai. In 1865, while a student in Montreal, he became, physically and psychologically, the embodiment of a dispossessed people. As Sebastian Klaus Littmann (1931-1986), a German Canadian psychiatrist, relates,

> Louis Riel believed himself to be David Mordecai, a Jew from Marseille, who had been brought to Canada at an early age. David resembled Louis Riel like a twin, but Louis Riel had been thrown into the Mississippi, and he, David Mordecai, had been substituted by his guardian. His parents, according to the fantasy, had left immense wealth, but he was not the rightful heir. He also discovered his duty to redeem the Jews and to be a second saviour.

In "The Jew from Marseille," written in Mile End, a neighbourhood in Montreal, Quebec, between 1865 and 1866, Louis Riel echoed this experience." As he related in the first person,

> I was born on a beach in Marseille
> I was deprived of any parent...
> I was instructed in Judaism:
> My soul served it for a long time.
> I loathed Christianity.
> Jew: enemy of Jesus Christ.

As Glen Campbell notes,

> In a letter addressed to Monseigneur Taché, he admits that he had claimed to be Jewish when he was "still young",... What is more, Dr. Daniel Clark, a specialist in mental illness from Toronto who testified at Riel's trial, relates that Riel wrote to a friend in 1865 that he was not Louis Riel but rather David Mordecai, a Jew born in Marseille, and who came to Canada while still a child.

In his "Letter to Ignace Bourget," written at Longue-Pointe, Quebec, on April 20, 1876, Riel wrote that the Spirit of God told him that he had committed the greatest of sins, a probable allusion to claiming to be Jewish by religion. Despite his written repentance, Riel would find himself irresistibly drawn to Jews, Judaism, and Jewish nationalism throughout his life.

5.3 Louis Riel and the Jewish Indians

While it might seem preposterous for a so-called "French Indian mixed-breed" to claim that he is Jewish by race, Louis Riel found the perfect solution: the claim that the Indigenous inhabitants of

North America were of Jewish origin. In February of 1876, Riel received a series of revelations regarding the Jewish and Egyptian origin of the Amerindians which are reminiscent of similar claims made in the *Book of Mormon*. The myth that the First Nations represented the Lost Tribes of Israel has been claimed by many, including whites and blacks. Some quacks have even claimed that they were of African, Arab, and Turkish ancestry, thereby denying First Nations their identity, history, and accomplishments. Some amateur linguists purport, preposterously, that Native Indian languages all derive from Arabic.

In his "Letter to Ignace Bourget," dated April 20, 1876, Riel claimed that "the Holy Spirit revealed to me that the Indians from North America are Jews from the purest blood of Abraham, except for the Eskimos who come from Morocco." As much as he was fascinated with the Old Testament and Judaism, Louis Riel ignored that Abraham was neither Jewish nor Christian; instead, he was a lone monotheist. As for the claim that the "Eskimos" are of Moroccan origin, it might amuse or offend both the Inuit and the Moroccans. Camels apparently originated in the Arctic, so one should suppose that the Inuit brought them to North Africa and the Middle East.

In the letter in question, and a subsequent one dated May 1, 1876, Riel traced the origins of Native North Americans to the Lost Tribes of Israel. He was still invoking this belief during the final year of his life. As was revealed in the "Prophecies" found in his *Journal*, which was written in 1885, "the Indians from the North of our continent are of Jewish origin." "The Indians from the South of this continent," however, "are Egyptians." Equating the Métis with the Jews, Louis Riel once told a trader for whom he worked between 1880 and 1882 that "these people of mine are just as they were, the children of Israel, a persecuted race deprived of their heritage. But I will wrest justice for them from the tyrant. I will be unto them a second David." This truly falls into the category of invented knowledge, false history, fake science, and pseudo-religion. To be fair, however, the Bible is no more historical than the revelations of Riel. They are both, shall we say, sacred history as opposed to actual history that is evidence-based, verified, and empirically established.

5.4 Louis Riel, the Hebrew Prophet

On December 8, 1875, while Riel was in Washington, D.C., he experienced a vision of God after attending mass. According to Riel, God appeared to him as He had done to Moses on Mount Sinai. Speaking to him in Latin, (the liturgical language of Roman Catholicism as opposed to Hebrew, the language of the Jewish prophets), God told him to: "Rise up, Louis David Riel, you have a mission to fulfill."

To Riel, this visual and auditory revelation confirmed his prophetic mission. He was convinced that God had chosen him to deliver the Métis, the New Chosen People, in the same fashion that He had appointed Moses to deliver the Jews, the Original Elect. Henceforth, he adopted the middle name "David," after the Jewish figure who was both a prophet and a sovereign, and professed to be an Infallible Pontiff, a Priest-King, and the Prophet of the New World. As Thomas Flanagan notes, Riel "modelled himself on Hebrew examples: Moses, Elias, Daniel, and above all David." He claimed that the prophet Elijah was with him. "As the first Chosen People," explains Flanagan, "the Jews provide an ever-ready model for prophets who wish to constitute a new people as God's elect in the present age."

Although he no longer claimed to be Jewish by faith, Louis Riel continued to claim that he was Jewish by blood. As Thomas Flanagan points out,

> Riel ... thought of an ingenious genealogical similarity between David and himself. He was seven-eighths French-Canadian and one-eighth Indian, his father's grandmother having been a Chipewyan woman. David was seven-eighths Hebrew and one-eighth Gentile (his great-grandmother was Ruth, from Moab).

Consequently, Riel went on to claim that,

> [B]y the Indian blood which flows in your veins, you are Jewish. And through your paternal great-grandmother, you belong to the Jewish nation as much as the first David belonged to the Gentiles, through his paternal great-grandmother. And as the first David belonged to the Jewish nation through all his other ancestors, so you belong to the Gentiles through all your other ancestors.

Even though he was a Roman Catholic Christian of ultramontane orientation, Louis Riel, like some Protestant denominations, placed a tremendous emphasis on observing many of the laws of the Old Testament, including the practice of polygyny, a married clergy, circumcision, observing the Sabbath, and the stoning of adulteresses, all of which he expounded upon in his "Revelations Pertaining to the Laws of the Old Testament," written in Beauport, between May 20, 1876, and January 23, 1878. In his words, "The laws of Moses are the laws of life because they come from the immutable God. They were made for the entire world."

As for the plurality of wives, Riel was clear: "God wants polygyny... Without a doubt, polygyny is pleasing to God." This Old Testament influence, however, appears to have come through the medium of Protestantism. As Thomas Flanagan notes, "the Saturday Sabbath recalls the Seventh-Day Adventists, and polygamy brings to mind the Mormons." It could also have come from his contact with the Cree, who practiced polygyny. Since Islam was the first religion to place a limit on wives in polygynous marriages, namely, a maximum of four, Riel's limit of five wives for most men might be inspired by Muslim practice. However, this seems highly unlikely.

5.5 Louis Riel, the Jewish Messiah

Not only did he view himself as the Prophet of the New World, but Louis Riel also believed that he was the Messiah. In the words of Thomas Flanagan: "He claimed to be the earthly messiah whom the Jews expected." In a revelation he received while confined to the *Asile des lunatiques* or Lunatic Asylum, in Beauport, Quebec, and which he shared with Ignace Bourget in a letter dated May 1, 1876, God reportedly told Riel:

> You are the David of Christian times of which the former was only the figure. You are the Messiah of human glory that the house of Jacob has awaited in the Word Incarnate. However, it was unable to find that Messiah in the person of Jesus Christ, whose kingdom is eternity and who came to teach men perfection and to practice it according to human nature... It is true that the Jews, as a nation, failed to recognize

> the first coming due to their corruption which prevented them from following the son of God hidden in the mystery of gentleness and perfect humility. However, according to the mercy of the prophecies that are still in their possession, and according to which they still await the coming of a humanly glorious Messiah, they will find in you the one who fulfils all their wishes.

In "Do you Come to Inquire, Looking at My Appearance," composed in Beauport in 1876 or 1877, Riel wrote: "Do you come to inquire, looking at my appearance / If God can send a prophet in a shirt / O sons of Chanan, I will return to visit you." As Glen Campbell notes,

> The Jews occupy a special place in millennialist beliefs. Riel, who calls himself the Messiah of the Jews, believes that their salvation will form part of the salvation of all nations. During the Apocalypse, they should be reunited with the Christians.

In "I Can Sing in My Poetry," composed in Helena between June and September 1882, Riel asserted:

> I have good friends amongst the Jews
> How I love them, they'll know one day.
> If I ever publish my view,
> Lots of them will give me fair play.
> Hebrews are men of business.
> Their success rests on great virtues.
> Oh! when will their uneasiness
> Give way to the happy issues!
>
> Nation! You are amongst us all
> A perfect model of good hope.
> When will your destinies so tall
> Succeed again and develop.
>
> If it's not imagination
> If it's not cruel flattery
> The world's present situation
> Is after your recovery.
>
> O people! Why would you not smile
> And in your hearts gather up cheers

> When perhaps in a little while
> God will choose to dry up your tears
> The tears of eight hundred years.

As Glen Campbell noted,

> 1876 years according to Riel's scenario: that is, 1876 years of the Christian era, from the birth of Christ to the proclamation of Riel's mission on 1 May 1876. As the "David of the Christian era," Riel would found a new kingdom for the Jews in Poland. The drying of the Jews' tears signifies that a new era has begun for them. They will recognize Christ as their saviour and be re-established as a people.

As Louis Riel reported in his "Letter to Ignace Bourget," written on April 20, 1876, God revealed to him that,

> A third of the Hebrew people will now be converted [to Roman Catholicism]. By means of Henry V, the Triumphant and the Victorious, you will give Poland to the House of Jacob so that ... I still consider the throne of David.

And in his "Notebook," dated between 1884 and 1885, Louis Riel prayed for the Jewish people: "O Immaculate Virgin Queen of the Hebrews, bless the Jewish people."

5.6 Louis Riel and the Jewish State

As part of his plan to colonize North America with immigrants, while ensuring that portions of land be allocated to the First Nations, the Métis, and the French-Canadians, Louis Riel was convinced that "Mr. Dumont ... will enter into negotiations with ... Jewish corporations" and would grant them enough land to form a province of their own. As he expressed in his "Letter to R.B. Deane, Edgar Dewdney, and John A. MacDonald," written on July 6, 1885,

> He does not ignore that the Jews are rich, that they suffer bitterly the fact that they are devoid of a fatherland; and if they could prepare to leave one for their children, they would get to work with unprecedented patriotism.

In his "Letter to A.-A. Taché," dated July 24, 1885, Louis Riel proposed to give Vancouver Island to the Belgians and parts of mainland British Columbia to the Jews. In his words,

> Would it not be charming to see, on the mainland, across from Her, a New Judea arise, in favour of the Jews who would consent to recognize Jesus-Christ as the Only Messiah and to recognize you, Monseigneur, as the authorized leader of the faith?

Evidently, this was a Jewish State without Judaism; a Jewish State for Christian Jews who believed that Louis Riel was the Second Coming of Christ and that Monseigneur Taché was the Pope. Louis Riel made the same proposal during his "Address to the Court" on August 1, 1885. As he expressed,

> [O]n the other side of the mountains, there are Indians and as I have said Half-Breeds, and there is there a beautiful island, Vancouver, and I think the Belgians will be happy there, and the Jews who are looking for a country for 1,800 years, the knowledge of which the nations have not been able to attain yet.

This Jewish State came with a cost: conversion; renouncing the Jewish religion, and embracing Riel's arguably heterodox or heretical form of Roman Catholicism. As Riel repeated once again during his trial for treason: "If the Jews will help us, on condition that they acknowledge Jesus Christ as the son of God and the only Savior of humankind, and if they help us with their money, we will give them a seventh."

As empathetic as he was toward the plight of the oppressed, Louis Riel failed to recognize that the Jewish people were persecuted precisely because they were Jewish, they practiced Judaism, and they refused to convert to Christianity. Moreover, even when they did, they were viewed with suspicion and persecuted all the more. Riel's so-called love for the Jewish people was not unconditional nor was it devoid of value judgements and stereotypes: the Jews as rich and powerful businessmen; the Jews as a corrupt people; and the Jews as enemies and killers of Christ. It was a strange kind of love.

While Riel's call for the creation of a Jewish State in Poland and the Northwest of Canada, particularly in British Colombia, could have been intriguing and even appealing, the requirement for Jews to convert to Christianity and embrace Louis Riel as the Prophet of the New World, the Messiah, and the Second Coming of Christ, condemned it to complete and utter failure. Louis Riel's political plan was never taken seriously and dismissed as the ravings of an "illuminated" or "enlightened" madman who was prepared to dispossess and displace Indigenous people to create a Jewish Homeland. In so doing, he would have been compounding problems rather than solving them while creating new ones. What is more, his religious exclusivism and absolutism were utterly un-Indigenous. In the words of Ohiyesa:

> We know that all religious aspiration, all sincere worship, can have but one source and goal. We know that the God of the educated and the God of the children, the God of the civilized and the God of the primitive, is after all the same God; and that this God does not measure our differences but embraces all who live rightly and humbly on the earth.

5.7 Conclusions

As Thomas Flanagan rightly notes in *Louis "David" Riel: Prophet of the New World,* "Riel's infatuation with the Jews went to great lengths." As we have seen in this study, Louis Riel claimed to be a Jew when he was a young man. Although he repented for having reneged momentarily on Christianity, he reclaimed an imaginary Jewish ancestry by claiming that Native North Americans were of Jewish stock. Riel, who was mostly French, one-eighth Indigenous, and of perhaps remote Irish ancestry, claimed to be Jewish by race but not by religion. Although he professed to be Catholic, *sui generis* that is for sure, Riel asserted that he was a Hebrew messenger of God like Moses. He even professed to be the Prophet of the New World, the Messiah, and the Second Coming of Christ. The Provisional Government of the Métis Nation, in a motion that passed unanimously, declared that:

> The French-Canadian Métis Exovedate recognize Louis "David" Riel as a prophet in the service of Jesus Christ the Son of God and the only Redeemer of the world; as a prophet at the feet of Mary Immaculate under the powerful and most favourable protection of the Virgin Mother of Christ; as a prophet under the visible and most comforting protection of St. Joseph, the chosen patron of the Métis, the patron of the universal church; as a prophet humbly imitating in many ways St. John the Baptist, the glorious patron of the French-Canadians and the French-Canadian Métis.

Although his ideas did not appear to have aroused the interest of a single Jewish person during his lifetime, perhaps due to lack of dissemination, it is nonetheless remarkable that a Métis man like Louis Riel, who was so far removed from the Jewish Question, was calling for the creation of a Jewish State in Poland and North America up to his execution in 1885. This was years before Baron Maurice de Hirsch (1831-1896), the European banker, railway builder, and philanthropist, formed the Jewish Colonization Organization in 1891 to facilitate the mass migration of Jews from Russia and Eastern Europe and settle them in agricultural colonies on purchased land in the Americas and Ottoman Palestine. Furthermore, it was years before Theodor Herzl (1860-1904) organized Zionism as a political movement in 1897. As Abraham Arnold observed, "The first and only Canadian politician ever to include the Jews on a list of prospective immigrants was Louis Riel." Louis Riel, an Aboriginal Christian who advocated for a Jewish State. Who would have thought?

Chapter 6

LOUIS RIEL AND ISLAM

"Le Seigneur dit aux tyrans / Qu'il va mettre en lambeaux tous leurs maudits corans." Louis Riel

6.1 Introduction

Louis Riel is one of the most enigmatic, controversial, and polarizing figures in Canadian history. As the popularly acclaimed leader of the Métis people of his time, namely, the so-called "Half-Breeds" whose ancestors included Indigenous women from various First Nations and men of mostly French ancestry, Riel played a central role in both the Red River Rebellion of 1869-1870 as well as the Northwest Rebellion of 1885.

Charged with high treason for defending the rights of the Métis, French-Canadians, and First Nations of the Northwest, whose lands were being usurped by the Anglo-Canadian government and whose traditional way of life was being disrupted by white Anglo-Saxon Protestant settlers, he was condemned to death by hanging by the Canadian government, an event that further entrenched the historical, political, and cultural divide between English and French-speaking Canadians.

Although Riel was much maligned by a majority of English Canadians for over a century, he was idealized by most French-Canadians, Métis, and First Nations, who held him up as a hero. With the rise of neo-liberalism, multiculturalism, and pluralism in Canada, spearheaded by policies implemented by Prime Minister Pierre Elliott Trudeau (1919-2000), who was in office from 1968 to

1979 and from 1980 to 1984, the arrival of millions of non-European immigrants, and the spread of neo-liberalism and leftism, the image of Louis Riel has improved considerably among Canadians of all backgrounds.

Although Louis Riel was vilified for over a century, and many Métis were forced to occult their origins due to violence, discrimination, and systemic racism, by the twenty-first century, many Canadians—including Prime Minister Justin Trudeau (b. 1971), who assumed office in 2015—have come to view the Métis leader as a hero, a human and minority rights activist, a proponent of inclusiveness and equality, an icon of the left, a precursor of liberation theology, and a righteous revolutionary. Some Canadians have even called for his posthumous exoneration over the objection of certain Métis leaders who resist cancel culture, whitewashing, and the rewriting of history. They believe in remembering the past: both the good and the bad. They refuse to support *1984*-style revisionism in which "every record has been destroyed or falsified, every book rewritten, every picture has been repainted, every statue and street building has been renamed, every date has been altered."

As any serious academic or historian will acknowledge, the image of Louis Riel as conceived by some Métis and non-Métis social activists is superficial, anachronistic, factually incorrect, politically motivated, farcical, and fictitious. "In the wake of Riel's execution in 1885," writes Lauren T. Basson, "US anarchists and labourers ... declared him ... 'hero to human liberty.'" He has been described as a traitor, Canada's Joan of Arc, a mad Messiah, Canada's own Che Guevara, the David Koresh of his day, a saint, and a martyr, and even as the precursor and modest Canadian counterpart to Ayatollah Khomeini. Basson writes,

> Thomas Flanagan (1986), a Canadian political scientist who has devoted most of his career to studying Louis Riel, concluded that Riel's unique vision of Catholicism and its relationship to politics was similar to Islam. Flanagan (1986, p. 227) portrayed Riel as an adamant foe of secular liberalism and compared him to the Ayatollah Khomeini... Based on the available evidence... Flanagan's interpretation of Riel's religious and political views is probably more accurate than those who

> have sought to construct Riel as a symbol of leftist political causes. The only aspects that Riel seemed to share with certain leftist political movements were an opposition to the government in power and an attempt to represent and fight on behalf of the interests of a disenfranchised minority. In most other respects. Riel's radical political and religious movement seemed to share more in common with what some have termed "messianic, millenarian" movements such as the Sioux Ghost Dance movement and contemporary Islamicist movements (see Martel, 1986; Flanagan 1996).

For the sake of historical accuracy and academic objectivity, Louis Riel must be understood on his own terms and in the context of his time and place. He must be presented—warts and all—in a fair and balanced fashion. As George Stanley warned, "historians... cease to be historians the moment they attempt to impose present-day values and ways of thinking upon the past." "The historian," he stressed, "must always endeavour to see past events in the context of the moral concepts of their time."

Riel was not some sort of "social justice warrior." For example, his views regarding Islam, like those that dominated the Western world at the time, were hardly favourable. And although there are many interesting parallels between the words and actions of Louis Riel, and figures like the Prophet Muhammad (570-632) and Imam Husayn (626-680), something which should be the subject of further study, the notion that the Métis leader was a natural ally of Muslims is misguided. And while there are Métis who are Muslims—some of whom are chaplains in the Métis Nation of Ontario and other Métis nations and organizations—and there are Muslims who support Aboriginal Peoples, any friendship and solidarity must be based on honesty and transparency. With this in mind, let us examine Louis Riel's image of Islam.

6.2 The Image of Islam in the Works of Louis Riel

Louis Riel received a Catholic education dispensed by priests in Saint Boniface, now a city ward of Winnipeg in the Canadian province of Manitoba. Alexandre-Antonin Taché (1853-1894), the

Archbishop of Saint Boniface, sent the talented and promising Riel to study for the priesthood at the Petit séminaire at the Collège de Montréal, Quebec, which was under the direction of the Sulpician Order, in 1858. There, the young Riel excelled as a student of languages, science, and philosophy. After his father's death, however, Riel lost interest in the priesthood and became a law clerk in Montreal. His worldview, however, would be forever shaped by the Bible, Christian teachings, and Western law. A brilliant man, Riel could only operate intellectually within the parameters of his educational formation and its points of reference.

According to Western or any other standards, Louis Riel was an educated man. He was a person of class and culture. He was an intellectual. At the same time, he had a traditional Métis education and upbringing. He was well-versed in Indigenous ways. As a result of his knowledge and wisdom, as well as the fact that he spoke French, Cree, Métis French, and English, he came to be regarded as a leader and elder among Aboriginal People. As a veritable crossroads of culture, Riel produced a voluminous body of literature, including letters, diaries, declarations, prose writings, political tracts, and poetry throughout his life. As surprising as it may be for a man who participated in buffalo hunts in the prairies in the nineteenth century, Louis Riel addressed Islam in some of his works.

In "Revelations Regarding the Nations of the Earth," written in Beauport, Quebec, between 1876 and 1878, he states that:

> The four great empires of Mahomet, Photius, Luther, and the English colossus, appeared before my eyes like the fourth sparks that you would see coming out together from four fireflies lost in the night.

In "The Strength that God Gives Me," written in Beauport, Quebec, in 1876-1877, Riel writes:

> The strength that God gives me
> Can knock down the firmest column.
> I am greater than Samson.
> And my genius resents the success of Nelson.

In the Mediterranean
I come after him again this year.
It has now been sixty-six years
That I wish to put an end to the Protestants.

I detest their commerce
Since it betrays me. The greedy who engage in it,
Side with the Sultan
As if I were, myself, on the side of the Mahometan.

When Riel claims that God gives him strength, he speaks as the self-described "Prophet, Infallible Pontiff, and Priest-King," as well as "a prophet of the New World." As far as Riel was concerned, supporting Protestantism and British imperialism was a form of defending the Ottoman Sultan, the Prophet Muhammad, and Islam. Later on, he speaks of "The Tiger of Byzantium... Behold Turkey: Is She Not Immense?" In the words of Riel,

Christianity places itself,
Via Liberalism, under the yoke of Mahomet.
One God digs the Dead Sea
To make a place for the Sublime Porte.

The Lord tells tyrants
That He will tear all their damn Korans to shreds;
May the Czars fall by the thousands.
Only Jesus-Christ is King, that is the gospel.

I carry out what is required.
The Truth of God is displayed by His Holiness.
I come from the land Above.
Follow me so that you shall live for I am both poor and rich.

These quatrains sound in some ways like the prophecies of Nostradamus (1503-1566). Perhaps they inspired Riel. They were popular and well-circulated. Though they were written in the nineteenth century, verses like "Christianity places itself, / Via Liberalism, under the yoke of Mahomet" would possibly apply more appropriately to the twenty-first century.

As Glen Campbell points out, the poem in question finds two other sources of inspiration: 1) a letter Riel received from Bishop Ignace Bourget in 1875, and 2) the quarrel between liberalism and ultramontanism that was taking place in the Catholic Church in Quebec. Ultramontanism, a current in the Catholic Church that rejected any compromise with modernity and demanded the supremacy of religion over civil society, took root in Canada in 1820-1830. Bourget, who belonged to the extreme ultramontanes, played a central role in imposing the movement's ideas throughout most of Catholic Canada. As Glen Campbell writes,

> Riel attacks the enemies of the Catholic faith who, according to him, include liberals, Protestants, and Muslim tyrants, along with others he lists with precision. The poet will fight against all these adversaries because God has given him the necessary strength to defeat them. He has a mission to accomplish, he says, and he invites the reader to follow him.

In Riel's view, Islam was the enemy, Muslim despots were the enemy, and the Ottoman caliphate was the enemy. Even the Russians were the enemy, on account of the moderate liberalization undertaken by Tsar Alexander II (1811-1881), who permitted the secularization of education. Riel further condemns Alfonso XII (1857-1885), the king of Spain, calling him a "bad dog" for establishing a constitutional monarchy which was the antithesis of the Catholic theocracy proposed by the Métis leader. He attacks Joseph II (1741-1790), the German emperor, for his anticlericalism. He criticizes the Prussian Bismarck (1815-1898) for trying to limit the independence of the Roman Catholic Church and seeking to place it under the control of the secular State. He also attacks Victor-Emmanuel II (1820-1878), the king of Italy who made Rome the capital of a united Italy, an act Riel viewed with opprobrium.

Louis Riel was no liberal. He was vehemently opposed to liberalism and secularism. As a nationalist and a traditionalist, as well as an obsessively and fanatically religious person, Riel was a staunch supporter of Catholic theocracy for most of his life. As the *Canadian Encyclopedia* notes, "The extreme ultramontanes fought for the immediate application of ultramontane principles in the control of education, the reform of laws in conformity with canon law, and the surveillance of civil legislation by the episcopate." "Among the Métis," wrote Riel, "the State, the Church, have always been one." In the twentieth and twenty-first centuries, the only proponents of the union of Church and State or Mosque and State have been Christian fascists and radical Islamists. Moreover, let us not forget that many Moroccan Muslims supported Franco (1892-1975) in the Spanish Civil War (1936-1939) because they saw the Communist and anarchist attack on the Church as an attack on religion per se.

In "Temperance," composed in Montana in 1882, Riel condemns the use and abuse of alcohol at a time when he was campaigning against the sale of intoxicating beverages to Indians and Métis. As he admitted in a "Letter to the Editor of the Helena *Daily Herald*," written in St. Peter's Mission, Montana, on April 12, 1883,

> The Half-Breed is a man who has a strong passion for intoxicating drinks. He spends most of his earnings in whisky. If he is a mere hunter on the prairie, liquor is one of the principal causes which makes him poor and prevents him from settling. If he is trying to settle, the use of spirituous liquors empties his purse and makes him sink more rapidly into poverty, and poverty drives him away from his little farm.

Ironically, the poem, actually a song with a chorus, is modelled upon the popular bacchanalian songs of the French-Canadians and Métis. Perhaps he wished to speak to the people in the language of the people. It is unlikely, however, that such a reproachful song would have appealed to listeners in bars, dances, and festive Métis gatherings where alcohol used to flow in abundance. Since they seek to escape their worries and sorrows, most partiers do not like to be preached to. Curiously, Riel dedicates the end of the piece to Islam, combining criticism and praise. The lines of verse read:

> If one must say so,
> The Turk practices temperance.
> However, his empire
> Was also great.
> His terrible brigades

Appeared everywhere.
Even after eight crusades
Europe could not overcome them.

In a nineteenth-century context, it seems that such allusions, with rare exception, would have been lost on a Métis, French-Canadian, and Native American audience. Although some of them, like Riel, were erudite, the Métis were predominantly parochial people with little formal education who lived in a church-dominated, self-contained society. How many of them had even heard about Islam, the Qur'an, Muslims, Muhammad, and the Ottomans? They lived in a different world.

Oddly, rather than invoke Protestant proponents of temperance, like the Quakers, Riel preferred to take Ottoman Turks as an example. Riel's praise for Muslims soon shifts to criticism, lamenting that eight crusades failed to defeat them. As Glen Campbell notes,

> The Seljuk Turks conquered Jerusalem in 1098. To liberate the city and to protect the pilgrims, Christian Europeans initiated a series of religious wars (the crusades) that lasted approximately two hundred years.

Riel moves between the Arab and Turkish world, praising the sobriety that was spread from the holy city of Islam:

O Ancient Mecca
Your sobriety,
Which is a Christian virtue,
In truth,
Made you rule strongly
For twelve hundred and sixty years.
Your Sublime Porte
Opened as double doors.

Ironically, Riel identifies alcohol abstinence as a Christian value when Islam was the first world religion to prohibit its use. In fact, he attributes the twelve-hundred-year-old success of Islam to Muslim sobriety. Riel, it would seem, was under the assumption that temperance was a practical reality in Muslim societies when, in fact, it has only been prohibited in theory and codes of law. Alcohol use and abuse have been as common in the Muslim world as they have been in the Christian world. Hence, such praise appears to be unwarranted and undeserved. Prohibition failed to show its fruits in the Islamic world just as it would in the United States between 1920 and 1933.

In his poem, Riel also invokes the "Sublime Porte" as the symbol of the success of Islam. As Glen Campbell writes:

> Built in 1478, the Sublime Porte of Istanbul was found at the entrance of the palace of the Grand Vizier. This monumental door subsequently became the synonym of Ottoman power. Since the caliph, the successor of Mahomet, reigned in the Turkish city, Riel implies here that the Sublime Porte would be the veritable point of entrance to the Muslim world.

Louis Riel, portrayed by his partisans as some sort of freedom fighter who defended the oppressed of the earth, which is true, also supported and encouraged European Christian and secular imperialism against the Ottoman Muslim empire. He describes the Ottoman empire as having double doors, namely, an entrance to Europe and an entrance to the Middle East and Asia. Riel intimates that the conquest and domination of the Muslim world depend on the fall of the Ottoman empire. The "Prophet of the Great Plains" proceeds to condemn the Qur'an and wish farewell to the Ottomans without opprobrium:

> You were born
> Of the hazardous Koran
> In the year
> Six-hundred and twenty-two.
> As an abstemious Power
> I bid you farewell.
> You die without disgrace
> Precisely in '82.

For Glen Campbell, Riel views the Qur'an as *hasardeux* or "dangerous" "because Mahomet, in order to save himself, had to flee from Mecca." While this is possible, I find this interpretation to be unlikely. In French, the adjective *hasardeux* means both risky and hazardous. The term also means something happenstance, the product of chance or coincidence, namely, a work of doubtful origin. It is the synonym of perilous and improper, namely, embarrassing, inconvenient, indecent, obscene, and shocking. To avoid offence, it seems that Campbell opted for the gentlest meaning even though it does not necessarily fit the context. It seems that Riel wanted to slight the Qur'an. His use of *hasardeux* to describe the holy book of Islam is disparaging. While no religious scripture is beyond criticism and even reproach, one should have the decency of reading it entirely and carefully before disparaging it. Otherwise, like Riel, one's criticism lacks all credibility.

Despite his ill-will toward the Turks, Riel stresses that the Ottoman Empire would die without disgrace in 1882. In other words, the fact that the Ottomans opposed alcohol offered them partial redemption in his eyes. As Riel writes,

> The Apocalypse
> Has well described the course
> Of your ellipse.
> Count your days.
> You are the comet,
> That beautiful, remote, celestial body
> That passes by and casts
> Its light upon us as well.

For Riel, the year 1882 was of great importance. As Campbell notes, Riel

> [S]peaks of 622, the first year of the Muslim era or hijrah. (On July 22, 622, Mahomet had to flee the Meccans who wanted to assassinate him). From that date onward, Mecca reigned for 1,260 years... The number 1,260 also has a great significance; the poet considers it sacred because John, in his Apocalypse (11:2), alludes to it. We can see why Riel, according to his calculations (622+1260=1882), insists so much on this date, writing it down four times in his draft.

In "Philosophical and Theological System: Only the Mysterious Cooperation of God Can Validate My Doctrine," written in Montana, at some point between 1881 and 1884, Riel writes that,

> I do not wish to lead anyone astray. God has given me a genius that is much greater than the one given to Mahomet. I know it. I can establish, without authorization, a religion, and empires far more famous than his.

In "Philosophical and Theological System: The Transfer of the Papacy," which he also wrote in Montana during the same period, Riel expresses the same thoughts in slightly different words:

> 64. God has given me a genius that is much greater than the one given to Mahomet. And I can establish a religion and empires even more famous than his, even if I wished to work as he did, without going to the trouble of obtaining divine authorization.
>
> 65. But this glory does not tempt me. I prefer to be without influence and to obey God rather than to make myself great through the distractions of pride, to the detriment of the submission that I owe to my creator.

The peak of Louis Riel's anti-Islamism and anti-Muslimism is perhaps found in "Revelation of the Sublime Porte," written in Longue-Pointe, Quebec, on March 10, 1876. The full text, in French and English, is included in the notes to this book. However, since it is so long, only the key segments are included below. In the words of Riel,

> The spirit of God has chosen a prophet... Here are the words that the Word Incarnate deigns to pronounce by my mouth...
> "The Muslim forces have worked, exerted, and exhausted themselves without calling me for help. They have worked against Me. The care that I took to keep them in contact with the Cross did not affect them...
>
> "I stood next to the Porte like a friend. My patience lasted for over one thousand years. My strokes of glory went unrecognized, as did my threats...
>
> "The Muslim forces did not want to be healed from sin. At last, the father in me gives way to the judge.
>
> "I knock on the Sublime Porte. My wrath is ignited. The fire of my wrath will reduce to ashes the powerful locks and padlocks, the bolts and bars of steel, the strong hinges, and the handles of the Sublime

> Porte. My two feet tread upon the sand, the shackles and the obstacles that the sultans have placed on my path.
>
> "The Sublime Porte is overthrown. Who will place the empire of Mahomet under his protection?
>
> "On the day of his vengeance, the Son of Man abandons the great empire of Mahomet in the Sahara Desert in the middle of burning sands, so that it is consumed by the storm.
>
> "Jesus-Christ forever deprives it of the services of the dromedary and forever removes its best Arab horses, which he turns over to other hands.
>
> "The Koran erases itself in the face of my irritated eyes. I place it among the iniquities, the great iniquities of the Dead Sea.
>
> "I open the Sublime Porte. I open the Door to the Orient. Dawn already starts to rise.
>
> "Since God is God, Mahomet is not His Prophet.
>
> "The largest part of the great empire of Mahomet passes to Russia. I allocate a second part to the House of Austria and the rest I give to England.
>
> "Since the House of Austria is my only Catholic, Apostolic, and Roman Church, I grant it the honour and the care of forming the army that must fight the Ottomans and divide up their empire, according to my goodwill and pleasure....
>
> "God wants Austria to preside over all powers when settling the difficulties that will ruin the Turkish government....
>
> "As proof that this is the divine will, Jesus Christ predicts to the world through his prophet, on this tenth day of March 1876, that the Sublime Porte will lose three great battles, the first of which is March 19, the second of which is April 19, and the..."

The "Revelation of the Sublime Porte" was written by Riel while he resided with his uncle John Lee in Longue-Pointe, Quebec. In February 1876, while staying with his uncle, Riel had also received a series of revelations regarding the Jewish and Egyptian origin of

Amerindians, [cf. the *Book of Mormon*] the "two gloves," and the "statue of Cavour." On March 6, 1876, Lee brought his nephew to a mental asylum in Longue-Pointe where he was interned and diagnosed as suffering from "delusions of grandeur." As Gilles Martel reports, an anonymous reporter published an article in *La Minerve* titled "Is Riel insane?" on May 23, 1885. The article explains that a reporter visited Riel in March of 1876 and brought back the strange document on the Ottoman Empire.

In the "Revelation of the Sublime Porte," Riel commences by claiming that God has chosen him as a prophet. Only the first two sentences are his, the rest of the work—which is between the opening and closing quotation marks—is said to represent the Word of God, who supposedly selected Riel to be the first prophet of the American continent. God, it is claimed, has focused His gaze on the Levant, lambasting Muslims for working against Him and for being impervious to the Cross. Neither did they learn anything from Christian contact nor Jewish influence.

After over one thousand years of patience with the Ottoman Porte, God has had enough. Apparently, God is not a historical buff nor exceptionally proficient in mathematics. Founded in 1299 and dissolved in 1923, the Ottoman Empire lasted six-hundred and twenty-four years. At the time of Riel's revelation, the Sublime Porte had existed for five-hundred and seventy-seven years. That being said, the "Revelation of the Sublime Porte" claims that God tried to guide and correct the Ottoman Muslims in ways that were both gentle and strict, efforts that ultimately proved futile. In fact, the sultans are accused of obstructing the guidance of God. The Father, claims the work, has given way to the Judge. In other words, the time of Christian mercy has come and gone. The God of Wrath replaces the God of Love of the New Testament.

The "Revelation of the Sublime Porte" prophetically predicts that the Sublime Porte will be overthrown. The empire of Muhammad, it claims, will be confined to the middle of the Sahara Desert, where it will be ravaged, decimated, and destroyed in an apocalyptic sandstorm. Those remaining Muslims will be forever deprived of camels, dromedaries, and Arab stallions. (At least, they were not deprived of their oil.) Even the sacred scripture of Islam shall come to an end: "The Koran erases itself in the face of my irritated eyes. I place it among the iniquities, the great iniquities of the Dead Sea," an apparent allusion to Sodom and Gomorrah. The Qur'an, the Word of God according to Muslims, and a literary masterpiece of universal quality, is vaporized and cast into the recycling heap of history. God proclaims that He is opening the Sublime Porte, the gateway to the Orient.

As the work conveys, the dusk of Islamic rule will bring about a new dawn. "Since God is God," states the work startlingly, "Mahomet is not His Prophet." This play on the Islamic profession of faith—There is no god but God, and Muhammad is the Messenger of God—is sure to offend Muslim sentiments. However, freedom of speech and religion entitle Louis Riel to express his opinions and convictions.

The "Revelation of the Sublime Porte" foretells that most of the Ottoman empire would be absorbed into Russia, that a second segment would be integrated into Austria, and that the rest of its territory would become a part of the British empire. God, it would seem, supports Austria because it has remained faithful to the Roman Catholic Church. God, however, expresses enormous hostility toward a great, German-named, red-head. According to Gilles Martel, the man in question was none other than Bismarck (1815-1898), who is accused of waging war against God. According to the text, God loathes him more than the Crescent, namely, Islam and the Ottoman empire. Alluding to Apocalypse 5:5, the text warns that the Lion of Judah, the Messiah, will ultimately be victorious.

The "Revelation of the Sublime Porte" calls upon Joseph to remember a series of apocalyptic prophets such as Isaiah, Jeremy, Ezekiel, and Daniel. As Martel points out, the person in question is François-Joseph I (1830-1916), the emperor of Austria (1848-1916), and the king of Hungary (1867-1916). The God of the text calls upon the Russian leadership to wage war against the Ottomans to expand the empire of Peter I, the Great (1682-1725), implying that the Czar is the successor of Saint Peter.

As evidence that the revelation is genuine, the divine narrator predicts that the Ottomans will meet with three defeats in 1876, on March 10 and March 19... the final date is missing, an apparent oversight by God, who was presumably resting at the time. Despite Riel's prophetic conviction, history tells a different story. There was a minor rebellion in Ottoman Macedonia in 1876, the Razlovtski insurrection, and the Turks suppressed it. The Montenegrin-Ottoman War took place between 1876 and 1878 and resulted in a decisive Montenegrin victory. The crucial battles took place in 1877 and 1878, not in 1876. In short, the Sublime Porte did not suffer three defeats in 1876; therefore, the "Word of God" is false. One can claim, however, that God changed His will, the classic argument used by religious manipulators when prophecies fail to come true.

While he can be admired for defending the rights of the Métis, French-Canadians, and First Nations, Louis Riel's views on the Prophet Muhammad, the Qur'an, Islam, and the Ottoman empire were, from a Muslim perspective, prejudiced, ill-informed, incorrect, and offensive. As he makes abundantly clear in his poetry and prose, Louis Riel was openly anti-Muslim. He viewed Islam and liberalism as common ideological enemies of the Roman Catholic Church. He said that God would destroy the cursed Qur'ans of the Muslims and tear them to pieces. He lamented the fact that the crusades of the Christians were unable to defeat Islam and Muslims. He described the Qur'an as a dangerous book of dubious origin even though there is no evidence that he ever read a Latin, French, or English translation. When it came to Muslims, the only things that Riel admired were their supposed abstinence from alcohol and the crescent flag of the Ottomans. As the Spirit of God had told him: "They have picked something nice." Had he known the truth, namely, that alcohol is as widely consumed in the Islamic world as it is in the Christian world, despite its religious and often legal prohibition, he would not have had a single positive thing to say about Muslims.

As part of his delusions of grandeur, Louis Riel claimed to be a greater genius than Muhammad, that Muhammad was devoid of divine authority, and that he could found a religion and empires greater than him. While Riel was brilliant, he pales in comparison to the Prophet Muhammad in terms of output and impact. After all, the Messenger of God was ranked number one in *The 100: A Ranking of the Most Influential Persons in History*, a work by Michael H. Hart. Riel's influence was local, regional, and bi-national. Muhammad's influence was global. Riel had thousands of followers in his lifetime. The Prophet's followers are now counted in the billions.

Louis Riel claimed that Muslims had failed to call upon God, fought against God, and refused to be saved from sin. Muslims, however, have always prayed five times per day, fought in the path of God, and asked for forgiveness. The fact that they did not believe in original sin, the Trinity, or redemption through crucifixion does not mean that they do not seek salvation through faith and deeds. Riel claimed that God had lost patience with Islam and Muslims and would rain his wrath upon them. God would punish them in myriad ways. While this might be true considering the consequences of colonialism, Muslims remain mighty, and the Métis have been reduced to a marginalized minority. Even the most impoverished Muslim nation is more powerful economically, politically, and militarily, than all the Métis people combined.

For Riel, God was so annoyed with the Qur'an that He would erase it from existence. After all, the work was an iniquity. Had Riel read it, he would have been astonished at how similar it was to the Old and New Testaments of the Bible. Ironically, in some regards, Riel's religious reforms drew him closer to the Qur'an and Islam than to Catholicism.

To add insult to injury, Riel mocked the Muslim profession of faith by insisting that "since God is God, Mahomet is not his prophet." This statement, which is not even original, was inspired by works and sayings in circulation during Riel's life and which he learned directly or indirectly. In *Étude élémentaire du décalogue* (1845) Augustin Laurent Montandon wrote that "Certainly, there is no god but God; but Mahomet is not His Prophet; and by associating truth with falsehood, you destroy the former."

In *Nouveau voyage dans le pays des nègres* (1856) [*New Voyage to the Land of the Negros*], Anne Raffenel used the expression, "God is Great, and Mahomet is not His Prophet." In *Physiologie de l'opinion*

(1867), Gustave Loüis wrote that "Only God is God, my brothers; and Mahomet is not His Prophet." In *La morale* (1883), Yves Guyot wrote that "Allah is not Allah, and Mahomet is not His Prophet." And Comte Régie de Trobriand (1816-1897), the French aristocrat, attorney, poet, and novelist who served as the commander of Fort Stevenson in Dakota Territory from 1867 to 1870, wrote that "God is Great! And Mahomet is not His Prophet!"

Although the expression was common in French-speaking quarters on both sides of the Atlantic, and was used by Catholics, Protestants, and secularists, it would seem that the ultramontanes, the Catholic ultra-conservatives, and fundamentalists with whom Riel studied, were the most responsible for instilling such ideas in his mind and soul. The statement that "God is one and Muhammad is not His messenger" is pro-Christian in its affirmation and anti-Islamic in its negation. Opposing Islam was a form of defending Christianity. The more anti-Islamic a person was, the more Christian they were thought to be. Few Christians and Muslims of the nineteenth century sought common ground between their respective faith traditions.

Finally, in an act of irony supreme, Louis Riel, a freedom fighter and anti-imperialist, called upon the Austrians, the Russians, the British, and other European imperialists to join forces to destroy the Ottoman empire. Ironically, despite his animosity toward Islam and Muslims, many of his contemporaries associated him with them. As Krisztina Kodó notes,

> John A. Macdonald ... made a reference to Riel as "some sort of half-breed Mahdi" in the Canadian House of Commons on 26 March 1885 ... Behind this striking comparison lies the figure of another anti-imperial resistor, Muhammad Ahmad of Sudan, who "declared himself 'the Mahdi' prophesied in Islamic doctrine to be the 'guided one' who would redeem the Islamic faith and purify the community of the faithful in preparation for Judgement Day"... Riel, then, was also deemed "the Catholic Mahdi of the North West" by the international press.

Riel may have been ahead of his time in some areas; however, he was no interfaith activist. He saw little value outside the Christian tradition. While he expressed some fleeting ecumenical sentiments toward the end of his life and brief openness toward other Christian denominations, he soon reverted to his old intransigent self. There was no place for Judaism, Islam, or other religions in Riel's New World. That being said, Riel did, however, embrace many republican ideals from the Founding Fathers of the United States. He clearly did not view them as secularists but as theists. He would have been startled to learn that Thomas Jefferson was inspired by the Qur'an and the Covenants of the Prophet Muhammad with the Christians and that the Founding Fathers were influenced by Islam.

In part of his revealed scripture, the *Massinahican*, Riel compared the plight of Irish Catholics under British Protestant dominion to that of Spanish Catholics under Arab and Islamic rule. He points out that, despite their constant defeats, the Irish were able to maintain their homogeneity, and national autonomy, even under the iron fist of Cromwell. He wonders whether the Irish would have been able to do so under Qur'anic law. As I have shown in *The Covenants of the Prophet Muhammad with the Christians of the World*, *Islam and the People of the Book*, and *The Messenger of Mercy*, among other works, true, Qur'anic and Muhammadan Islam protects and defends the rights of other faith communities.

6.3 Conclusions

As can be appreciated from the above, Louis Riel was no friend to Islam, the Qur'an, the Prophet Muhammad, and Muslims. To claim that Riel "merely shared the dominant views of the time" does nothing to redeem him, as these were his sincerely held beliefs. Paradoxically, although Riel eventually espoused the principle of religious freedom, he treated the Qur'an with contempt and envisioned its desecration and destruction. He viewed the crusades with nostalgia and lamented that the Christians had failed to conquer the Muslim world. He also yearned for the overthrow of the Ottomans due to their Islamic imperialism.

From an Islamic point of view, it is clear that no believing Muslim can accept Louis Riel as a spiritual or religious leader, much less as a

Prophet, Priest-King, and Infallible Pontiff. Muslims can, however, accept him as a socio-political leader while rejecting his views on all matters related to Islam. The question is, would he have accepted them in his midst whether they were Métis or not? How, for example, would he have reacted to the conversion of his secretary, Honoré Jaxon (1861-1952), born William Henry Jackson, from Riel's newly revealed religion to Bahaism in 1897, a faith that flowered from Islamic foundations? As Jaxon expressed, he embraced the "Bahai Revelation" since "it seeks ... the renewing of that Truth in all religions which constitutes the bond that ties religious people together" (Smith 2008: 103).

Considering that some Métis Nations and organizations have adopted neo-liberalism, leftism, secularism, and illiberalism, that they support the LGBTQ and transsexual movement, and that they have a lovey-dovey relationship with Muslim immigrants and Islamists, Louis Riel, an ultraconservative Christian who was hostile to Islam and whose statements against the faith were even more offensive than those of Salman Rushdie (b. 1947), might be turning in his grave, especially when a conservative scholar like Thomas Flanagan, a controversial figure in his own right, associates the Métis leader's ideology with Islam.

While it is unfair to condemn a man from the nineteenth century based on twenty-first-century standards, it is equally unfair to use a man from the nineteenth century, selectively and deceptively, to promote twenty-first-century ideals that he never espoused. So let us view Louis Riel in the context of his time and place, without rewriting history, pretending that certain postures are not present in his work, or painting a false picture of his complex and compelling personality. People are judged based on what they said and did, not on what they might have said and done.

That being said, it should be stressed that the anti-imperialist struggle of the Métis and the Muslims was the same. By the nineteenth century, the tiny island nation of Britain had created an empire that covered one-fifth of the planet earth. Its supporters boasted that the sun never set on the British Empire. In the process of colonizing the Indigenous and Muslim people of the world, the British murdered and starved millions of human beings. As Robin

Philpot summarizes, the British engaged in "military conquest, bloody repression, massive colonization, and racist domination."

The first man sent to suppress the 1870 Métis uprising in Canada was Garnet Wolseley (1833-1913), who earned the accolades of the British Empire for participating in his murderous colonial wars in India in 1857 and China in 1860, including the pillage and destruction of the Summer Palace in Beijing, which was considered one of the wonders of the world. While governor of the Gold Coast, known today as Ghana, he burned the capital of the Ashanti Kingdom, Kumasi, to the ground. He also fought against the Mahdi rebellion in Sudan and other uprisings in South Africa. The British ended up being defeated in Khartoum by the Mahdi but Wolseley was not blamed. It was Charles George Gordon (1833-1885) who took the blame.

The second man sent to suppress the 1885 Métis rebellion in Canada, General Sir Frederick Dobson Middleton (1825-1898), had a long imperial military history. He served in the New Zealand Wars (1845-1872), where thousands of Maori lives were lost. He participated in the suppression of the Indian Mutiny of 1857, in which nearly one million Indians died due to warfare, famine, and epidemics. Finally, in 1885, he commanded over five thousand troops that were unleashed upon five hundred some odd Métis and First Nations freedom fighters in the Northwest Rebellion. Louis Riel understood that First Nations, Métis, French-Canadians, Irish Catholics, and Americans all shared a common enemy: British imperialism. With his intelligence, it would seem that it was only a matter of time before Louis Riel made common cause with the oppressed of the earth against their imperial overlords. Such recognition would have made the Métis the allies of all anti-imperialists regardless of race or religion. Many contemporary Métis people have come to that conclusion, namely, the need to work with other populations on issues of joint concern.

Chapter 7

LOUIS RIEL'S PSYCHO-SPIRITUAL STATE

7.1 Introduction

Louis Riel was convinced that he was in communication with God and that he received divine revelations. While some of his followers believed that he was a prophet in Indigenous and/or Biblical fashion and converted to his new creed, others concluded that he was mentally insane. The matter, however, is not cut and dry. So, what are we to make of the "revelations" of Riel? A series of sporadic events throughout his life may hold the key.

7.2 Riel's Mental State: Sane or Insane, that is the Question

According to his uncle, John Lee, reports Flanagan, the first time Riel showed "signs of mental alienation" was after the death of his father, whom he adored, in 1864. As Lee put it,

> [H]is heart ... was inconsolable... this profound sorrow was affecting his brain and ... he was delirious. That was obvious in his exaggerations and religious eccentricities; for he threw himself into excesses of piety and spoke on religious matters in a language I found unreasonable. Afterwards, he remained very melancholic.

In 1865, at the age of twenty-one, while he was studying in Montreal, Riel suffered a strange loss of identity experience and started to identify as a Jewish person. From a clinical point of view, this incident might also mark the onset of mental illness. As both Stanley and Littmann report, between February 24 to 27, 1870, at the age of twenty-six, Riel fell ill with "brain fever." What exactly befell him? Did he suffer from meningitis, pneumonia, typhoid fever, or tuberculosis? Or was this some sort of psychological or spiritual crisis?

It should be recalled that Wovoka (c. 1856-1932), the Paiute prophet and second leader of the Ghost Dance Movement, started to have visions after falling into a coma, possibly due to scarlet fever, on January 1, 1889. And when Black Elk (1863-1950) was nine years old, he also became unresponsive due to a life-threatening illness. It was when he fell into a coma due to extremely high fever that he experienced a series of visions. Call it brain damage or the opening of neural gateways, it was fever, in the case of Wovoka, Black Elk, and Louis Riel, that permanently altered their way of seeing the world. A physician, psychologist, or scientist would argue that the physical illness altered the psychological state. A shaman or a mystic would argue that the physical illness was a side-effect of the spiritual awakening.

In any event, on July 14, 1875, Louis Riel received a letter from Bishop Bourget that became "the foundation of his prophetic mission." On December 8, 1875, reports Littmann, Riel underwent "a spiritual experience in Washington, D.C, which he will later consider the commencement of his mission. Other mystical experiences follow in rapid succession." It was there that God appeared to Riel, as He had done to Moses, saying: "Rise up, Louis David Riel, you have a mission to fulfill."

On January 2, 1876, reports Stanley, "Bourget writes to Riel, emphasizing that he should never leave 'the path which divine Providence has laid out for you.' Riel takes this as further proof of his mission." During that same month, notes Martel, Riel's uncle, John Lee, wrote that his nephew would bellow, howl or roar at night. This moaning coincided with the receipt of Riel's revelations which were both auditory and visual. Not surprisingly, notes Stanley, on March 6, 1876, "Riel is committed to the Hospital of St. Jean de Dieu at Longue Pointe." From March to May, notes Stanley, "Riel writes repeatedly to Bishop Bourget about his revelations and implores to be set free. He struggles violently with hospital authorities." On May 19, 1876, writes Stanley,

> Riel is transferred ... to the asylum at Beauport, near Quebec City. At first, he struggles with the hospital authorities, but gradually he becomes more subdued until he is allowed many privileges, such as attending meetings of the ultramontane *Cercle catholique*. He writes prolifically in the hospital about his revelations.

In one of the poems he wrote at the time, he proclaimed that:

> When I speak to you, it is the voice of God that rings.
> And everything that I say is essential to you.
> I am the happy telephone,
> That transmits to you the songs and discourses from heaven.

Between 1884-1885, Stanley reports that "Riel has numerous and intense spiritual experiences... He goes through extremes of exaltation and depression." In 1885, notes Stanley, Riel wrote that his "communication with God" was "continual and taken for insanity." He was convinced that God had granted him a mission: to establish a new Métis Nation in the Northwest where he would be a leader like the biblical David. As Glen Campbell writes, "One of his more important revelations deals with the transfer of the papacy from Rome to Montreal, and ultimately to St. Vital, [Manitoba,] where the Riel family resided... Anyone attempting to thwart this ambitious goal was seen by Riel as an enemy and attacked accordingly."

In his "Revelations Regarding the Laws of the Old Testament," written in Beauport, Quebec, between May 20, 1876, and January 23, 1878, Riel sanctified polygyny, but by the authority of Jesus only permitted men to have a maximum of five wives. In some instances, he even allowed brothers to marry their sisters. As he wrote,

> Has a man delayed marriage until the age of forty? If, perchance, one of his sisters, who has been previously married, becomes a widow: he can ask her in marriage, on the condition that he views the children of his sister as his own.
>
> Has a girl reached the age of thirty without getting married? Let her then see if her brother has the five wives he is permitted to have. If he has less, she has the right to offer her hand to him, for it is the will of God that he takes her in marriage.

> All the marriages that our Lord Jesus Christ permits are filled with blessings.

As Gilles Martel notes, quoting Leviticus 20:17 and Deuteronomy 27:22, "Mosaic law harshly condemned this type of incest" and notes "the situation invoked by Riel was exactly his own." As Flanagan points out, "Riel's theory of polygamy seems to be the fantasy of repressed sexuality... his doctrine of plural marriage emerged like the gluttonous daydreams of a starving man."

Whether he was temporarily healed of his messianic revelations as a result of medication or sedation or whether he had learned to conceal them from those who thought he was insane, Riel was released from Beauport on January 23, 1878. He spent some time in New York, Minnesota, and the Dakota Territory, and then made his way to Montana. During the winter of 1880-1881, while travelling with a band of Métis buffalo hunters in Montana, he started working on a Cree-titled work, the *Massinahican,* which simply means "the Book" or "the Bible." Although the title was in an Indigenous language, one that he spoke, the text was written in French. Perhaps the Cree title indicated the intended audience: Métis and First Nations of the Americas. In any event, only bits and pieces of this work appear to have survived. It was to include the overtly anti-Islamic texts espousing his "Philosophical and Theological System." As Gilles Martel observes,

> The *Massinahican* was intended to be a vast synthesis encompassing a cosmogenesis and a political-religious history of humanity divided into three periods: Mosaic religion, Roman religion, the new religion of the New World, one of ecumenical nature, in which the Métis, and especially the French-Canadian Métis, would play a privileged role.

It was "supposed to have outlined his ideas for a theocratic utopia in western North America." As a prophet of a new religion, some sort of renovated or reformed Catholicism, Riel believed that he needed a new sacred book to guide God's chosen people, the Métis, in the formation and administration of their mixed-blood nation. Riel's doctrine shared similarities with that of Joachim da Fiore (1135-1202), who taught that the Age of the Father (the Old Testament) and the

Age of the Son (the New Testament) would be followed by the Age of the Holy Spirit.

Riel's religious views are also reminiscent of Mormonism. If Brigham Young (1801-1877) saw himself as a "Mormon Moses" who led his followers in an exodus to a promised land in the desert, Riel viewed himself as a Messiah who led the Métis, God's chosen people, to a promised land in the prairies. Joseph Smith (1805-1844), Brigham Young, and Louis Riel all professed to be prophets. They also promoted polygyny. Moreover, if Joseph Smith claimed to have received golden plates from an angel, which were published in English as the *Book of Mormon*, so did Riel claim to have received revelations that were intended to form a scripture, the *Massinahican*. In a prayer to the Virgin Mary, Riel asks her to accept the writings he has produced in good faith, particularly, the *Massinahican*. He adds that the book's publication is destined to cast "fear, dread, and terror" throughout the world.

As Gilles Martel notes, "Riel's *Massinahican* has never been discovered. Probably it never will; if only because we cannot be sure, on such slim evidence, that it even existed." Whether they were all written down, Riel's revelations continued to guide him. Perhaps, like the Qur'an, the *Massinahican* existed in a Heavenly Tablet, was received in auditory fashion, and revealed orally, only to be recorded in writing in stages. By 1885, he was at the head of the Northwest Rebellion, and the diary he kept at the time was filled with "visions, revelations, and prophecies." In a part of the *Massinahican*, likely written between 1880-1881, Riel envisaged an ecumenical New World in which religious denominations were closely connected. There would be a place for Catholics, Episcopalians, Methodists, Lutherans, and Universalists. Riel, it is evident, fluctuated between tolerance and intolerance. By 1885, however, he demanded absolute submission to his leadership and creed.

After declaring a Provisional Government on March 19, 1885, Riel broke with Rome on March 25, declared a four-day fast starting on April 24, established Saturday as the Day of the Lord on April 25, along with declaring that hell was not eternal as this opposed God's mercy. He denied the infallibility of the Church, rejected the

Catholic understanding of the Trinity, and claimed that he was the Comforter, namely, the Paracletes who had come to reform religion following the example of Jesus and Moses.

Some Muslims, it should be noted, make the same claim for the Prophet Muhammad. Many of Riel's Métis followers were convinced he was a prophet like Joshua. He insisted that they only take mass from him. Those who wished to remain faithful to Catholic doctrine were reportedly subjected to insults of all kinds. Rather than focus on issues of importance, Riel devoted an inordinate amount of time to renaming the days of the week as well as the stars. He wanted to change the pagan names to Christian ones.

After the failure of the Northwest Rebellion (March 26-May 12, 1885), Riel recanted his "heresies" in writing and "tried to reformulate his doctrines so as to make them compatible with Catholic orthodoxy." Although this amounted to a "major restatement of his prophetic teaching," he admitted, in writing, that his retraction was "only exterior." In fact, he continued to claim that his writings were divinely inspired. He engaged in pious dissimulation. Such behaviour is also common among esoteric cults and secret societies based on initiation.

When speaking about his revelations, Riel preceded them with words such as "It was said to me" or "The Spirit told me." This is reminiscent of Qur'anic verses that commence with the command: "Say." As Thomas Flanagan notes, Riel "still experienced revelations almost every night. He recorded his perception of these spiritual events in a psychologically interesting note... which compares the communications of his inner voice to the bubbles tremulously rising in a pan of heated liquid." He still insisted that he was a "prophet of the New World" in his defence. As he stated in his "Address to the Court" on August 1, 1885: "I think that, to a certain number of people, the verdict against me today is a proof that maybe I am a prophet, maybe Riel is a prophet, he suffered enough for it." Louis Riel was adamant that he was not insane. He summarized the situation as follows:

> Up to this moment, I have been considered by a certain party as insane... do I appear excited? Am I very irritable? Can I control myself? ... Should I be executed—at least if I were going to be executed—I would not be executed as an insane man.

After the close of the trial, Louis Riel was interviewed by a correspondent of the *Montreal Star* in Regina on August 2, 1885. According to the article, "Riel related his revelations with apparent pride."

On October 31, 1885, a medical commission was appointed to assess Riel's sanity. It should be pointed out that psychology was still in its infancy. Psychology, as a formal field, was established by Wilhelm Wundt (1832-1920) when he founded his laboratory in Germany in 1879. As evidence of Riel's supposed insanity, one of the specialists who testified at his trial, Dr. Daniel Clark, included the claim that he was an "inveterate masturbator." (Flanagan 15-16). At the time, "self-abuse" was viewed as a dangerous mental illness and got people committed to mental asylums. All that was required to lock Riel up in a madhouse in Quebec in 1876 was the certification of a physician that he was a lunatic, an insane person, an idiot, or a person of unsound mind who needed to be confined.

On November 9, 1885, the commission submitted its reports to the Prime Minister. Since the experts were divided, the Canadian Cabinet decided to proceed with the death penalty on the grounds of high treason. As S.K. Littmann has rightly noted, "His ultimate fate was ... not a simple matter of differential psychiatric diagnosis, but of differential political expediency." Riel was hanged at Regina, Saskatchewan, on November 16, 1885, while piously reciting the Lord's Prayer. He faced death calmly, courageously, and with dignity.

The psychological state of Louis Riel has been the subject of serious analysis by physicians and psychiatrists from 1885 to the present. The consensus has been that Riel suffered from megalomania, a chronic, cyclic illness of hypomania and depressive symptoms without episodes of major depression, which in the case of Riel included the following comorbid psychiatric conditions: eating disorders, ADHD, conduct disorders, panic disorders, social phobias, and adjustment disorders. In this, he closely resembled the Jewish false Messiah, Shabbetai Zevi (1626-1676).

After a thorough examination of the case, of which I have only provided a fraction, S.K. Littmann, a professor of psychiatry from the University of Toronto, excluded many conditions and concluded as follows:

> Paranoid schizophrenia typically begins after 30 and is characterized by the presence of persecutory and grandiose delusions, often associated with hallucinations. Excessive religiosity is not uncommon. Behaviour tends to be consistent with the delusions. Personality organization is less frequently disturbed than in the other forms of schizophrenia, and there are remissions. Hostile, grandiose, and hallucinatory sub-types have been recognized. Riel appears to fit the grandiose sub-type of paranoid schizophrenia...
>
> The relationship between prophets and mental illness and the nature of inspiration are beyond the scope of the present pathography. Prophets of the Old Testament were very unusual people. Hosea, Isaiah, Jeremiah, and Ezekiel professed to be, and undoubtedly were ecstatics, and their ecstasy was accompanied or preceded by a variety of pathological states and acts. These included remaining solitary, giving strange symbolic names, having contortions, and falling to the ground or walking naked and barefoot for three days, and others. They were not regarded as mad in their time, but many so-called prophets since then have ended their days in mental hospitals. As regards Riel's claim to be a prophet of the New World, the jury, as it were, is still out until such a time that the relationship of prophecy and psychopathology is examined more closely.

The issue of mental illness, however, is more complex than many scholars have assumed. From a Western perspective, Riel seems to have suffered from some serious psychological issues. He was not, however, legally insane as he was not unable to distinguish between right and wrong. Consequently, from a legal standpoint, he could be held accountable for his actions. However, from an Indigenous perspective, Riel could be seen as an inspired individual who was in communication with God. In fact, Riel pointed out that in Aboriginal culture, people who had visions and could see the future were revered. As he explained,

> If I am insane, of course, I don't know it, it is a property of insanity to be unable to know it... It is said that I had myself been acknowledged as a prophet by the Half-Breeds. The Half-Breeds have some intelligence... It is not to be supposed that the Half-Breeds would have acknowledged me as a prophet if they had not seen that I could see something into the future. If I am blessed without measure, I can see something into the future, we all see into the future more or less... An insane man cannot withhold his insanity, if I am insane my heart will tell what is in me... the Half-Breed hunters can foretell many things... I have seen Half-Breeds who say, my hand is shaking, this part of my hand is shaking you will see such a such thing today, and it happens. Others will say I feel the flesh on my leg move in such a way, it is a sign of such a thing, and it happens... the Half-Breed by the movement of the hand, sometimes of his shoulders, sometimes his legs, can have certain knowledge of what will happen.

Interestingly, up to fifty percent of people who have schizophrenia are not cognizant that they have a mental disorder. However, as a person marinated in a Biblical worldview, it was normal for Riel to interpret his experiences in light of Old Testament prophets and Christian saints. Had he been more familiar with the Islamic tradition, he would have seen that he shared many of the same symptoms as Muhammad.

When the Prophet of Islam would receive a revelation, he would hear the ringing of a bell, which caused him pain or the buzzing of bees around his face. At times he saw the vision of a man, who spoke to him, and the Prophet would remember his words. He would suffer from a crushing feeling so much that if his thigh was on another person, the weight was so great that it felt like it would be crushed. If he were riding, his mount would be compelled to lay down due to the pressure. Even on cold days, the revelations would turn his face red and make him soaked in sweat.

The revelations that Muhammad received were involuntary, and their onset was sudden. When he wanted them to come, they did not come. When he felt they were coming, and he received some during decidedly inconvenient and awkward times, he felt a need for solitude. He had both clear visions and auditory revelations. They took place when he was awake and in a state of sleep. They caused him to tremble and shake. While some non-Muslims have accused

Muhammad of being possessed or suffering from epilepsy or some sort of mental illness, which is offensive to those who believe in him, the point here is that Louis Riel's symptoms of revelation were shared by the Jewish prophets, Christian saints, and Muhammad, the Messenger of God. The experience and its interpretation belong to the same tradition.

In light of these mental health assessments of religious figures, other experts believe these diagnoses do an injustice to both psychology and religion. After surveying the Old Testament, some have provided a psychopathological profile of the Biblical God Yahweh, concluding that the being described probably suffers from a "group/cluster B" personality disorder, highly probably "narcissistic." Not only were these prophets insane, claim certain psychologists, but their God was also a being that for all intents and purposes was a projection of themselves. This places a different interpretation on the saying "To know God is to know oneself."

According to this line of psychological thought, which is irreligious and atheistic, revelation is interior. While it might seem like it comes from above, the voice in one's head comes from one's head. The Greek attributed inspiration to the muses. For Arab polytheists, inspiration came from the jinn or demons. The poets were thus said to be possessed by the jinn. Since Muhammad did not believe in pagan gods, he rejected such a claim. Since he believed in but one God, the inspiration could only come from Him. As a Christian, Catholic, and Indigenous person, Louis Riel could only interpret the voices he heard and the visions he saw in the context of his own particular culture. For religious people, this is a shallow and hollow explanation of spirituality devised by those without faith.

So, what are we to make of Louis Riel's psychological state? Except for some of his "revelations," which might seem insane to certain readers, but only make up a small portion of the thousands of pages that he wrote, the near totality of his literary output is perfectly sane. In fact, it is brilliant.

Had his revelations not been published, there would have been scant evidence to claim that he was insane. Although it can be claimed that Riel suffered from mental illness, and had psychotic episodes, it can also be claimed that he formed part of a long line of mystics and messianic figures. The literary works he produced when he was supposedly insane seem far too lucid and coherent to be the product of a person with serious, negative, psychological issues. Moreover, the revelations Riel recorded are no more insane than those found in the scriptures of many world religions. To be quite fair, they are sometimes even saner.

Although some psychologists have retroactively diagnosed Biblical figures as suffering from psychotic disorders, they admit their behaviour does not exclude a role for the supernatural. Perhaps the same parts of the brain are activated during the revelatory experience, the creative process, and certain mental illnesses. Case in point, "as many as sixty percent of those with schizophrenia," notes Evan D. Murray, "have grandiose religious delusions consisting of believing they are a saint, God, the devil, a prophet, Jesus, or some other important person." Consequently, while truth can be found in the positive revelations that certain people receive, psychologists warn that it would be wise not to take them too literally.

The link between creativity and schizophrenia has been studied extensively. The findings suggest that full-blown schizophrenia is not associated with higher creativity, unlike milder forms. Hence, the distinction between negative and positive schizotypy. What is more, people who are bipolar tend to be more creative. Hence, "there is a grain of truth to the notion that creativity and mental illness are related." In fact, creative people are more likely to carry genes associated with schizophrenia and bipolar disorder.

Was Louis Riel hearing voices? Or was he hearing his inner voice? Was he a madman? Or was he an inspired, enthusiastic, charismatic, and illuminated person? Riel suffered from extreme highs and lows. Was he bipolar? Such people can become euphoric during their manic phase. Or was he consciously adopting a prophetic voice for literary and political purposes? This was not the case. He channelled his creative impulses and original thoughts in a way that made religious and cultural sense to himself as a Métis and a Christian. Had he been raised as a Muslim his spiritual experiences would have taken on Islamic dimensions. He might have been a Sufi sage.

As Riel clearly stated himself, he believed that the New World needed a new prophet, a new scripture, and a new religion. Abandoned by the Church, which purportedly placed profits over principles, Riel tried to fill a socio-spiritual void by inspiring and uniting the Métis people. He had advised his followers not to love the priests since they did not follow God's law. In his words, "They only want to convert the world to make money." The hypocrisy of the Christians was observed and condemned by many Native American wise men, not the least of which was Ohiyesa. Gabriel Dumont had also come to the same conclusions after Catholic priests had betrayed the Métis, excommunicated their combatants, and transmitted their battle plans to their enemies. "At that time, we were ignorant," he stated, "and the words of priests were synonymous with truth." "Since then," he added, "we have learned a few things and we know that they are perfectly capable of lying to us."

When it comes to the psychological state of Louis Riel, Charles Upton, the metaphysician, expressed the following:

> Sane and insane are relative. The Sufis have always recognized the existence of holy madmen who bring news from Allah but who are too imbalanced to keep the shariah, [namely, Islamic law], and so should never be taken as murshids [or spiritual guides].
>
> Schizophrenics are sometimes known to possess real psychic talents. There are stories of their ability to see demons, know who in the asylum a particular demon is attacking, and have paranormal insight into the state of other inmates. Jungian analyst Marie-Louise Von Franz said that many schizophrenics resist treatment because they know that if they are cured, they will lose their psychic powers.
>
> It seems that Louis Riel had a "sub-personality" that was psychically imbalanced and also able to see beyond ordinary reality, but since the greater part of his personality was sane and stable, he was able to function on a fairly high level. He was clearly not a prophet of God, but he was a visionary, and some of his visions seem to have had a kernel of truth. He also appears to have been bipolar to a degree. Qualities that would indicate insanity if they were dominant in an individual's personality can sometimes prove useful if they are kept in check by

> a strong character and a clear intelligence, though not without cost in terms of personal suffering. This describes the psychic makeup of many artistic types.
>
> Riel's "brain fever" episode exhibits some of the characteristics of a shamanic crisis. As for his hearing voices, sometimes this only indicates that one is unusually sensitive to one's own thoughts and so able to recognize the largely autonomous character of thought. We believe that we think our own thoughts, but the phrase "it occurred to me" demonstrates that this is not always the case. Huston Smith, I think following Bergson, described the brain not as an organ that generates thought but as an apparatus for receiving thoughts from the surrounding psychic medium: "The brain breathes thoughts like the lungs breathe air."
>
> Wovoka's visions did not turn out very well for the Lakota when they believed in them, yet the return of the buffalo is now beginning to be a reality... visions usually have a negative result when taken literally; taking visions literally is perhaps one of the definitions of insanity... yet we ignore them at our peril. With the right kind of interpretation, they can provide an important extra dimension to our lives....

Louis Riel, after all, was like a shaman to some of the Métis. He was a prophetic figure. So long as he could function, so long as he was practical, so long as his visions were good, as opposed to evil, and so long as he could function in society, and lead men, he was viewed as a messianic visionary. Even the American Psychological Association distinguishes between adaptive and maladaptive expressions of religious experience. The summary of *Louis "David" Riel: Prophet of the New World* says it all:

> Louis Riel believed that on 8 December 1875, he received a divine commission authorizing him to save the Métis and reform the Catholic Church. He was a prophet, inspired by the Holy Spirit, and the Métis were the new chosen people. A new branch of the Catholic Church would be founded in North America, with its first Holy See in Montreal and its second in Riel's birthplace of St Vital. When Riel expressed these views in 1876, he was committed to a lunatic asylum. After his release, he suppressed his ideas for several years, only to reveal them again to his Métis followers during the Northwest

Rebellion. The Rebellion thus became as much a religious as a political movement; to the end of his life, Riel believed himself a prophet, and he went to his death thinking that he, like Christ, would be resurrected on the third day. Earlier writers about Louis Riel noted his religious beliefs but did not take them seriously. They usually dismissed Riel's attempt to found a new religion as a symptom of a deranged mind. Thomas Flanagan takes Riel's religion seriously and analyses it using categories developed in the literature about millenarian movements. He shows that Riel's religion, far from being simply individual madness, is typical of the nativistic and millenarian movements described by one author as the "religions of the oppressed."

7.3 Conclusions

Louis Riel was a man of superlative talent and ability. He was intelligent, talented, gifted, creative, passionate, and charismatic. He was very much a leader of men. Upon examining his case, some psychologists would conclude that, like many geniuses, Riel's brilliance verged on mental illness, and, on some occasions, he seems to have crossed the line from sanity to insanity. This was the diagnosis of the medical authorities who examined him in Quebec. In their view, he suffered from delusions of grandeur.

For S.K. Littmann, a psychiatrist who examined his case in the late nineteen seventies, Riel fit the profile of a paranoid schizophrenic of the grandiose subtype. Other specialists concluded that he suffered from megalomania and some comorbid conditions. Other scholars, who are not medical professionals, psychologists, psychiatrists, or licensed mental health therapists, have attempted to dismiss allegations of mental illness as a strategy used by his legal defence and a tool used by his enemies, claiming instead that Riel was simply "excitable." Such people have never read the entirety of his writings. Although they are not remotely qualified to diagnose, they do so based on a glance as opposed to meticulous study and analysis.

Riel, like many gifted and creative people, exhibited symptoms of Bipolar I Disorder. During the manic episode, he would have manifested decreased need for sleep, increased or faster speech, rapid cycling, uncontrollable racing thoughts or quickly changing ideas or topics when speaking; distractibility, increased activity, and increased risky behaviour. In his case, this would have been accompanied by disorganized thinking, false beliefs and/or hallucinations. During the major depressive episode, Riel would have suffered from intense sadness or despair, loss of interest in everyday activities, feelings of guilt, fatigue, increased or decreased sleep, increased or decreased appetite, restlessness, pacing, or slowed speech or movement, difficulty concentration, and frequent thoughts of death. By Jove, I think we've got it. If the hat fits, then let him wear it.

As can be appreciated from his behaviour and writings, Riel manifested all these aforementioned symptoms. He regularly contemplated death so much that it can be said he had a death wish. This was well-known to his close companions. As he told his wife after Batoche, "I know the Good Lord wants me to die." If Gabriel Dumont refused to surrender at the battle, stating that "I will not lay down my arms—I will fight forever. And the first who comes for me, I will kill," Riel was determined to die a martyr, believing he would be resurrected on the third day. If my psychological analysis is correct, then Louis Riel was not insane or a madman, as he has been made to be to stigmatize and delegitimize him.

Terms like "crazy" are pejorative. Bipolar people may think differently and have different emotional responses. They may have dramatic shifts in mood, energy, and ability. However, they are not insane. Those who are "insane," a term largely abandoned in psychology, and used mainly in law, suffer from severe mental illness. They cannot distinguish fantasy from reality. They cannot function due to psychosis. They are subject to uncontrollable impulsive behaviours. People who are bipolar have a mental health disorder that is caused by the central nervous system and the brain. Compared to other disorders, it is one that is more desirable.

If he was indeed bipolar, Louis Riel was like many artists, authors, and musicians that we admire. He was not like calm, flat, water, that looked like glass. He used to ride the waves with their regular ebb and flow. Occasionally, their crest was considerable, and the ups and downs that he experienced could be extreme. Overall, despite days in the dungeon of darkness and wild nights of euphoria, he was able to function at a very high level, work, write, organize, lead, and wage war. He was not spiritually, emotionally, and psychologically inert. He was not a corpse. He was a living, breathing, and vibrant human being filled with feelings. It was the conquerors, colonizers, imperialists, enslavers, exploiters, plunderers, rapists, and mass murderers who perpetuated genocide who were truly insane, morally insane, sociopathic, and psychopathic.

From a religious perspective, be it Indigenous, Jewish, Christian, or Islamic, Louis Riel was an illuminated, enlightened, and inspired man in the mold of prophetic, messianic, and apocalyptic leaders such as Joseph Smith (1830-1844), William Miller (1782-1849), Muhammad Ahmad (1844-1885), Mirza Ghulam Ahmad (1835-1908), Wodziwob (d. c. 1872) and Wovoka (c. 1856-1932), leaders of the Ghost Dance Movement, as well as W.D. Fard (disappeared in 1934) and Elijah Muhammad (1897-1975) from the Nation of Islam, among many others. Obviously, Riel cannot be considered part of the orthodox tradition. At the very least, he was heterodox, if not heretical, according to the mainstream of these faith traditions. Ultimately, in matters of religion, success or failure is what distinguishes between a true prophet and a false prophet and between sanity and insanity. Faith prevails over reason, and spirituality trumps science. Whether or not he was a divinely inspired prophet or the Messiah, Louis Riel was most certainly a remarkable revolutionary leader and a martyr for the Métis people. Flaws can be forgiven. He put his principles into action and gave his life in defence of the destitute and dispossessed. Consequently, his accomplishments outweigh any of his shortcomings.

Chapter 8

LOUIS RIEL AND QUEBEC

"Québec! Province chérie! Oublieras-tu jamais tes Métis-Canadiens." Louis Riel

8.1 Introduction

Louis Riel viewed Quebec as the mother of the Métis, the cradle and bastion of Métis culture, a source of cultural and Catholic inspiration, the political defender of the Métis people, and a symbol of the quest for sovereignty and self-determination as a French-Canadian nation within an English-dominated nation. It was the land where his father, born in the Northwest, had lived most of his childhood. It was the land of all his grandparents. It was also the land where Louis Riel himself went to college.

Gabriel Dumont, whose grandfather had come from Quebec, insisted that French-Canadians and Métis French-Canadians had indissoluble ideological and religious ties, as well as a shared identity tracing back to the arrival of the first settlers in Eastern Canada. "Since I left Batoche, after the war," affirmed Dumont, "I always wanted to come to this beautiful Province of Quebec, to be with our people." Likewise, Louis Riel considered French-Canadians from Quebec to be his cousins, and Quebec to be the land of his ancestors and family members. The Métis, in his mind, were the children of Quebec.

8.2 Quebec: The Mother of the Métis

True to history, in which he was well-versed, Louis Riel recognized that the Métis originated in New France, in Lower Canada, in the Province of Quebec. He sang its praises in "O Québec," a poem he composed in St. Joseph, between the months of September and December 1870. It reads:

Quebec! Mother Colony!
You were loved by our ancestors!
And throughout my life
I will love your sweet name, always pronouncing it.

Quebec! Dear province!
Will you ever forget your Métis [French] Canadians!
Of Manitoba betrayed
Your children, O Quebec, are nevertheless the supporters!

Enemies to be feared
Threatening the cradle of your darling children.
But they won't be able to reach,
O Quebec! Despite you, never our country!

May holy Providence
Inspire your men from Ottawa to favour us.
Remember how much France
Hurt you, O Quebec, when she forgot you!

Noble country! Your courage
Makes you look great after a century of fighting!
Accept the beautiful omen
Immortal Pius-Neuf blessing your soldiers!

You who provide zouaves
For the Church, would you never suffer
to see your brave ones crushed,
Your proud children of the North who are heirs to your Heart!

As Riel acknowledged, Quebec was the Mother Colony of the Métis. As it is only natural for children to love their mothers, the ancestors of the Métis of Riel's time had a great love for the Province of

Quebec. Riel himself shared this love. He loved the name *Québec*. He took pleasure in pronouncing its name. It was his dear province. Invoking Quebec, he wonders whether the province will one day forget the Métis Canadians from Manitoba betrayed, reminding Quebec that its children, the Métis, are its very foundation. Ironically, the opposite would come to pass. Instead of Quebec forgetting about the Western Métis, some of the Western Métis have forgotten about Quebec, their place of origin, genesis, dispersion, and exodus. Quebec, however, has always shown great concern for the rights and conditions of French-speaking people throughout Canada and the survival and transmission of the French-Canadian language and culture. The people of Quebec strongly supported Riel and his rebellion against English Canada. As Adolphe Ouimet notes,

> As was its right and its duty, the Province of Quebec placed itself at the head of the movement, and we saw, for a certain time, like the good old days of our glorious political struggles of the past, reign unity among the descendants of the great French-Canadian Catholic family.

In the mind of Riel, the enemy of the Métis were the enemy of Quebec: British Canadians. They were what Gabriel Dumont considered to be the natural enemies of the French-Canadians and the Métis. And while Riel was concerned about the plight of the Métis of the West, he was confident that English-speaking Canadians would never dominate Quebec, our country, as he described it, namely, the country of the French-Canadian Métis and French-Canadians. He prayed that Holy Provenance would inspire the politicians from Quebec, who served in Ottawa, to remember the French-Canadian Métis from the West. He reminded the people of Quebec how painful it was for them when France forgot about them, abandoning them to the English conquerors and occupiers.

For Riel, Quebec was a noble and courageous country, a distinct nation that has struggled to survive linguistically, religiously, and culturally for over a century of British rule. He urged Quebec to accept the blessings of Pope Pius XIX (1792-1878). He was confident that Quebec, a province that provided zouaves or light infantrymen for the Church, would never suffer to see its brave and proud children of the North, the Métis, crushed, as they have inherited and embody the very heart of Quebec.

8.3 Quebec: A Source of Cultural Inspiration

In his "Letter to Ignace Bourget," written in Montreal in April 1875, Louis Riel acknowledged that "the province of Quebec exerts all its influence on the Métis people and makes them submit to it. The Métis of Manitoba cannot help copying Lower Canada." Riel viewed Quebec culture in a positive light. It was a source of inspiration and emulation for the Métis outside their Motherland. It could be argued that the Métis of Quebec should also continue to inspire Western Métis and the Métis of the United States for the simple fact that they have preserved their language and culture to a greater extent than some of the Métis from western lands, with obvious exceptions, of course. Consequently, they can help reconnect the English-speaking Métis with their original French language, as well as other aspects of their culture that were lost due to various degrees of assimilation and acculturation. The more French-Canadian they become, the more Métis they become.

8.4 Quebec: A Fountain of Catholic Inspiration

If the Métis of the West looked to Quebec for cultural inspiration, they also looked towards it for religious guidance and instruction. As far as Louis Riel was concerned, Quebec played a crucial role in ensuring that all French-Canadians and Métis adhered to the Catholic program. Riel understood the central role played by religion in matters of identity. The Métis shared the same French blood as the people of Quebec. They shared the same language and much of the same culture. Moreover, they shared the same Catholic religion, which helped encourage group cohesion. While some Métis have changed their religious affiliations over time, and others have become increasingly secularized, a greater proportion of Quebec Métis identify as Catholic as opposed to the Métis of the West. Some, however, in response to the Quiet Revolution, the rise of secularism, and the virtual abandonment of Catholicism on the part of Quebeckers, have decided to follow the "Red Road," embracing the spirituality of the Indigenous people from the Eastern Woodlands and the Prairies, and adhering to the Grandfather Teachings.

In his poem, "The French-Canadian Métis People," written down at St. Peter's Mission, Montana, in August 1883, Riel expressed his confidence that the French-Canadian clergy, ostensibly emanating from Quebec, would play a central role in uniting the Métis people: "The clergy who build us up / Will unite us of course." After all, as he wrote in "Some Good French People from Overseas are Our Hosts," written at St. Peter's Mission, Montana, around 1883,

> The Métis are charitable.
> And the [French] Canadian is manageable.
> The good French have grown up
> To defend the church. Beautiful is her page in
> History! He must spread
> His faith that has not failed him.

8.5 Quebec: The Political Defender of the Métis

Ironically, while some Western Métis political organizations and leaders have essentially disowned the Métis of Quebec, Louis Riel praised the province of Quebec for defending the Métis people. In his "Letter 'To the Electorate of the District of Provencher and to my Fellow Compatriots from Manitoba,' written in Worcester on June 16, 1875, he expressed his gratitude to the solidarity shown by the province of Quebec:

> The province of Quebec stood up to defend us and made its most eloquent voices heard in our favour. Its generous and powerful support has been invaluable to us, and it is through it, I have the firm hope, that justice will one day be rendered to us.

In a letter that he wrote to Louis-Rodrigue Masson (1833-1903), Minister of Parliament for Terrebonne, Riel described Quebec as a province "which is all our support, which loves us and which we love: this is the country of our fathers." "Given the bond between language and religion in Quebec," notes Raymond Huel, "Riel could not but associate the Métis to the French Catholic element and count on the latter's support."

8.6 The Nation of Quebec: The Precursor of the Métis Nation

While Western Métis political organizations claim nationhood, sovereignty, and its privileges, some apparently ignore, willfully or cunningly, the fact that the Nation of Quebec inspired the very concept of a Métis nation. Riel did not look to the First Nations for inspiration when he wanted to build a nation for the Métis people. What he took from the Métis and the Cree was democracy. For a fuller, more complete, political model, he looked to Quebec. Although it was colonized, it was, very much, in his mind, a distinct society linguistically, culturally, and religiously. Although it was not politically independent, and remained occupied and colonized by the British, in his estimation, Quebec was a nation, albeit a nation within a nation. In this regard, his "Letter to Paul Proulx," written in Beauport on May 10, 1877, is revealing. It reads:

> I would like, with the help of God, to work to make the French-Canadian Métis people great enough to be the heirs of Lower Canada [i.e. Quebec], in the same way that a good son receives and benefits from the goods that are bequeathed to him by his parents...

As Riel expressed, he wanted to build up the French-Canadian Métis people so that they would be worthy to inherit the heritage of Quebec like a son receives and benefits from the property bequeathed by his parents. For Riel, the Métis were the product and progeny of Quebec.

8.7 Conclusions

As can be appreciated from a study of his writings, Louis Riel loved Quebec to the core. He considered Quebec to be the Motherland of the Métis. It was like Israel to the exiled and dispersed Jews: the ancestral homeland that one longs for even after establishing oneself in other lands. Regardless of where the Métis would be found, they would view Quebec as a source of cultural and religious inspiration. What is more, in the mind of Riel, Quebec served as a political and economic model for nation-building. New France may have been conquered. Lower Canada may have become a British colony, and Quebec may have become a province of English-dominated Canada. However, the Canadians, namely, the French-Canadians, who later identified as Québécois, were able to preserve their language, culture, and religion. They were like a French-speaking island in an English ocean. Increasingly they would control their political and economic destiny, and despite thwarted attempts at independence through sovereignty referendums, they remained a distinct culture and a nation within Canada. The vision that Louis Riel had for the Métis Nation was inspired by his vision of the Quebec Nation. A people seeking sovereignty needed support. For Riel, the natural ally and advocate of the Métis people and their national aspirations was none other than Quebec.

Chapter 9

LOUIS RIEL AND THE FRENCH-CANADIANS

"Dieu veut se servir de nous tous pour fonder le peuple Métis-Canadien-Français." Louis Riel

9.1 Introduction

Louis Riel loved Quebec: its history, its geography, its language, its people, its religion, its literature, its music, its food, and its culture. It was his ancestral homeland and the land of his relatives and family. It was a cultural anchor, a source of pride, and a shining beacon of political inspiration in the struggle against colonialism and imperialism.

9.2 The French-Canadians and the Métis: All for One and One for All

In his "Letter to N.-J. Ritchot," written in Montreal on October 5, 1774, and addressed to a priest who was deeply involved with the activist Métis from the Red River Settlement, Louis Riel criticized a group of French-Canadian politicians who refused to advocate on behalf of the Métis of the Northwest. In his words,

> When the French-Canadians deal with the question of the Northwest, by telling themselves and showing that they do not want to make it a question of race and religion, the organized fanaticism of Ontario resumes its usual uproar... The Province of Quebec would only have to frankly accept the question of race and religion and say to Ontario: You attack me as such, I defend myself as such.

To further consolidate the "small Métis people," Louis Riel encouraged the large-scale immigration of French-Canadians from Quebec to the Province of Manitoba. In his words:

> I told Monsieur Royal to take the autonomy of the Métis people to mind and heart, to encourage all possible French-Canadian emigration to Manitoba, with the firm and avowed goal of protecting the Métis people founded in the Northwest by the Province of Quebec and ensuring that they multiply. This will have the great advantage of eliminating a great deal of mistrust between the Métis and a certain nucleus of French-Canadians. The arrival of [French] Canadians among us will please us. Consequently, the contented Métis will adopt a greater sum of French-Canadian mores and traditions in such a way that while calling us the Métis people, we are in fact, effortlessly and with the best grace in the world, identified with the Province of Quebec, through education. Which is very desirable, it seems to me.

9.3 French-Canadian: The Family Name of the Métis

In his "Letter to Paul Proulx," written in Beauport on May 10, 1877, Louis Riel was adamant that the Métis people belonged to the French-Canadian family. As he explains,

> And if you ask me why I don't want our people to be called French-Canadian, quite simply, I will answer you that this name is already its last name. Consequently, it is befitting to give it another name, one that designates it specifically and which is, in a way, its baptismal name as a people.

For Riel, French-Canadian was a family name. The Métis, the Acadians, and all the Francophone population of Canada and North America belonged to the French-Canadian family.

If Riel opted for Métis, accompanied by French-Canadian, as an identifier, it was precisely because it was an inclusive name, as opposed to an exclusive one. He did not want the Métis to be parochial in perspective or to limit the term to a small or specific historical or geographical community. He wanted the Métis community to be large and strong as there is strength in numbers. Riel wanted the "little Métis flock" to think vast and compared the foundation of the French-Canadian Métis people to that of a fabric yet to be quilted. It is possible that he was imagining the Métis sash with its threads of diverse colours. As he explains,

> And when the material is finished, it will be French material, because the workers of the beautiful profession of France will have worked there. It will be a truly Canadian fabric because our weavers were true Canadians at heart. It will be a French-Canadian Métis fabric. Let us not have worries. French, [French] Canadians and Métis, let us work together, not only without suspicion, but with a great deal of friendship, as God wishes to use us all to create the foundation of the Métis-French-Canadian people.

In the eyes and mind of Riel, the final product of this process would be a French fabric since the French contributed to it. It would be a [French] Canadian fabric as the weavers were [French] Canadian in their moral fibre. It would thus be a French-Canadian Métis fabric. He believed that the French, French-Canadians, and Métis needed to work together, without mistrust, to jointly pour the foundation of the French-Canadian Métis people.

In "Some Good French People from Overseas are our Hosts," written at St. Peter's Mission, Montana, around 1883, Louis Riel described the Métis as "three-bloods." He stated that the Métis drew the best out of the righteousness of the Indians. He believed that "our good French-Canadian qualities / correct the shortcomings of our Indian blood." He felt that the virtues that the Métis received from the First Nations kept some of their bad qualities in check. When all is said and done, Riel asks:

> In the three-blooded race, is it the [French] Canadian,
> the French or the Métis whose example
> Deserves more to be admired?
> Which of the three does the most good?

Consequently, Riel valued the contributions that the Métis had received from the First Nations, the French, and the French-Canadians. In "The French-Canadian Métis People," composed at St. Peter's Mission, Montana, in August of 1883, he praised the qualities of the three-blooded race:

I love beyond measure, and I admire
the French-Canadian Métis.
This new people
that has already made great accomplishments.

Since their ethnogenesis was relatively recent, dating back to the seventeenth century, he viewed the Métis as a "new people" which had already accomplished incredible feats. Case in point:

It makes its glory known
To the Indians of Minnesota.
It was always victorious
Over the tribes of Dakota.

Although the Métis eventually made peace with the Lakota people, who originated from Minnesota, but were pushed out by the Ojibwe, settling in the Dakotas and Manitoba in the 1700s, this was only after a period of conflict, including the battle of Grand Cocteau, located southeast of what is now Minot, North Dakota, which took place between July 12 and 14, 1851.

Among the achievements of the Métis, and the priests that always guided them, Riel recalls the foundation of the province of Manitoba:

Although it is young
Manitoba is great because it was founded
Under the beautiful guidance of the Priesthood
Which has always guided it so well.

The mixed origins of the Métis, and the hyphenation of Métis and French-Canadian, are not negatives in the eyes of Riel: they are a positive:

If a hyphen is placed
Between Métis and [French] Canadian;
Both races assure
that it will be all for the better.

The Métis leader praises the qualities of the French-Canadians, including their knowledge of politics and governance, which they learned from Anglo-Saxon rule. Although he adamantly opposed Anglo-Protestant imperialism, Louis Riel was an admirer of the Anglo-Saxon race. He viewed them as a great and glorious race and believed that "the English constitution is an institution which has been perfected for the nations of the world." It was due to Anglo influence, Riel believed, that French-Canadians made good, firm, diplomats. He was very clear when it came to the French and Francophone identity of the Métis. For him, both Métis and French-Canadians were French:

> Métis and Canadians are together
> French, if our three elements
> Fuse together well, it seems to me
> That we will one day be greater.

He also accepted the cultural contributions from Ireland and Scotland, as some Métis were of partial Celtic ancestry from their paternal side.

> The three leaves of the clover can
> Exist on the same footing.
> All three, pretty, move
> In unison, as they see fit.

Riel was well aware that the Métis people has suffered considerably in their struggle to create the nation of Manitoba which he viewed as a French-Canadian Métis nation:

> Its big heart takes a lot of pain
> To consolidate, I know it,
> The Manitoba Nation
> French-Canadian Métis.

Consequently, he wanted "the French-Canadians to come and help us there today, tomorrow." After, he states that the Fathers of the Métis were "les Francs et les Canadiens" [the French and the (French) Canadians]. Clearly, the nation that Louis Riel founded was inclusive of French-Canadians. In 1885, Riel had the Métis warriors of Batoche, Saskatchewan, swear before God that they would be "faithful to the movement of the French-Canadian Métis and their Provisional Government."

9.4 French-Canadian Métis Unity

Louis Riel was not one to divide. He was one to unite. He expressed his dislike for those who tried to play the Métis and the French-Canadians against one another. As he expressed in his "Letter to Pierre Lavallée," written in St. Vital, Manitoba, in August of 1883,

> At all costs, the Métis and French-Canadians must cease maliciously reproaching one another for their faults. "The kindness of the Métis and the generosity of the French-Canadians are called to come together; so that the Métis become more [French] Canadian through [French] Canadian virtues, and the [French] Canadians become more Métis through the admirable virtues which the Métis possess as a primitive people. This is a must: let's be Métis [French] Canadians."

Not only did he want French-Canadians to become more Métis, but he also wanted the Métis to become more French-Canadian. He wanted them to honour both sides of their heritage: the First Nations and the French-Canadian. They were a synthesis, not polar opposites. They existed in symbiosis.

9.5 Conclusion

As far as Louis Riel was concerned, the Métis were tri-racial: French, French-Canadian, and First Nations. They were the product of racial and cultural amalgamation. The result was a New People, and a New Nation, the Métis, who belonged to the French-Canadian family. They were not just French. They were not just French-Canadian. They were not just First Nations. They were French-Canadian Métis. As a proud people, who honoured their ancestors and relations, no part of the family could be ignored, and the bridges between any of these groups could not be burned. Being Métis was not about severing ties of kinship: it was about strengthening them while, at the same time, asserting one's unique characteristics.

Chapter 10

LOUIS RIEL AND THE FRENCH LANGUAGE

"Notre langue française... La langue de nos chers aïeux." Louis Riel

10.1 Introduction

Although he was multilingual, speaking English, Cree, and French, Louis Riel had a profound and undying love for the French language. After all, it was his maternal language, the language of his family, the language of his people, and the central language of the Métis Nation. It was a unifying factor and the means through which Métis culture was predominantly transmitted. Consequently, it was only natural for Louis Riel to be a staunch defender of the French language in North America. A nation, he had learned from Europeans, was built upon language, borders, and culture. He was intent on building one, and it would be a French-speaking one in the heart of North America.

10.2 Louis Riel's French-Canadian French

Although Riel spoke Métis French with other Métis, a dialect of French-Canadian with some substrata from Indigenous languages, "Canadian French was the language of the family home." As Roger Motut explains,

> His Lagimodière grandparents both came from Quebec. Their daughter, Julie, mother of Louis Riel, had learned her language from her parents. Louis Riel, Sr., had been brought up in the East and had studied

> for two years with the Oblates newly arrived from France. We are allowed to believe that in this family environment, the French that was spoken was a little more refined than that of other families in Red River. This was not always the case for Louis' little comrades from mixed marriages, who often spoke both the languages of their fathers and mothers, and whose languages influenced each other in that bilingual environment, producing a French dialect with its own identity.

Although he spoke the Métis variety of Canadian French that was particular to the Prairies, "nothing in the writings of Louis Riel, except perhaps, a few words and expressions ... suggests any knowledge that Louis Riel had of the language of the Métis." As Motut explains, "If he called himself Métis, it was because he belonged to this people by other ties than those of the spoken language."

It would even seem that the Riels were proud to speak good French. Sara, the sister of Louis, who was educated in Western Canada, learned to read and to write in the little school founded by Mgr. Provencher, which was under the direction of nuns, and seems to have acquired a rather snobbish attitude toward Métis French. In linguistically elite fashion, she complained that the Métis "speak a French jargon which is ugly to hear." Likewise, Louis Riel had a sound mastery of the standard French language acquired from elementary school under the direction of monks and nuns, a year of Latin under Father LeFloch, and studying at the College of the Sulpicians of Montreal, which later became the Collège de Montréal. His grades indicate that he was an intelligent and gifted student. As Motut points out,

> The reader who has taken the trouble to read the entire work of Louis Riel, as commented on and set out in the pages written in French, of the four volumes, will quickly realize that Louis Riel mastered his mother tongue. He mastered it to the point of being able to use it to express himself in verse, despite all the complexities of French versification that make it difficult to compose a clear and understandable message.

10.3 French: The Language of the Métis

Riel acknowledges the centrality of the French language to the Métis. He writes:

Let us endow our French language
With beautiful foreign words
So that it may be even richer
In these new parts.

Let us borrow choice expression
From the Indian languages
Some of their images
Some of their beautiful phrases.

These novelties will strengthen
The language of our dear ancestors.
Let's embellish it that way

While he spoke French, Cree, and English, "Louis Riel... did not speak Michif." As far as Riel was concerned, the language of the Métis was not Cree, Cree Michif, or even French Michif: it was French. He called for spicing up the French language with words and expressions drawn from Indigenous languages. At no point did he promote the creation of a pidgin, a mixed language, or a new language as that would have disconnected the Métis from other Francophones, isolating them and making them an even smaller minority. As Louis Riel stated in his "Letter to Pierre Lavallée," written in St. Vital, Manitoba, in August 1883: "Let's be proud to be French. The French language is one of the most beautiful languages in the world and certainly the most polite of all. We love the French very much. Let's be Métis-French-Canadian."

10.4 Conclusions

As much as certain Western Métis may wish to promote some mythical Michif as the language of the Métis, neither history nor linguistics support this contentious, politically motivated claim. The primary language of the Métis people, throughout most of their history, has always been the Métis variety of Canadian French. It is French Métis, not Cree Michif, and certainly not Michif, a mixed language that was only spoken by a small number of semi-nomadic bison hunters in the prairies. These are indeed Métis languages; however, they were always peripheral and local, with no literature of any significance, not something that should be promoted at the expense of French, a global means of communication, with a rich and vast literature. The language of the vast majority of Métis was French Métis, namely, a form of Canadian French with its own unique characteristics.

Chapter 11

LOUIS RIEL AND THE IRISH

"Connaissez-moi: Presque tout mon sang vient de la France; j'en ai de l'Irlande; et j'ai du sang sauvage." Louis Riel

11.1 Introduction

As a person of professed Irish ancestry, who suffered not from hatred of self and was a person of pride and dignity, Louis Riel loved the Irish people, identified with them as fellow victims of British imperialism, and supported their just struggle for sovereignty and independence. To the best of his ability, he strove to unite First Nations, Métis, French-Canadians, and Irish Catholics in a common front against Great Britain and its Commonwealth.

11.2 Irish Pride

As we saw in chapter two, Louis Riel claimed to have Irish blood and praised his sister's "Métis-Celtic spirit." We also noted that his purported Irish ancestry, which traces back to Limerick, Ireland, was genealogically problematic. It is possible that his European ancestors were Franco-Irish, people of French ancestry who lived in Ireland. However, it cannot be excluded that they were genuinely Irish. That being said, statements made by Riel in his "Address to the Court," dated August 1, 1885, further complicate matters. On this occasion, he claimed that his forefathers originally came from Scandinavia. In his words,

> I don't abandon my ancestors... My ancestors were amongst those that came from Scandinavia and the British Isles 1,000 years ago. Some of them went to Limerick, and were called Reilson, and then they crossed into Canada, and they were called Riel; so in me there is Scandinavian, and well rooted; there is the Irish, and there is the French, and there is some Indian blood.

Either way, Riel admired the "originality, wit, and unsurpassed courage" of the Irish and praised them for their attachment to the Catholic faith.

11.3 The Fenians: The Irish Republican Brotherhood

Louis Riel entertained a long relationship with Irish Catholic nationalists. In fact, he appointed William Bernard O'Donoghue (1843-1878), an American Canadian born in County Sligo, Ireland, and Fenian leader, as treasurer of the Provisional Government that was established at the Red River Colony during the 1869-1870 Red River Rebellion.

After the collapse of the Provisional Government, Riel fled to the United States in the company of O'Donoghue where they had a falling out. The Irishman argued that they should ask the American government to intercede on behalf of the Métis. Riel, however, was adamantly opposed to the idea as a violation of sovereignty. O'Donoghue viewed Riel as too soft on the British, whereas Riel was concerned that O'Donoghue cared more about striking out at Britain than the plight of the Métis people. In time, however, Riel would change his attitude and emphatically asked the United States to invade and liberate Northwestern Canada.

The patriotic Irish Fenians, who were based in the United States, had launched several small, armed attacks against British targets in Canada between 1866 and 1871. Hoping to obtain the support of Louis Riel, the Fenians, under the leadership of John O'Neil, crossed the Manitoba border at Emerson. Rather than support them, Riel rallied fighters to defend the border. This amounted to the final blow to the Fenians.

In his "Memoir to Ulysses S. Grant" from 1875, Riel called for a common front comprised of Métis, French, and Irish American citizens. "With a strong Irish movement," reasoned Riel, "we would not only have Quebec to countenance our politics, in the East, but all the Irish from Canada would give us their support." If the Irish could not be free in Ireland, he proposed the creation of an Irish province in the Canadian Northwest.

In his "Letter to Deane, Dewdney, and MacDonald" written in 1885, he expressed hope that Gabriel Dumont would reach out to the Irish Land League. Founded in Ireland in 1879, its goal was the nationalization of land. It is possible, noted Thomas Flanagan, that Riel viewed the aspirations of the Land League as similar to his, namely, the establishment of land rights for the Métis.

As Glen Campbell notes, while in New York in September of 1878, Riel had attempted to negotiate an accord with the Fenians to liberate the Métis and Irish in Canada. His support request failed, perhaps due to the fact that Louis Riel had himself defended the Manitoba border from a Fenian raid in 1871 and had them handed over to American authorities. The Métis leader, however, would continue to call for Métis and Irish unity. As he expressed in "Sir John A. MacDonald," written in August of 1879, the offspring of indomitable Ireland had a purpose in the United States. The day they united under a proper leader, Riel being implied, they would walk, side by side, as brothers with sincere French-Canadians and Métis people.

11.4 Conclusions

Louis Riel was proud of his Irish ancestry. He seems to have been racially, ethnically, and culturally dexterous, pragmatic or, some would suggest, even opportunistic. He emphasized his indigeneity among Indigenous people. He focused on his French ancestry with French-Canadians. He insisted on his Irishness among the Irish. And he even claimed to be Scandinavian when it suited him. He was playing the cards that he was given to build rapport with different individuals and communities. An admirer of the Irish Republican Catholics, Riel placed an Irishman as a treasurer in his Provisional Government. In an act that he came to regret, he repelled a Fenian incursion into Manitoba in 1871, since they did not fly the Métis flag, and opposed American intervention in Canada. Later, however, he would change his stance and actively call upon Americans of French-Canadian and Irish heritage to support the struggle of the Métis, the Irish, and the French in Canada. He even went so far as to encourage the government of the United States to invade and annex Western Canada. He claimed that this command had come from God Himself. As an incentive to the Irish, and as a reward that he offered any ethnic groups willing to support the Métis liberation struggle, he offered the Irish a portion or province of land in the Canadian Northwest.

Chapter 12

LOUIS RIEL AND THE UNITED STATES

"The cause of the States is a great one. It is the cause of civilization; the cause of humanity itself." Louis Riel

12.1 Introduction

Although the British and English Canadians were viewed as the enemies of the Métis and French-Canadians, Louis Riel did not stereotype all English speakers. The Fenian Irish, for example, were viewed as friends and allies of the Métis, sharing the same heroic history of struggle against British imperialism and its derivatives. He even threatened to create an alliance of Métis, French-Canadians, and Irish Catholics from the United States.

While many Americans were of English stock, and virtually all Americans spoke English, and despite the devastation they heaped upon First Nations, and both enslaved and emancipated Africans, Louis Riel held them in high esteem since they had fought for independence against the British and succeeded. This feat was an inspiration to both French-Canadians and Métis people.

Not only was Riel deeply impressed with the *Declaration of Independence*, but it is also possible, despite his aversion to liberalism, that he found the *Constitution of the United States* and the *Bill of Rights* to be beacons of rights and freedoms. If one thing is sure, it is that Riel did not conceive of the United States as a secular-liberal political entity but as a Christian nation that placed its trust in God.

12.2 Louis Riel: The Métis Ambassador to the United States

In his "Memorial of the People of Rupert's Land and Northwest," written in the Red River on October 3, 1870, Louis Riel asked Ulysses S. Grant (1822-1885), the President of the United States (1869-1877), to intervene on behalf of the Métis. He noted that "not a single pledge given by the English and Canadian Governments to our people, and to the Government of the United States, has been kept or performed, but on the contrary, each and every one... has been ruthlessly and revengefully violated and trampled upon."

In his "Memoir to Ulysses S. Grant," which he wrote in Washington, DC, probably between December 10-15 of 1875, Louis Riel informed the American President that "The Métis people ... entered the Canadian Confederation, on faith of a treaty which, Canada, as one of the two contracting parties, does not fulfill." He implored: "Mr. President, if you please, help me get justice for my people, the new nation, the Métis." Riel's cry for American intervention in resolving the Métis Problem fell on deaf and indifferent ears.

12.3 Louis Riel: The American Citizen

In his "Letter to Joseph Riel," written in Wolf Point, Montana, in July of 1880, Louis Riel declared that he was becoming an American citizen:

> As for me, I have decided to become an American citizen. I have declared my intention to do so according to the law. And I received my papers on May seventeenth. I think I can help the Métis better this way than not.

As far as Louis Riel was concerned, the Métis Homeland was wherever the Métis lived. He encouraged them to relocate to Montana and apply for American citizenship if they could no longer live in Manitoba. As can be appreciated, Riel believed that First Nations and Métis people should be full citizens with full rights. They were free people, not wards of the state to be confined on reservations and left landless. "Historically," notes John Weinstein, "one finds that the Métis Nation of the West rejected treaties and reserves and demanded that the Government accord them a special recognition as a distinct people."

Louis Riel became an American citizen on March 16, 1883. And he was a proud one at that. In so becoming, he insisted that he was not rejecting his origins, vindications, and aspirations. "When I was an American subject," he explained, "I retained my land rights... my American naturalization papers erased the border between the Northwest and the United States." As a Métis, Riel argued that he had land rights in English Canada and the United States and that acquiring another nationality in no way represented a relinquishment of such rights. As he further noted,

> As an American citizen I believe that, without infringing in any way international law, I am part of the republic with my people, the Métis and with my Indian country, like so many other American Indian chiefs who are part of the United States with their tribes and lands, even before dealing with the government in Washington.

In Riel's mind, as Aboriginal people, the First Nations, and the Métis held inalienable rights. These rights were not predicated upon treaties; they predated them. They had a right to the land by birth and by blood. As he asserted in his "Address to the Court" in Regina, Saskatchewan, on August 1, 1885: "It is constitutionally acknowledged in the *Manitoba Act* by the 31st clause of that Act, and it does not say to extinguish the Indian title." The right of the First Nations and Métis to the land was granted by God Himself:

> Who starts the nations? The very one who creates them, God. God is the master of the universe, our planet is his land, and the nations and tribes are members of His family, and as a good father, he gives a portion of his lands to that nation, to that tribe, to everyone, that is his heritage, that is his share of the inheritance, of the people, or nation, or tribe... God cannot create a tribe without locating it. We are not birds.

12.4 Louis Riel: The American Activist

As an American citizen, Louis Riel advocated on behalf of the First Nations and the First Métis People. In fact, he presented himself, perhaps paternalistically, as the sole viable intermediary between Americans and Indians. As he professed in "The Future of the French-Canadian Métis Chiefs in the United States," written in Big Bend between October of 1879 and March 1880: "Louis is the only one who can bring the Blackfoot, the Crow, the Gros-Ventre, the Pend d'Oreille, and the Flathead, etc."

In his "Letter to H.M. Black, Fort Assiniboine," written in Montana on March 16, 1880, Riel advocated on behalf of the Métis hunters of the Big Bend of Milk River who were asked to leave the Indian reservation. He adopted a grateful, non-belligerent, humble, and submissive tone, one which he rarely used when dealing with Anglo-Canadian authorities. While he appealed to his Métis warriors to treat Canadian soldiers with mercy, he also called for a "war of extermination." In the US context, he wrote:

> They consider that the American authorities have conferred a great favour on their children, ... their families, and ... themselves, in allowing the Métis Hunters, to winter on Indian reservations at the Big Bend of Milk River. Having no other way to acknowledge efficiently such a favour, those Métis have exerted themselves during the whole winter to pacify the Sioux, Sitting Bull himself and all his band.

Riel, it would seem, wanted to give the impression to the American military that he was on their side, helping to pacify the Indians. He signed off, meekly, as follows: "I have the honour to be, Colonel, your humble and obedient servant." We know, however, that while he was in Montana, Louis Riel had attempted, in vain, to unite the American Indian tribes in revolt with the stated aim of creating an Indigenous Republic. On December 26, 1878, he had vowed to "round up the cruel nations," namely, the Indians, to support the Métis nation-building revolution.

Riel was a keen and cunning politician, diplomat, and strategist. Being predominantly European, he understood the white man and his ways. This proved to be a great advantage. He could not be duped and deceived by white leaders like so many Indian chiefs. He understood that war was deceit and that one should never let the adversary know what one is thinking and planning. As Gilles Martel notes,

> Throughout this wintering of 1879, Riel remained in contact with a large contingent of Métis, and a large population of Indians from multiple tribes, many of whom came from the Canadian Northwest Territories. He tried, but in vain, to organize an alliance with these Indians against Canada.

The displaced, devastated, and decimated Indians refused to have anything to do with Riel's grandiose dreams or delusions of rebellion and nation-building. In their view, it was simply suicidal. The First Nations were already stuck in survival mode. They were broken and dejected. Their needs were more immediate. They needed food and shelter.

If Riel had struck a supplicative tone with American military authorities, it was strategic in purpose. He wanted to be in their good graces as he had a request to make, one for land on a reservation. As he wrote in his "Petition to N.A. Miles, Musselshell River," penned in Montana on August 6, 1880,

> We ask the government to set apart a portion of land as a special reservation in this territory for the Half Breeds as, scattered among other settlers, it becomes a very difficult matter for us to make a living and owing to our present limited means and want of experience in economy, we cannot compete with the majority of our fellow countrymen.
>
> We ask the government to kindly consider that as Half Breeds we stand between the civilized and uncivilized man and are closely related with the several tribes of the northwest, owing to which fact we indirectly exercise some influence and from the Indian blood in our veins, we are inclined to believe that Indians will listen to us more favourably than to the majority of those who are not connected by family ties with them.
>
> If the government would wish to use our influence, such as it is among the Indians, we freely offer it and will always be ready to do everything that lays in our power to fulfill [a] peaceful mission; and if it should be desired to have half breed scouts a willing answer to the call would be given.

Unable to secure land for the Métis people in the form of a reservation, Riel became increasingly desperate to find a home for his errant, semi-nomadic people, who were scattered between two nations, so much so that he reached a point where he was willing to content himself with portions of existing Indian reservations. During this low point, he was asking for crumbs from birds.

In his "Letter to N.A. Miles, Fort Keogh," written in Montana on August 20, 1880, Riel asked for "two small half-breed counties in the Crow reservation, or in some other large Indian reservation, near the buffalo region between Musselshell and the Yellowstone." There is no evidence that Louis Riel consulted with the Indians in question when trying to negotiate some of their land away from them. However, since there were ties of blood between the Métis and many of these First Nations, it is possible that Indigenous hospitality would have been expected. A case in point is that of the Métis of North Dakota who were not recognized as an Indian tribe or granted a reservation. However, their Cree relations welcomed and enrolled them in the Turtle Mountain Reservation to ensure that they received federal recognition and rights. Riel, however, was opposed to settling Métis on the Turtle Mountain Reservation. As he expressed in his "Memoir on the Half-Breeds of Dakota," written perhaps in St. Vincent, Minnesota, between June and August 1883:

> Dakota ought not to allow their Half-Breeds to go back to the simple Indian condition, at least those, who have been up to this time American citizens. Do not allow them to go back on the Turtle Mountain Reservation.

In hindsight, this was a major mistake on the part of Riel as the Turtle Mountain Reservation permitted the Métis to survive as a people, and to perpetuate their language, culture, and customs. Ironically, while Riel opposed its establishment, he is listed as the first chief of the Turtle Mountain Reservation, followed by Gabriel Dumont.

As for the Métis who did not settle on the Turtle Mountain Reservation, many of them were left landless eventually assimilating into white Anglo-American and Anglo-Canadian culture. Riel, it could be argued, was wrong to place his faith in politics, but what other options did he have? While he admired democracy in theory, he soon realized that it did not function as intended by the Founding Fathers. Consequently, he came down hard on the Democratic Party in his "Memoir on the Indian Question," calling it "immoral."

12.5 Louis Riel: The American Imperialist?

Louis Riel believed in American exceptionalism, not in its imperialistic manifestation, but in its foundational principles. "The cause of the States is a great one," he proclaimed, "it is the cause of civilization; the cause of humanity itself." He went so far as to call the country "the United Moral States." Rather than oppose American expansionism and its belief in Manifest Destiny, Louis Riel encouraged it but with an emancipatory ethos. In his "Manifesto to my Fellow American Citizens," written in Regina between August and November 1885, he wrote:

> As an American citizen, I urge the government in Washington to erase the international line from Lake Superior to the Pacific Ocean, to deliver me from tyranny, and to remove the entire [North] West from oppression.

Instead of viewing the United States as an imperial threat, as perhaps he should have done, Riel believed it would "protect New France and the Northwest against the malevolent powers who would like to rule them." In "Revelation Regarding the American Annexation of the Northwest," which he wrote in Regina, Saskatchewan, between August and November 1885, God commanded:

> Annex the Northwest from Lake Superior to the Pacific Ocean; Place the Métis and the Indians of the United States in the Northwest; Guarantee the Métis one-seventh of the Northwest Territories; Take for yourself a seventh of the Northwest Territories; Organize in the Northwest Territories named after our nationalities.

Riel's call for the Americans to invade and annex northwestern Canada was not rhetorical or hyperbolical. It was not an empty threat. He was actively lobbying American politicians to support an invasion of Canada. As Raymond Huel notes,

> In October 1875, Riel went to Indianapolis where he met Oliver P. Morton, Republican senator from Indiana. During these meetings, Riel put forth his plan for an American-based invasion of Manitoba. Morton did not commit himself to this proposal... Riel met other American statesmen, including President Ulysses S. Grant, and discussed his plan with them... Riel later prepared a map ... showing the main entries into Manitoba and containing information on the revenues and population.

In concrete terms, Louis Riel proposed that the land be divided among different ethnic groups, with the Métis receiving one-seventh. This was a considerable concession and one that was not made in consultation with other First Nations. While he was entitled to negotiate on behalf of the Métis, as he was their uncontested and popularly acclaimed leader, he did not have the right to represent the interests of other Native peoples. Riel, however, would have viewed this not only as his right but also as a divine duty. God, in his mind, was guiding his every action. He was, after all, the self-professed Prophet of the New World. The confidence this brings is considerable.

Considering the devastating and traumatic relocation of Indian tribes from one part of the United States to the other, asking the Americans to place "the Métis and the Indians" of the United States in the Canadian Northwest, which then encompassed the current prairie provinces, was arguably desperate and reckless. Perhaps it was the last resort to avoid absolute annihilation. However, can one imagine the consequences of moving the Apache of the Southwest to the freezing cold of the Canadian Northwest? Surely Riel should have seen the devastation wrought by the Indian Removal Act of 1830-1847, in which approximately sixty thousand members of the Cherokee, Muscogee, Seminole, Chickasaw, and Choctaw nations were forcibly removed from their ancestral homelands, resulting in ten thousand or more deaths. It was traumatic enough to move the Seminole from the Florida Everglades to Oklahoma. Can one imagine moving a tropical tribe like them to Alberta, Saskatchewan, the Northwest Territories, or the Yukon? If Riel wanted to create an Indigenous-Métis Nation for the Chosen People, they would have been the Frozen Chosen.

If Riel could not get a Métis Homeland from the Anglo-Canadians, he thought the Americans could conquer the Canadian Northwest and turn over a portion of it to the First Nations and Métis. However, why would the Americans have done so when they could have kept it for themselves? After all, they never honoured a single treaty they made with Native American tribes. Of the three hundred and seventy-one treaties that the United States made with Indigenous Peoples, the government broke all of them in one way or another. For Aboriginal people, the white man truly spoke with a forked tongue. His word was not worth the paper upon which it was written. For Indigenous people, however, a treaty was an eternal word. It was not a mere pact or contract between two parties that could be broken; rather, it was a covenant that the Great Spirit witnessed. Only one without faith and fear in God would violate it.

12.6 Conclusions

While Louis Riel may have had the best of intentions, and may have been politically naïve or exceedingly idealistic, his love for the United States, and his faith that it would protect the Métis and First Nations from Anglo-Canadian colonialism was arguably misplaced. After he was found guilty of treason, and condemned to death, he "himself wrote to J.W. Taylor to ask for American intervention on his behalf." He asked the US consul at Winnipeg "to investigate the claims of the Half-Breeds and Indians on one side; and to investigate thoroughly whether the Federal government [of Canada] has prominently inaugurated some principle which they themselves afterwards conspicuously disregarded." On March 11, 1889, President Benjamin Harrison (1833-1901) issued a message in response to Senate Resolution regarding the case of Louis Riel. He shared a letter from Thomas F. Bayard (1828-1898) from the Department of State concluding that Riel's "alleged United States citizenship did not give him any immunity from Canadian laws for offences committed within their jurisdiction." So much for supporting its citizens abroad.

In August or September of 1885, Riel "prepared a petition to President Grover Cleveland [1893-1908], asking for American annexation of the Northwest," an act which, from the Anglo-Canadian perspective, could only have been perceived as treasonous and worthy of the death penalty. Riel's admiration for the United States was not reciprocated. The nation he held up high abandoned him in the same fashion it abandoned its Indigenous and African populations. As Malcolm X once asked, "What does a white man call a black man with a Ph.D.?" "A nigger," he answered. As curious as it may have been for white Anglo-Saxon American Protestants to hear Louis Riel invoke the founding principles of their republic, he was, in the end, but a racially inferior savage infidel in their minds. After all, for such people, "the only good Indian is a dead Indian." The fact that he was primarily white meant nothing. Appealing to whiteness brought nothing but darkness.

Chapter 13

LOUIS RIEL AND WOMEN

"Leur seul moyen d'être agréable à Dieu, de plaire à leur mari et d'être longtemps honorées dans le monde, c'est de pratiquer sincèrement la modestie, l'économie et les amabilités de la vertu." Louis Riel

13.1 Introduction

Although he wrote over four volumes of prose and poetry and addressed a wide variety of topics, Louis Riel had little to say when it came to women. Perhaps, like many religious, conservative, and Christian men, Riel viewed it as unbecoming and uncouth to openly discuss matters regarding the other sex. For many such men, women should be concealed, covered, and confined in their homes, caring for their children, cooking, cleaning, praying, and making themselves pretty for their husbands. The minute amount of material regarding women that we find in the works of Louis Riel paints a traditional portrait of patriarchy with firmly delineated gender roles. A revolutionary he may have been, but a feminist, he was not. When it came to women, he was firmly a French-Canadian conservative Catholic of the nineteenth century. While they might have had more freedoms than French-Canadian women, if we judge by the writings of Louis Riel, Métis women had fewer rights and lower status than First Nations women. Let us see what the Métis leader had to say about them.

13.2 Barefoot, Pregnant, and Pious

As a fervent Catholic for most of his life, except for periods in which he had falling outs with the Church and created his own renewed religion, it comes as no surprise to learn that Louis Riel held conservative ideas regarding the place of women as mothers and housewives. However, the Métis leader adopted an even more illiberal attitude toward women, inspired by the Old Testament in which polygyny was permitted. In so doing, he drew closer to Judaism and, dare say we, Islam. In "Revelations Regarding the Laws of the Old Testament," written in Beauport, Quebec, between May 20, 1876, and January 1, 1878, Riel wrote that:

Our Lord Jesus Christ now allows a man to marry up to five women. He wants it to be so

> 1. for more girls to marry;
> 2. so that women, being several together to seek the favours of the husband, feel more emulation in the household and the Christian education that they should give to their children;
> 3. to teach women again that their only way to be pleasing to God, to please their husbands, and to be honoured for a long time in the world, is to practice modesty, economy, and virtue, sincerely.

Like all men who promote polygyny, Louis Riel presents the practice as beneficial and advantageous to women: it is good for them. What a convenient argument for men. Polygyny, they claim, allows more girls to get married. Since the proportion of men to women is roughly the same, this claim does not hold and would only apply in times of war when there is a major reduction in the number of marriageable men.

Riel also claims that co-wives would compete in favouring the husband making them better housewives and mothers. Studies on the subject, however, show that the opposite is true. It produces rivalry and jealousy. Research conducted worldwide and published in peer-reviewed journals reveals that polygyny is detrimental to women, children, families, and societies. Finally, in the mind of Louis Riel, polygyny pleases God as it teaches them that the only way to please God, please their husband, and be honoured in this world is through modesty, frugality, and virtue.

For women, reason many in our times, the path to God does not have to pass through the agency of men. For many conservative men, however, modesty applies primarily to women, as does chastity. As critics contend, it is a means of controlling female sexuality to safeguard male insecurity. And while women were expected to be frugal penny-pinchers, argue modern thinkers, their husbands typically had free rein over finances and could squander them as they pleased, often spending the funds on women of the night, gambling, and booze. The blame for mismanaging money, however, always fell on women.

While a limit of five wives was placed on ordinary people, Riel wrote that a lieutenant governor could have six, a governor of several provinces could have seven, the presumed heir to the throne could have eight, and kings could have a total of fifteen. Louis Riel's rules made Islamic law, which allows for a maximum of four wives but a limitless number of sex slaves, look prudish. It was not enough that conservative French-Canadian Catholics insisted that a woman's place was in the home, caring for her children and her husband. If Riel had his way, it would not be a woman, but women, five or more, who would be bearing children, educating them, and attending to the whims of their husbands.

While a man could sow his wild oats as he pleased, with five to fifteen wives at his disposal, a young girl, however, was expected to remain chaste. In Riel's words "a young girl, while remaining chaste, can have inclinations, without admitting them to others." In other words, it was not becoming of a female to express interest in a male, even in matters of marriage. It was the man who had to make the first move. And of all the things he could praise of his sister, he complimented the modest way she walked and carried herself. Riel, of all people, shares the cherished conservative belief that women are responsible for the family's honour. A man's indiscretions, however, are invariably excused in this traditional system of double standards.

When viewed from the twenty-first century, some would suggest that Louis Riel sounds like a polygynous Mormon, a traditionalist *sede vacante* Catholic, a Traditionalist-Perennialist follower of René

Guénon or Frithjof Schuon, a conservative Muslim, or even a radical Islamist. For some, there is nothing in his works that shows the slightest sign of Indigenous beliefs regarding the sacred status of women. Louis Riel's views of women were those that were espoused by ultra-Catholic French-Canadians in the nineteenth century. He may have been proud of being part Indian; however, he adopted very few Indigenous beliefs and values regarding women.

The situation was even direr among some First Nations who were taught by priests that husbands should control their wives and that they should beat them into submission. This was part and parcel of the Western Christian assault on predominantly matriarchal Indigenous family structures. The trauma caused by this tragedy continues to this day, with Indigenous women suffering from the highest domestic violence incidents in Canada and the United States. They have the Church and the State to blame for that. However, as critics counter, they can also blame themselves for failing to address and resolve these problems. Most First Nations, however, have no interest in the pity of others, nor do they like to blame others. They assume responsibility for their present condition and strive to improve their situation. It is a matter of individual and collective accountability and responsibility. That does not mean, however, that others are off the hook.

Although Riel wrote many romantic and arguably corny poems and letters to various women during his lifetime, they were filled with demands and expectations. In "If My Love Pleases You: If My Joys are Agreeable to you," written in Glen's Falls in April of 1878, he told Evelina that "the more your life is exemplary / The more you will know how to please me." "Be firm and wise among all women," he counselled her. "A woman is great with aspirations / which give her a taste for holy deeds." In his words, "You who want to serve your God, you know / What it takes for a Christian woman to have wisdom / To escape the world and its dangers." As Riel put it plainly, "I am looking for a good woman." Religious and righteous, that is how he liked them. If they have the fear of God in them, they do not need as much fear of man. In the case of Riel, fortunately, he showed every indication of being a tender, loving, caring, responsible, and affectionate husband and father. He provided for his wives and children and raised them in stable homes. If only the same could be said of many men in our day and time.

13.3 Conclusions

As advanced, forward-thinking, and progressive as Louis Riel may seem to contemporary readers on such issues as republicanism, Indigenous rights, anti-racism, and anti-imperialism, the same cannot be said of his ideas regarding the roles and rights of women. For Riel, and most men and women of his day and age, a woman's value resided in her beauty, piety, and fertility. She was expected to be chaste, religious, and God-fearing. She had to manage household finances carefully. To please God, she had to please her husband. The man, however, apparently had no obligation to please his woman. Her place was soundly in the home as a wife and mother. The coverage of women in the works of Louis Riel commits a grave injustice to Métis, First Nations, and French-Canadian women. They were strong women who made significant contributions to their communities. In the works of Riel, however, they have not received the credit that they duly deserve. Perhaps it was unintended and an oversight. Riel has many other pressing matters on his mind. Let us forgive him for this lapse.

Chapter 14

LOUIS RIEL AND LIBERALISM

"Mon Dieu: délivrez-moi du noir libéralisme." Louis Riel

14.1 Introduction

As much as the image of Louis Riel has been hijacked and appropriated to serve anarchist, leftist, socialist, liberal, and illiberal causes, the Métis leader was an inveterate enemy of liberalism throughout his life. As Thomas Flanagan has noted, "Riel's political ideas were an exaggerated form of ultramontane thought, in which the fundamental concepts of liberalism and theocracy were extended to their ultimate limits." The situation was so severe that "liberalism became synonymous with evil itself." Anyone who opposed him, the pope and priest-king, was a liberal, and anyone who was a liberal was an enemy of God. Either you are with me, or you are against me. It was black and white. There was no gray. However, as Obi-Wan Kenobi warned, "Only a Sith deals in absolutes." The wise have always warned against extremes and polarization and have called people to moderation, tolerance, and the middle ground. In the case of Louis Riel, however, the people he defended were in a quandary. When it came to their plight and predicament, options were few. Since most of the Métis at the time were committed and convinced Catholics, Riel rallied them around the Roman Catholic Church and retrenched himself behind ultra-conservative Catholicism in its combat against godless liberalism and secularism.

14.2 Liberalism

In "The Strength that God Gives Me," written in Beauport, Quebec, between 1876-1878, Riel claimed that "Christianity places itself, / via Liberalism, / under the yoke of Mahomet." Riel was convinced that the Roman Catholic Church was weakening itself by adopting the liberal ideas that coalesced as a distinct movement in the Age of Enlightenment in the seventeenth and eighteenth centuries.

It is worth remembering that those who ran Canada at the time were Orangemen, members of the Loyal Order of Orange, a Protestant sectarian, triumphalist, and supremacist fraternal society founded in the Irish province of Ulster in 1795. The Order reached North America via Irish-born Protestant immigrants. From 14,000 members in 1834, membership rose to 60,000 by 1900. John A. MacDonald and several other Prime Ministers were Orangemen as were countless mayors across the country. They wanted to turn Canada into a Protestant North American Ulster: one queen, one language, one religion. They were violently opposed to Catholicism, Catholic education, and the French language.

Ontario was run by Orangemen where they had 930 lodges by 1870. The St. Patrick's Day parade was prohibited in Toronto for nearly a hundred years. As Michael Wilcox relates in the *Canadian Encyclopedia*,

> From the mid-19th until the mid-20th century, members exerted significant political influence, particularly at the municipal level. In Toronto, for example, almost every mayor of the city was an Orangeman between 1850 and 1950. The power of patronage was evident: scores of Orange-friendly administrators, aldermen, police, firemen, and public works employees were appointed, and members were pressured to vote for Orange officials. In fact, during the late 19th century, Toronto was sometimes referred to as the "Belfast of Canada," a designation referring to its sectarianism and the Orange influence in municipal governance.

During Riel's days, Western Canada was being overrun by Orangemen. The First Nations, Métis, and French-Canadians were under siege. The Catholic Church was under siege in Canada as was the case in much of the United States. As an educated and politically astute person, Riel understood that the only religious power capable of confronting Protestantism was Catholicism and that the only language that could compete with English was French. He lived in the midst of a religious, cultural, and linguistic war between English Protestants and French Catholics. First, it was New France that fell. Quebec came under British rule. These English-speaking Protestants then started to expand westward, eliminating, assimilating, and replacing everyone in their path. Riel revolted. Had he spoken Spanish, he would have cried: *¡no pasarán!* The enemy shall not get past! For Riel, anything that weakened the Roman Catholic Church, such as absorbing liberal and secular influences, or making alliances with Islam and Muslims, was suicidal.

For Christianity to defend itself from Islam, which many conservative or traditional Christians of the time considered its greatest threat, Riel believed it had to remain true to its principles. This might explain why Riel's religious teachings were mostly devoid of syncretism, unlike other nativistic movements, which borrowed from Christianity and Indigenous beliefs. Since the Métis were already Catholic, he drew his inspiration from Christianity. According to Flanagan, Riel may have modified his teachings when he presented them to his people, drawing conceivably from Indian tradition or lore; however, as he admits "there is no record of this, except for his brief allusion in his trial speech to Métis traditions of prophecy."

In Riel's view, by bending principles, changing them, eliminating them, or replacing them, as the Church was doing, and which would culminate in the Second Vatican Council of 1965, Catholic liberals were corroding the very foundations of the Christian faith. For traditional, conservative Catholics like Riel, it was a complete capitulation to secularism. Rather than align society with Catholic values, morals, ethics, and principles, they were compromising and casting away fundamental Christian doctrines. Under the guise of religious liberty, idols were being placed on par with the one true God. Under the guise of equality, the wicked were to be treated like the righteous. Under the guise of tolerance, intolerable sins were supposed to be tolerated and normalized. Riel would have none of it. Principles were pillars that upheld the Church. Tear them down, and the entire edifice collapses.

Since the political and moral philosophy of liberalism is purportedly based on individualism, secularism, constitutionalism, and the consent of the governed—and opposes state religion, absolute monarchy, and the divine right to rule—Riel reacted by stating that "Only Jesus-Christ is King; and only the Gospel is Law." The Métis leader refused to place Man above God. It was God, and not Man, who was the Lawgiver. The hierarchy in Riel's mindset was God, the Church, and Man.

While secularism and liberalism are presented in a positive light in the Western world, they have historically excluded the "others." The principles invoked by political liberalism only applied to the chosen few: in England, the English, but not the Welsh, the Scottish, and the Irish; in the United States and Canada, the WASPs, but not the First Nations, the Métis, the blacks, the Hispanics, the Chinese, the Japanese, and the French-Canadians. Human rights were for them, the elites, not others. The principles of liberalism never applied to the millions of people that its proponents colonized and enslaved. It was like the Herrenvolk democracy, a system of government in which only a specific ethnic group participates in government, while other groups are disenfranchised. Case in point, the rise of liberalism in England was parallel with the biggest rise in slavery and the Trans-Atlantic slave trade. Civil and human rights were only for them, the privileged elites, not those they oppressed, exploited, and enslaved. Riel was not opposed to rights; he was opposed to hypocrisy. He was fighting against that double standard as it was applied to the Métis, First Nations, French-Canadians, and the Roman Catholic Church.

As an opponent of liberalism, which supposedly supported individual rights, including freedom of speech and freedom of the press, Riel insisted that free thought was fatal. In a letter to Monseigneur Alexandre Taché, the Archbishop of Saint Boniface, Manitoba, written from the Lunatic Asylum, the actual name of the facility in which he was institutionalized, a term that has long been deemed inappropriate, he humbly implored:

> Lead us, all the Métis, and by the government of your mind and by that of your hand. We no longer demand the freedom to hold opinions that are contrary to your outlook. Free thought is fatal. She is the mother of libertinism or liberalism. It is obedience to the Holy Hierarchy of the Church of Saint Peter that leads individuals, families, and peoples to life.

In another "Letter to A.-A. Taché," written in Beauport, Quebec, between October and November of 1876, Riel wrote that,

> [W]orldly governments are not conservatives of evangelical law, they are all Liberals. I know that constitutional governments are governments of bondage and slavery. I see clearly that the representative government is the government of the locusts which the apostle Saint John describes in the ninth chapter of his apocalypse from the third verse until the twelfth.

For Riel, it was very clear that the liberals talked the talk but did not walk the walk. They did not deliver upon the rights and freedoms that they promised. They were merely tools at their imperial capitalist service. In "The Man from the Catholic Circle," written in Beauport, Quebec, in 1877, he praised the priesthood in the following terms: "The priest ... is Liberty. / He has his catechism. / It's enough to overcome error / He resents liberalism / the terror of which he exposes."

For Riel, at least during that period in his life, freedom was not to be found in democracy but in the guidance of the clergy. To be faithful, one had to follow them faithfully as they acted based on moral principles and not material and political interests. As Glen Campbell notes, "Liberalism was one of the great enemies of the Catholic faith according to Riel and the ultramontanes. The Catholic Circle had certainly attacked this political doctrine during its discussions." Riel appears to have absorbed their philosophy during that vulnerable time. Like a Thanksgiving turkey, they stuffed the drugged up and sedated man with their Catholic ideology. It was more than most could digest. According to current standards, Louis Riel's human rights were violated. He was confined against his will and he was subjected to torture, spiritual abuse, and brainwashing as opposed to sound medical treatment. Since he was locked up due to his insane views on Métis liberation, it could be argued that he was very much a political prisoner.

In "Oh! How I Have Paid Attention," written in New England and Beauport, Quebec, between 1874 and 1878, Riel prayed: "My God: deliver me from darkness of liberalism. / And all the evils it produces." As Glen Campbell notes, "As defender of ultramontanist thought, Riel considered liberalism to be one of the greatest of sins."

In his "Letter to Ignace Bourget," written in April of 1875, Riel stated that he wanted to identify the Provisional Government as conservative. However, he feared that his opponents among the Métis would then claim to be liberals without fully understanding the underpinnings of that ideology. As he asserted, "I want to save this segment of the Métis people from the evil of liberal ideas." He stressed that he wanted all political parties to adopt the conservative Catholic socio-political program. In another letter to Bourget, written in Longue-Pointe, Quebec, on April 20, 1876, Riel wrote that "the good Lord chooses you among all the bishops of the world! His Providence has preserved you so that in these unhappy times when liberalism is introduced everywhere, everywhere, everywhere."

In another letter to Ignace Bourget, written in Longue-Pointe, Quebec, on May 15, 1876, Riel quotes God as saying: "What! ... my prophets and my sovereign Pontiffs would not be infallible if the highest authority of liberalism assumes infallibility to rule and govern as it wishes." Gilles Martel notes,

> The struggle of the ultramontanes, and in particular of Bishop Bourget, against liberalism was in full swing. On February 1, 1876, Bishop Bourget had published his famous pastoral letter against liberalism...

In "Revelations against Beauport," written on May 22, 1876, in Beauport, Quebec, Riel attacked Monseigneur Alexandre Taschereau (1820-1898), cardinal and archbishop of Quebec, whom certain ultramontanes viewed as tainted by liberalism: "Who is this man who sings loudly the Psalms of the Church? But who has both hands tied and still wrapped in coarse red leather, with the coarse red leather of liberalism?" As Riel wrote in his Prayer, written in Beauport on May 5, 1876: "Lord! Jesus Christ! O living God! There are many camps and advanced positions of liberalism in the world. Deign to kill only 45 now."

In his "Letter to A.-A. Taché," written in Beauport, Quebec, between October and November of 1876, Riel warned that,

> Worldly governments of all shapes and colours are only good to put men outside the law of God, to wage war against them, to persecute them, to expatriate them, to throw them in prison, to judge them satanically and to condemn them to death. When they can't help it, they just forgive them for being righteous. But they are careful to forgive them as little as they can. The bounties they pretend to practice are misguided. The graces they pride themselves on bestowing are as imperfect as possible when not accompanied by some insult or some derision.

In a letter to his confessor, written in Beauport, Quebec, probably in May 1877, Riel described a vision God showed him. As Riel describes, he chastised Mastaï-Ferretti, Pope Pius IX, who ruled from 1846 to 1878, repeatedly accusing him of being a liberal. He also condemned Old France and Italy for having prostituted themselves to the cause of liberalism and secularism.

In "Revelations that Jesus Christ Granted to His Poor and Useless Servant, Louis 'David' Riel," written in Beauport between May 20, 1876, and January 23, 1878, he said that it was the will of God to repel universal liberalism. In "Revelations Regarding the Old Testament," written in Beauport between May 20, 1876, and January 1, 1878, Riel swore that "I will never succumb to liberalism! That liberalism consists in turning one's back on God, fleeing the works of consistent virtue, in exchange for the love of ease, [moral] feebleness, and sensual pleasures."

As Gilles Martel notes, Riel believed that Mosaic law protected men from the evils of liberalism. Riel even believed that his physical ailments were the symbolic projection of humanity's ailments, and particularly the ailments of the Roman Catholic Church that allowed itself to be invaded by liberalism. He also condemned Victor Emmanuel II (1820-1878), king of Sardinia (1849), and Italy (1861), for dismantling the Papal States and creating a united Italy, which was a shock for many Catholics.

14.3 Conclusions

Louis Riel was a paradox. On the one hand, he opposed liberalism vehemently, considered it to be the greatest sin and an affront to God and the Church, and called for the creation of a religious theocracy. On the other hand, he sang the praises of the United States of America and the principles on which it was founded, principles which, perhaps unbeknownst to him, were philosophically and politically liberal.

Not only does the United States continue to advocate socio-political and economic liberalism, so do many Western European nations. Although the liberal world order is being challenged by Russia, China, and Iran, in the twenty-first century, nation-states that are exploiting the internal and inherent weaknesses of liberalism to debilitate it, the system created by liberals continues, for the time being, to function although it appears to be in decline and risks eventually collapsing. According to some political analysts, the West is essentially being coerced into committing suicide. Thanks to the globalist elites, they argue, it is casting itself into destruction as empires past have done.

Although Riel evoked some liberal notions such as liberty, equality, and democracy due to his exposure to American ideals and time spent living in the country, he remained, at his core, an opponent of liberalism and secularism. He believed in freedom for his people, not individual freedom. Liberalism, for him, was self-indulgence and sensual pleasures. For him, salvation could only be found in submission. The regime Riel espoused was the union of Church and State under the rule of the "priest-king."

Like today's Christian millenarians and radical political Islamists, Riel wanted to create the kingdom of God on earth. However, God, Christ, or the Awaited Mahdi are always conspicuously absent for all such endeavours. They may be on the guest of honour list, but they never show up. The throne remains empty.

Consequently, the clerics conveniently rule on behalf of the absentee ruler. This is spiritual abuse taken to its extreme, a vile, opportunistic use of faith and religion for personal political purposes.

Ironically, despite opposing liberalism, and encouraging censorship, Riel asserted his freedom of thought, faith, and expression to such an extreme that the Church treated him like a heretic and an apostate and required him to repent, in writing, for his wrongdoings before his death. And while he told them what they wanted to hear; Riel also made it clear in his writings that he had not changed his views. In his mind, the Church was simply not ready to hear the truth that he had proclaimed.

Although, for pragmatic reasons, he became slightly more ecumenical towards the end of his life, catering to different audiences, and recanted some of his theological excesses to ensure that he would receive a Catholic burial, Riel ultimately died as a believer in God, a believer in his divine mission and reformed Christian religion, and a political conservative who was opposed to liberalism and libertinism. Some sympathizers might claim that Riel died after repenting his heresies and receiving absolution. However, until the very end, he had continued to say one thing to appease Catholic clerics, but to believe another. As difficult as it was for him, Riel simply seems to have been biting his tongue.

If one thing is clear, it is that Riel was no liberal at any point in his life. One can always speculate how his ideology would have evolved had he lived longer. However, whether one likes it or not, Riel is who he was, and that is his legacy for good or bad, depending on one's worldview. The sole consolation we can offer to progressive people is that Riel softened his opinion about liberalism in 1885, admitting that "French-Canadian and Irish liberals have done me much good."

If Riel was a fervent, ultra-conservative Catholic, it was partly because most of his people shared the same spiritual sentiments at the time. Since faith is a powerful force, he rallied them behind God and the Church. When the Catholic Church waned in its support for the Métis cause, Riel developed his own reformed religion to meet the needs of his people. When the Church turned against the Métis fighters, betrayed them, and excommunicated them, Riel became more ecumenical and open to liberal influences. When he was defeated in life, and faced death by hanging, he turned back, strategically, to Roman Catholicism to ensure a dignified Christian burial, perhaps hoping for reconciliation between the Métis and the Church. The Church, however, never regained the trust of the Métis. The Quiet Revolution, namely, the break with the Church that took place in Quebec in the 1960s started among the Western Métis after the hanging of Louis Riel.

Louis Riel was a sincere man of faith who was committed to Christianity and opposed to secularism and liberalism. At the same time, however, he was a wise politician and tactician who had no choice but to play the cards that he was given. He did not believe in God because he followed the Church. He followed the Church because he believed in God. His faith was not hinged on a particular interpretation of the faith. He was quite capable of challenging doctrines and dogmas and developing ones of his own. If his religious beliefs could change, so could his socio-political views. Louis Riel was not a fossil. He was not frozen in time. He was a living, breathing, thinking, and evolving human being, a realist, and a political pragmatist. The fundamental principles in which he believed could not change, faith in God and the fight for freedom; however, their interpretation and application were malleable based on changing circumstances and the reality on the ground.

When it comes to Louis Riel, or any other human being, for that matter, one must sift the gold from the sand. Blindly and uncritically following any person, regardless of their claims to power, prophecy, infallibility, and even divinity is foolish, foolhardy, dangerous, and even deadly. It leads to fundamentalism, extremism, corruption, despotism, dictatorship, and totalitarianism. Riel remains great despite his faults. That does not mean that one should follow his faults. His qualities and virtues are those that should inspire us. Let us not pray to him as if he were a saint, as some have done. Hope should be placed in God, not humans.

Chapter 15

LOUIS RIEL AND MÉTIS UNITY

"Restons unis, et nous serons heureux." Louis Riel

15.1 Introduction

Sage and sagacious, Louis Riel encouraged Métis unity and not division. He knew far well that the oldest political tactic was *divide et impera*, namely, divide and conquer, and warned his people to be wary of the traps set upon them by their internal and external enemies. As he knew from Matthew 12:25: a "house divided against itself shall not stand." The Métis people had to set aside their differences and unite based on their collective history, similarities, culture, and what they shared in common.

15.2 United We Stand, Divided We Fall

In his "Proclamation to the People of the Northwest," written in Fort Garry on April 9, 1870, Louis Riel warned:

> Let us remain united, and we will be happy.... If ever we let the day come where we are divided just as outsiders have tried to make us, that day will be the harbinger of all the disasters we have been fortunate enough to avoid.

As Raymond Huel notes, "Riel counselled the Métis to avoid internal division and dissension." In the event of disputes, they were to act as brothers and quickly make amends. The Métis were to fear rancour and be united on the most important matters. Riel would have been livid to see Métis people bickering about who is a real Métis and who is a wannabe based on where their ancestors were born, the year of their birth, where they lived, and to which First Nations their ancestors belonged.

15.3 Conclusion

Louis Riel was one to unite, not to divide. He was one to strengthen, not to weaken. He was inclusive and not exclusive. Riel and his followers rose in revolt due to poor leadership. He promised that "our politics will be good governance for the people, as soon as we can establish it; and public prosperity by every means we can devise." The Métis people of Canada and the United States merit no less. May they receive the leadership, good governance, and prosperity they desperately deserve.

GENERAL CONCLUSIONS

"Malgré ses échecs, la cause métisse grandit sans cesse." Louis Riel

This journey through the *Collected Writings of Louis Riel* has provided a panoramic bird's eye view of numerous parts of his ideological ecosystem. It is hoped that this exploration of discovery and rediscovery will inspire other academic adventurers, travellers, and prospectors to survey more regions of Riel's intriguing intellectual habitat and environment so that we can understand and appreciate them better.

Our quest commenced with chapter one, in which we clarified Louis Riel's conception of the word *Métis*, a term that has become increasingly contentious in recent decades but which is imperative to understand and adequately define due to its centrality in matters of ethnic identity and collective rights. As Riel established, the Métis were predominantly the progeny of European settlers, voyageurs, wood-runners, trappers, and travelling fur traders of predominantly French, French-Canadian, and Acadian ancestry and Indigenous women of various First Nations.

Louis Riel, like Gabriel Dumont, and most of their people for that matter, understood that the Métis, as a distinct ethnic group with its collective consciousness, culture, history, and identity, arose in eastern Canada, in Acadia and Quebec, and spread to Ontario and western Canada, as well as large parts of what is now the United States, but which had belonged in the past to Spain and France. While the Métis formed communities throughout North America and along lakes and waterways of all kinds, it was in the Red River that a group of them first created an independent but fleeting political nation.

According to the Old Testament, the Jews did not become a people in the Promised Land. They were Jews both before and after Egypt. Likewise, the Métis were Métis before they settled in the Red River. They were Métis when they set out from Acadia and Quebec to spread throughout the rest of North America.

As we observed in chapter two, Riel recognized that the Métis had many names. Although they had First Nations ancestry, Riel never described his people as such, nor did he claim to be an Indian or an Indigenous person. He did, however, state that he was a Native of the Northwest with Indian ancestry and occasionally described himself as an Aboriginal. While Riel insisted that he had Indigenous rights due to his blood and birth, *droit de sol et droit de sang*, he admitted that the bulk of his blood was white. His heart, however, was with the half or mixed breeds, identifying overwhelmingly as a French-Canadian Métis. Moreover, while he insisted that he was a French Métis, he also recognized that the English Métis were part and parcel of the broader Métis family. It was their Indigenous identity that bound them, not their European one.

Following the same inclusive line of thinking, Riel had enough historical sense to recognize that, like himself, the Métis had used different signifiers to identify themselves, including French, *Métis*, *Canadien*, and *Bois-Brûlé*. Although he does not appear to have employed the terms *Métif*, *Michif*, *Chicot*, *Créoles*, *Gens Libres*, *Hommes Libres*, Freemen, Country-Born, Mixed-Blood, or *Otipemisiwak*, Riel recognized that they described the same ethnic group that was found throughout North America. For him, the Métis were a multiracial race, a people, a flock, a tribe, a country, and a nation. Whether the Métis, the Jews, the Kurds, the Berbers, and other groups, consist of nations is debatable. For Riel, however, the Métis were both a people and a nation, a position not shared by all of his people. In any event, in order to claim their rights, and to negotiate with the British, the Americans, and the English Canadians, Riel believed that they had to do so on a nation-to-nation basis.

Following this conceptual train of thought, we examined Louis Riel's view of the Métis Nation in chapter three. The Métis of the Red River and the Northwest may have had a particular history;

however, in Riel's mind, that did not deny the existence of other Métis communities, including the Eastern Métis, the Northern Métis, the Southern Métis, the West-Coast Métis, and others. Moreover, while he had struggled to create a Métis Nation in the Red River, Riel had also attempted to create a reservation or even an independent Indigenous Republic in the heart of North America. As Riel conceived it, this confederation would have provided a refuge and a national base for First Nations, Métis, and others. Whether in the American Prairies or the Canadian Northwest, it was the nation that mattered, the homeland of Indians and Métis, and not its geographic location. A person did not cease being a member of the Métis people if he or she did not live within the physical boundaries of the political Métis Nation. Outside of the Turtle Mountain Reservation in North Dakota, and the Métis settlements in Alberta, there is no Métis land base. The Québécois are more of a nation, albeit a nation within a nation. At least they own the land and control the government of the Province of Quebec, its economy, and its resources. Most Métis "nations" are merely virtual. They are cultural clubs and associations.

Although he did not identify as an Indian, Riel was proud to be Aboriginal, Indigenous, and Métis. He admired and honoured the First Nations but did not succumb to the myth of the "noble savage" that was spread by some Europeans and Euro-descendants. In the Latin American literary context, he was more *indigenista* than *indianista*. Riel praised what he perceived as positives and criticized what he considered negative. Whether we agree with his assessment, in whole or in part, his honesty and frankness are to be appreciated even though he occasionally succumbed to some stereotypes. However hopeful he was for the future of the Métis people, his outlook for the First Nations was dismal, gloomy, and depressing.

In Riel's mind, the First Nations were on the path to doom and destined to disappear forever. Their only hope was to marry into the Métis community and create a larger, more powerful, unified people and nation. After all, due to the population decimation that the First Nations had suffered—massacres, epidemics, and starvation—safety was to be found in numbers. Fortunately, the fate Riel foretold for Indian tribes did not come to pass. They have survived. Most importantly, before his execution, Riel received a revelation stressing that the legal rights of the First Nations to the land were deep, just, great, and profound, and their struggle surpassed all others in importance. Not only did the First Nations survive, so did the Métis and the Franco-Manitobans that Riel was so concerned about. They never merged as one, surviving as distinct minorities.

As difficult as it is to believe, and as surprising as it may seem to some, Louis Riel once claimed that he was a Jewish person. As a result of his Catholic education and his intimate familiarity with Scripture, Riel came to view the world in which he lived and his role in life through Biblical lenses. This curious Christian conception coloured everything. If there was one thing he did not absorb from his Catholic teachers, it was antisemitism. He simply could not relate to racism and bigotry. At a time when being anti-Jewish was the order of the day, Louis Riel was pro-Jewish. While Canadian politicians wanted to prevent Jews from entering Canada, Riel invited them and welcomed them. He even promised to establish a Jewish State in Western Canada if a country could not be carved out for them in Poland. The catch, however, was that they had to embrace Christianity. For a man whose mind spent more time in the Old Testament than in the New Testament, Riel's love for Jewish people did not extend to Judaism. If Riel identified with the Jewish people, it was because he found striking parallels between their plight and that of his people, the Métis. For Riel, the Métis were very much like the Jews of the New World and the New Chosen People of God.

As favourably inclined as Riel was toward the Jewish people—so much so that he called for Jewish statehood prior to Theodore Herzl, who founded the Zionist movement in 1897—the same cannot be said of his attitude towards Islam, as we observed in chapter six. With little knowledge about its faith and history, except for the presumably anti-Islamic comments made by Catholic priests and seminary professors, Riel spoke ill of the Prophet Muhammad, cursed the Qur'an, advocated tearing it to shreds, and called for a new crusade against the Ottoman Turks. In light of the ravages that alcohol was causing among the First Nations and the Métis, Riel admired but two things about Islam: its prohibition of intoxicating beverages and the crescent that the Turks had chosen for their flag. So, from a Muslim perspective, all was not lost. He was not completely closed off.

Ironically, John A. MacDonald, the Prime Minister of Canada, and the nemesis of Louis Riel, compared him to the Sudanese Mahdi or Islamic Messiah, and Thomas Flanagan, a conservative political activist with an agenda of his own, likened him to Imam Khomeini. Had Louis Riel read the Qur'an and studied some basic books about Islam and its history, he would probably have developed a more nuanced view of the faith and its followers, both good and bad, and found that they formed part of the same global struggle against Western European colonialism and imperialism. Just like his secretary, Honoré Jaxon, came to appreciate the value of Islam through the Baha'i faith, Louis Riel may have done so himself. While some of Riel's views about Islam, the Prophet, and the Qur'an are hurtful to the religious sensitivities of Muslims, the fact remains that there are Métis people who profess Islam and Muslims who work with Métis people on matters of common concern. Curiously, despite Riel's call to conquer Islam, it is Islam that has conquered the hearts and souls of some Métis people.

Louis Riel's psychological state has caused much ink to be spilled and many keys to be pressed. Once viewed as suffering from delusions of grandeur, paranoid schizophrenia, and megalomania, it now appears that his condition can be downgraded to that of bipolar 1 disorder or manic depression, a common occurrence among those who are brilliant and talented. Call it the cost of genius. Creativity requires energy. That energy is supplied during the manic phase. The process is quite draining and is followed by a depressive stage in which rest and recovery is required. People cannot operate at such a high level of intellectual and creative activity for long periods without crashing.

Oscillation is part of a natural process for those who are not flat liners, namely, so-called normal people who do not suffer from such mental and emotional fluctuation. Like the human heart's systolic and diastolic beat, their lives consist of a rhythmic cycle of ups and downs. As sensitive, emotional, and passionate people, who are in tune with their feelings and the suffering of others, many produce great art, music, and literature, not to mention rising in revolution out of energetic empathy. Riel was not the worst of us. He was the best of us. Despite his eccentricities, his struggle for freedom was sane. As one of their flags proclaims, the Métis defended their homes and altars, but mostly, their freedom: *maison, autels, surtout liberté*. As Riel wrote on April 2, 1885, "Ours is a battle for homes and human rights... Jefferson's sublime sentiment, 'life, liberty, and the pursuit of happiness,' is a living echo in our hearts."

At a time when some mostly monolingual English-speaking Western Métis leaders and their academic allies claim that the French-speaking Eastern Métis from Quebec, Acadia—and even the Anglophone ones from Ontario—are not real Métis, it is time to remember the regard that Louis Riel held for Quebec. Riel was clear that Quebec was the heartland of the Métis and the cradle of their birth from whence they spread to Western Canada and other parts of North America. In the eyes of Riel, Quebec was a model of nation-building and an inspiration to the Métis people. The people of Quebec, with their national aspirations, were the natural allies of the Métis. The vision that Louis Riel had for the Métis Nation was inspired by his vision of the Quebec Nation. A people seeking sovereignty needed support. For Riel, the natural ally and advocate of the Métis people and their national aspirations was none other than Quebec. Chapter eight is a wake-up call for the Métis who have forgotten who they are, where they came, and who have adopted the anti-French attitude of the colonial masters.

Considering that Louis Riel loved Quebec, it follows that he loved Quebeckers and French-Canadians. So much is evident from chapter nine. For him, the Métis were mostly the offspring of French-Canadians and First Nations. They were French-Canadian Métis. And since he loved French-Canadians, it goes without saying that he loved the lovely French language, as we saw in chapter ten. For Louis Riel, French, even peppered with Indian words and expressions, was, and would always be, the central and national language of the Métis people. After all, even where English and

Indian languages were spoken, French served as the *lingua franca* among the Métis. Riel's pride in the French language resonates with all the French-speaking people of Canada and the United States, from Acadia to British Columbia and from Quebec to Louisiana. Not only did he love the language, but he made notable contributions to French Canadian literature through his poetry and prose.

Riel loved the First Nations, the Métis, and the French-Canadians, and he also loved Irish Catholics, the republican Fenians for certain, and not the Protestant Orangemen and Ulstermen as we observed in chapter eleven. While he made a major *faux pas* and a military blunder by failing to support the Fenian attacks on Canada, which was a fatal blow to their militia, he realized that the Métis required allies and that it was vital for them to enlist the support of Irish Catholics. Despite his efforts to mend bridges, and Fenian attempts to use his name to attract supporters, Riel had alienated some vital allies. His diplomatic outreach in New York and elsewhere bore no fruit and was met with failure. However, this obstacle did not prevent him from continuing to call upon the support of Irish Catholics and champion their cause in Ireland, the United States, and Canada.

As an anti-imperialist, it is difficult for some to understand how Louis Riel could be so pro-American, even calling for the United States to conquer and annex the Canadian Northwest. It should be remembered and recalled that the United States was initially revolutionary and anti-imperialistic. The Founding Fathers waged war against British imperialism. It was only later that the imperial character of the United States started to surface. Riel, it would seem, was fixated on the ideals of the American War of Independence, the *Declaration of Independence*, the *Constitution of the United States*, the *Bill of Rights*, and the writings of the Founding Fathers. Still, the United States was engaged in an imperialistic and genocidal western expansion during his life. How else can we describe the Indian Wars and Manifest Destiny?

In chapter thirteen, we moved from the political to the social and scrutinized Louis Riel's view of women. It would do readers well to remember that the Métis leader lived in the nineteenth century and was the product of a conservative Catholic upbringing and education. He was even considered a dyed-in-the-wool conservative in his times. Consequently, he seems all the more so in our times. For Riel, like most men and women of the time, a woman's value resided in her beauty, piety, virtue, fecundity, and frugality. Her place was in the home. Her purpose was to please her husband and God. While he was respectful of women, treated them with courtesy, and appears to have been a loving and romantic man, he was, in the view of many current readers, old-fashioned, which is expected of a man from that time and place. Different times and circumstances produce different results.

It is unfortunate, from a twenty-first century perspective, that Riel wrote so little about women and that his works did not reflect the strong First Nations and Métis women who contributed to their communities and the struggle for their rights. This is a lasting lacuna. It might have been the product of conservative Christian ideas. It could also have derived from First Nations ones. Still, the affection he showed to his wives, mother, and sisters is touching. In that sense, Louis Riel can serve as a role model of a loving and responsible father and husband who does not engage in domestic violence and who cares and provides for his family.

As much as some liberals, leftists, and other activists wish to appropriate Louis Riel, chapter fourteen made it clear that the Métis leader was no friend of liberalism and libertinism. When he called for freedom, it was freedom for his people, the Métis, and not individual liberty. He believed that human beings should have the right to submit to God and God's law. Riel did not view freedom as an absolute right. After all, Riel was always quick to condemn "liberal Christians who refused to obey anyone while Jesus Christ was obedient up to his death." A staunch believer who held traditional, conservative, Christian values, Riel viewed liberalism as an evil affront to God and religion. Moreover, he viewed both liberalism and Islam as allies in a religious, cultural, and civilizational war against the so-called Christian West. Whether we agree or disagree with some of Riel's views, we must remember that many anti-imperialists of the time in different parts of the world held similar views to his. Like

Riel, Karl Marx loved the American revolution and the Republic and was a staunch supporter of Lincoln. People adjust, adapt, and evolve, for good or bad. Prior to his death, he admitted that French-Canadian and Irish liberals had been very good to him. This was a humble and important overture. It shows that he was willing to cross the aisle and work with others on issues of common concern. Things were not black and white after all. There was a spectrum. There was room for compromise.

Finally, in chapter fifteen, we saw the importance of Métis unity in Riel's mind. One can only hope that Métis leaders, non-Métis academics, and politicians will heed his call and stamp out the fires of internal division and dissension that only serve to debilitate the Métis people. The artificially created conflict between the Western Métis and the Eastern Métis is a classic case of divide and conquer. Riel's concept of a Métis Nation was inclusive and spanned from East to West, North to South, and from sea to shining sea. It covered the entire interconnected Métis diaspora of the northern part of Turtle Island, namely, Canada and the United States. The teachings of Louis Riel remain more relevant than ever. May they continue to inspire an awakening of Métis consciousness, pride, unity, and solidarity in Canada and the United States.

APPENDIX: WHAT MAKES A MÉTIS?

Being and Becoming Métis: A Complex Question

Who is a Métis, like who is First Nations, is a complex and contentious question that receives many different responses. For some, it is a matter of race, biology, and genetics. For others, it is a question of culture. And yet, for others, it is a political matter, an issue of membership and citizenship in a tribe or nation. For some, however, this does not suffice, in and of itself, unless it is federally recognized. This leaves most non-status native people in the lurch, including the Métis and all others whose ancestors did not sign treaties with the American or Canadian government. What is more, in the United States, many tribes, who had signed treaties, had their federal recognition rescinded. Although federal recognition can provide some rights, white men should never have been allowed to become the gatekeepers of Indigenous identity. People who own themselves have the inherent right to recognize themselves. What follows is an attempt at defining what makes a Métis person. Evidently, it all depends on one's definition of Métis. In this case, we operate on the premise that the Métis are a distinct people of European and First Nations origin who emerged in north-eastern North America in the early 1600s and who spread throughout North America propelled, in part, by the fur trade.

1) A Métis is a Métis by Race, Biology, and Genetics

Although their non-Indigenous ancestry may vary and is predominantly French-Canadian, a Métis, unless adopted, must have an

Indigenous root ancestor from North America, namely, Canada and/or the United States. A person of Spanish and Indigenous ancestry is a Mestizo, not a Métis. Although the Mestizos from Latin America are part Indigenous, they are not Indigenous people by identity or culture. They have not historically identified as such, nor have they been identified as such by others. They are Hispanic or Latino. Although it contains Indigenous elements, their culture is Western. They identified with their European ancestors in language, culture, customs, and religion.

The Indigenous root ancestors of the Métis inhabited numerous cultural zones, including the Eastern Woodlands, the Subarctic, the Great Plains, the Plateau, and the Northwest coast. Since the Métis are Aboriginal people, they must have an Indigenous ancestor. The Métis, however, have always rejected the imperially imposed blood quantum, which was designed to gradually diminish the number of status Indians as part of a process to breed them out of existence and assimilate them into white colonial culture. As Jack Hitt has pointed out, those who ridicule a supposedly lax sense of tribal membership "have retrofitted the old genocidal system of blood quantum—measuring racial purity by blood—into the new standard for real Indianness, a choice rich with paradox." In fact, as C. Matthew Snip, a Native American scholar, has noted, the Bureau of Indian Affairs, which grants the Certificate of Indian or Alaskan Native Blood, determines who is Indigenous, like the American Kennel Club judges which dogs are purebred.

That being said, regardless of degree, Métis must carry First Nations DNA. However, this does not suffice. And they do not need to be subjected to genetic ancestry testing to prove who they are. Moreover, as a people of mixed ancestry, their maternal and/or paternal DNA can be either Amerindian or European. What is more, genetic markers that are common among Indigenous Peoples are also found among other populations worldwide. Some Indigenous Peoples find blood quantum a useful fence to keep fraudsters out; others view it as offensive. As a Cree and Anishinaabe woman stated, in reference to the term "Half-Breed," "I don't like being talked about in a vocabulary usually reserved for dogs and horses."

Although blood quantum and an ancestor in a tribal roll are all that remain when it comes to determining who is legally an Indian in the United States, in the past the process also involved racial biologists scratching the skin of people to see whether it changed colour or not, measuring craniums and the height of cheekbones, and other techniques that were also applied to blacks to determine their degree of admixture.

To claim, as the Ontario Métis Family Records Center does, that "any person with an aboriginal ancestor" is a Métis is an oversimplification and a profitable one at that when it comes to granting paid pedigrees, that is only correct in a biological, or genetic sense as there is a distinction between race—which is a European concept imposed on Aboriginal people—in the sense of human genetics, and ethnicity, which refers to a shared cultural identity and heritage. Being Métis by race, namely, having mixed European and First Nations DNA, does not a Métis make. It is the essential foundation; however, it is not enough. It requires the home that was built upon it: Métis family, community, and culture. The First Nations never viewed themselves as members of a race. As the meaning of their original tribal and national names demonstrate, they viewed themselves as human beings and people.

A person with a Cherokee ancestor who lived two hundred years ago, and whose family has identified as white Americans ever since, is not a Métis. One must have a First Nations ancestor who married a non-First Nations person, in most cases a European, typically a Frenchman or a *Canadien*, and their children must have belonged to a Métis family, clan, or community. Many Canadians and Americans have a remote Indian ancestor who lived centuries past. However, their ancestors never developed a unique culture and never evolved into an identifiable ethnic group that was distinguished from others. They integrated into white, Hispanic, or black culture. They were not members of the Métis people.

Being Métis is not merely about race. It is about historical community connection, cultural continuity, and current identity. Métis are not merely "mixed-bloods." They are not entirely Native or European. Having a single Amerindian ancestor who lived in the seventeenth century and whose descendants assimilated into French or English culture does not make one a member of the Métis people any more than having a white great-grandfather would make an African American white. Who is your family? Who are your people? How did they identify? Where do you feel at home? How do you see yourself? As the 1996 Report of the Royal Commission on Aboriginal Peoples noted, "Many Canadians have mixed Aboriginal / non-Aboriginal ancestry, but that does not make them Métis or even Aboriginal... What distinguishes Métis people from everyone else is that they associate themselves with a culture that is distinctly Métis."

First Nations and Métis ancestry is the essential founding stone of Métis identity. However, Métis people, like First Nations people, are not expected to look a stereotypical way. Some may look very First Nations, whatever that means. Others may look very European, whatever that means. And some are even black, whatever that means. Some Métis, like some First Nations, have engaged in exogamy for decades or centuries, which shows in their facial features and skin colour. Their outward appearance does not determine their racial, ethnic, and cultural identity. This has never been an issue for most Métis and First Nations throughout history. Still, it has been made into an issue by non-Natives as a means of mocking Indigenous people for not looking Indian enough, whatever that means. As Jack Hitt has noted, "A lot of Indians haven't looked 'Indian' for quite a while, especially in the eastern half of the country, where there is a longer history of contact with Europeans." The Métis and the First Nations will not stand for such racist nonsense that requires them to look a certain way, dress a certain way, or act a certain way. They honour the past, but live in the present with eyes on the future. As Arikara chief, White Shield, stressed: "The colour of the skin makes no difference" as "the Great Spirit made all men brothers."

2) A Métis is a Métis by Ancestry and Genealogy

A Métis person should be able to trace his/her ancestry back to an Indigenous root ancestor and his/her Métis offspring. In most cases, these lines trace to a French-Canadian father and a First Nations mother. In some cases, they trace to a French or *Canadien* woman who married a First Nations man. The structure is patrilineal and/or matrilineal, marked with intermarriage with other Métis, and particular kinship ties. Having a single Indigenous ancestor who lived in the 1600s, and whose children assimilated into French or English Canadian society, demonstrates remote Indigenous ancestry and not Métis cultural continuity. Centuries of marriage between Métis people does demonstrate a clear cultural connection as there was a great deal of endogamy among them until the twentieth century. Métis people tended to marry other Métis people. Their kinship network was complex. They tended to be all interrelated and interconnected.

For Métis who have lived in majority Métis communities which are few and far between or larger minority communities, membership is easily established based on oral history and family connections. For those who have lived as scattered and dispersed minorities among Anglo-Canadians, French-Canadians, or Acadians, the situation can sometimes be more difficult. Rather than belonging to a specific, geographically bound Métis community, these individuals belonged to minority Métis families and/or clans. They are Métis, nonetheless. "This diasporic sense of community is necessary to the Métis," notes Katie K. MacLeod, "as their identities have been marginalized and dispersed." Some, however, belonged to families that suppressed their heritage, at some point in recent history, for reasons of shame or safety. Others were adopted by non-Métis families who raised them in another culture, typically the dominant English or French-Canadian one.

These reborn Métis have every right to take pride in their heritage and humbly reconnect with their culture. Human beings have the right to self-identification. Obviously, people cannot claim to be what they are not and what cannot be proven. If a person does indeed descend from the North American Métis people—not just people with a remote, mythical, or imaginary Indian ancestor—and whose ancestors were accepted as Métis, then their descendants have every right to be identified and recognized as such without being accused of being white settlers, wannabes, ethnic frauds, race shoppers or race-shifters. Although there might be some rare exceptions, they are not white Canadians or Americans who are pretending to be Métis.

Although some First Nations and Métis denounce this increased Indigenous self-identification, others like Clem Iron Will, a Lakota elder, "sees this flood of new ethnic claims as magnificent, a surge of Indians 'trying to come home.'" Rather than weakening and diluting First Nations and Métis communities, this influx of the reborn and revitalized can help revive and strengthen them, bringing education, wealth, skills, political acumen, legal knowledge, and a zeal to serve, help, organize, cooperate, collaborate, and lead.

Evidently, there is no place in First Nations or Métis communities for pretendians, people without proven Indigenous ancestry, who attempt to pass as Indigenous people in an extreme form of cultural appropriation. All bona fide Métis communities require their members or citizens to provide verifiable genealogical, historical, and legal documents proving their descent from a demonstrated Métis ancestor. Lineage, however, does not suffice. They must also be connected to historical Métis ancestors, families, and communities, and identify as Métis people.

3) A Métis is a Métis by Identity

As Joanne Nagel explains, "Ethnic identity is at the intersection of ethnic self-definition (internal identification) and ethnic attribution (external ascription)." As Elizabeth Sperry elaborates,

> Basically, identity is neither black nor white, and it cannot be measured by the composition of our genetic material. Rather, it is a grey area that resides somewhere along a continuum between how we see ourselves and how others perceive us.

Since the ancestors of the contemporary Métis used no less than thirty-five different ethnonyms to describe themselves in the Red River Colony alone, "the current strategy of demanding proof that one's ancestors used the 'Métis' ethnonym in a self-referential way is truly deceptive." So long as one's North American ancestors were of mixed First Nations and European ancestry and one meets the rest of the criteria required of the Métis, one can identify as Métis.

For unity and uniformity, a Métis must identify as a Métis person. If a person identifies exclusively as First Nations or French-Canadian, for example, and not as a Métis, in part or whole, then such a person is First Nations or French-Canadian. Since there is no singular Métis identity, as ethnic boundaries are not cut and dry, Métis identity represents a spectrum. Identifying as Métis, as well as First Nations and/or French-Canadian, negates none of these identities. For Bouchard, Malette, and Marcotte argue,

> The fact that the Métis were capable of participating in the cultural universe of both Euro-Canadians and Indians does not mean that they were assimilated into either community. As Louis Riel himself articulated, it is more accurate to conceptualize French-Canadian and Métis identities not as mutually exclusive but as at times overlapped: identities between which individuals can navigate, identities that can be reclaimed, and combinations thereof.

As Gaffney, Gould, and Semple note, there are many Métis peoples in Canada. This reality was recognized by the Supreme Court in Daniels v. Canada:

> There is no one exclusive Métis people in Canada, any more than there is no one exclusive Indian people in Canada. The Métis of eastern Canada and northern Canada are as distinct from Red River Métis as any two peoples can be. Yet all are distinct from Indian communities by ancestry, by choice, and their self-identification as Métis. As early as 1650, a distinct Métis community developed in LaHève, Nova Scotia, separate from Acadians and Micmac Indians.

Rather than "comprising a single people, speaking a single common language, occupying a single common territory with defined borders, having a shared psychological character, and striving for statehood... the documentary record... reveals an open-ended diaspora culture that is fluid and resistant." As Elizabeth Sperry notes, "contemporary scholars redefine the Métis as a 'people in motion' who never occupied a specifically bounded tribal region, but continuously evolved as distinct communities that utilized a variety of resource areas." They view the Métis as ethnically dynamic. For Foxcurran, Bouchard, and Malette, "Métis identity is not limited to just one region of Canada." It is not even limited to one region of the United States. As Elizabeth Sperry notes,

> The Métis, Cree and Chippewa people of Montana existed in a seamless web of overlapping and interweaving cultural variation, and their survival and persistence depended upon their ability to accommodate and incorporate the social, economic, and political changes they experienced through interaction with cultural others...

The same complexities can be found among the Métis of Acadia, Quebec, Ontario, western Canada, Louisiana, Maine, Illinois, Indiana, Michigan, Wisconsin, North Dakota, Montana, Oregon, Washington State, and elsewhere. They found themselves at a crossroads of cultures. They had to navigate cross-cultural currents.

Considering that Métis communities existed throughout many parts of North America, Foxcurran, Bouchard, and Malette argue that "other communities can legitimately claim a Métis identity of their own, in line with Louis Riel's inclusive political vision." In short, "Métis identity should be recognized as pan-continental."

The Métis are a people. They consist of nations, communities, and individuals. They, and they alone, should determine their identity. Their self-identity does not require political or judicial recognition. Outsiders have no say in the matter. While a Métis community can determine its criteria for membership or citizenship, they cannot impose those on others. An Acadian Métis is not a Red River Métis, nor is a Red River Métis a Northern Métis, nor is a Northern Métis a Michigan Métis. However, they are all Métis. Riel may have said that "the Northwest is our Mother;" however, he was referring to the Métis from the Northwest. It should be remembered, however, that he also stressed that "Quebec is our Mother." As Bouchard, Malette, and Marcotte assert, "the Métis exist today, as yesterday, regardless of what governments, scholars, and ideologues may say, and their voices, though muted, still resonate."

While people have the right to self-identify, this alone does not grant a person legal entitlement to recognition or collective rights from a political perspective. Recognition comes from family ties, kinship, and community, as well as membership and citizenship in Métis organizations and nations. It is not enough to claim to be Indian or Métis. One should also be claimed. There are, however, many Indigenous people, who proudly identify as such, but who have been disconnected from their families and communities of origin. They are like prodigal children and should not be left orphaned.

There are members of federally recognized tribes who are fully assimilated into American and Canadian culture. They are more colonial than the colonials. There are also non-status Indians and Métis people, with no federal or state recognition or rights, who are profoundly immersed in the Indigenous culture and worldview. There are people who are less than 1% native who are fully native while there are people who are 100 percent native who are white in culture, mindset, and mentality. Indigenous identity is essential; however, culture is also crucial.

4) A Métis is a Métis by Culture

Although there is diversity among the Métis community, and their experiences are different, some trace to explorers, voyageurs, hunters, trappers, fishermen, farmers, and loggers, and others to buffalo hunters, a Métis must be a Métis by culture. Cultural markers include race, ethnicity, self-identification, religion, common history, strong links to territories and nature, traditions, rites of initiation and passage, purpose, language, shared values, ethics, principles, norms, and boundaries, kinship structures, niche occupations, and professions, traditional knowledge, clothing, cuisine, music, dancing, art, ceremonies, hunting, trapping, gathering, and fishing, as well as agricultural practices and outdoor survival skills. In most cases, there is a living or ancestral connection to Catholicism and/or First Nations spirituality. Cultural identifiers include symbols, geography, learning styles, social behaviour, and a sense of self-determination. They create a sense of mutual trust and belonging. One fits in with one's people. One feels at home. Although overlapping elements can be shared between cultures, ethnic markers differentiate one ethnicity from others. Although they are diverse, they are distinct in specific forms and fashions.

People partake in their culture of origin to various degrees. Some are deeply engaged. Others are moderate or passive. And yet others treat their culture and ancestry as peripheral. Some Italian Canadians speak Italian at home, eat Italian food, watch Italian programs, read Italian books, listen to Italian music, and participate in Italian festivities. Others speak only English and are primarily Italian by heritage and lineage. Some Muslims pray five times a day, fast the month of Ramadan, read the Qur'an on a daily basis, and try to live their religion. Others are mostly nominal Muslims, attending the mosque only for the two major celebrations. People also grow more or less religious during their lives. Some become increasingly involved in their culture. Such things fluctuate during one's life. What applies to others also applies to the Métis. Who is authentically Indigenous? Who determines that? The fact is that it varies for each individual. What is clear, however, is that the failure to partake in particular cultural markers does not make one any less Métis.

During part of his adult life, Jean-Baptiste Richardville—the Métis son of a Miami chiefess and a French-Canadian fur trader, Jean-Antoine Drouet de Richardville, who settled permanently in Trois-Rivières, Quebec— identified as French which, in Miami, is *Meehtikoošia*. Although it is generally believed to mean "dugout canoe people," it sounds suspiciously close to the term *Métis*. According to Miami accounts, their ancestors first encountered the *Meehtikoošia* on Lake Huron, presumably before 1640. They also came across them in Wisconsin in the 1670s. It is possible that the Miami indigenized the term *Métis*. It could also argued, however tenuously, that the term is of Indigenous origin and was adopted into French as *Meehti* or *Métis*. A sound linguist would argue that the Miami coined the expression from the French word *Métis*. This would support the claim the French-Indians or Half-Breeds were already identifying themselves as *Métis* in the seventeenth century, placing their ethnogenesis in Eastern Canada and the Great Lakes well before they established themselves in the Northwest. We know for a fact that the *Bois-Brulés* had visited Sault Ste. Marie as early as

1654 and held a *rendez-vous* at Mackinac before 1670. This is precisely the period in which the Miami Indians encountered the Métis on Lake Huron. And they were not few and far between. By then, they represented such a sizeable community across parts of North America that they had organized a large gathering of their people.

In any event, Chief Richardville, the leader of the Miami, was proud of his aristocratic French ancestry and identified as such for a period of time, insisting on dressing French, speaking French, and taking an interest in European culture. Later, he asserted that he was a *Créole*, a French Half-Breed or a Métis, speaking both French and Miami. However, after seeing that he could only secure rights for his people if they identified as Indians, including a reservation for the Indiana Miami in Oklahoma, he started to stress that he was a Miami Indian, dressed in Miami clothing, and insisted on only speaking Miami. This is the spectrum in which many Métis have lived and continue to live. At times they emphasize their French side, while at others, they stress their First Nations side. However, they find more balance and equilibrium when they stand in the middle and straddle both sides. While the Miami may identify as Indians today, many, if not most, of their ancestors were French Métis. Likewise, most of the Chippewa Indians from the Turtle Mountain Reservation in North Dakota are ethnically of French Métis ancestry, although legally, they are classified as Indians. The same goes for the Little Shell Tribe of Chippewa Indians of Montana.

Culture is ever evolving. Twenty-first century Métis are not required to live in the nineteenth, eighteenth, or seventeenth century. They are not a people frozen in time expected to wear traditional dress, drive logs down rivers, hunt bison, live in cabins and tipis, eat without cutlery, and drive horse-drawn wagons. They do not live in a time bubble in which technology has ceased to evolve and progress and science has come to a halt, like many Amish and Mennonites. They are connected to their past, not constrained by it. They are neither a historic community nor relics of the past required to engage in a historical reenactment to obtain legitimacy or credibility in the eyes of outsiders. They are a contemporary community. Wearing Western clothing, eating sushi, practicing yoga or martial arts, listening to jazz, or attending the opera does not make one any less Métis or First Nations. Aboriginal people find it comical when whites ask them, "why don't you wear traditional clothing?" to which they respond, "as soon as you do so to go to work." First Nations and Métis wear regalia when they participate in a pow-wow or a *rendez-vous*, just like some people of European ancestry wear traditional ethnic clothing when participating in festivals celebrating their heritage. Considering the prohibitively expensive and exorbitant cost of such formal, ritual attire and its impracticality, it is not something they wear daily.

Since most Indigenous people live in urban settings, they have become urban First Nations and Métis and have adopted and adapted aspects of urban culture. Indigenous rappers and dancers are Indigenous. A Mexican does not have to play mariachi to be Mexican. He can play rock and roll if he so wishes. A Métis who lives in a city and works as an attorney is no less authentic and legitimate than one who works as a hunting or fishing guide. Their indigeneity is not compromised. Indigenous diasporic identities are fluid, not frozen. First Nations and Métis are not required to live up to imagined and idealized ethnic traits imposed by others. They have the right to reconstruct their identity, grow, flower, and blossom. They, and they alone, determine their identity, not outsiders, naysayers, and character assassins who assign themselves roles as ethnic inquisitors on a mission to out so-called imposters. The Métis should not be required to "show their papers" or prove who they are to people outside their families, clans, and communities. They do not appreciate being told who they are and who they are not. As one Ojibwe man joked, "I am part white, but I don't have the papers to prove it."

5) A Métis is a Métis by Language

Language is central to cultural transmission and identity. Since the earliest Métis were French-speaking, a Métis is a Métis by language or, in most cases, a descendant of French-speaking Métis people. Many Métis lost their French. Some of them abandoned the tongue out of shame. Others lost their French due to assimilationist government policies that prohibited free speech. As Robert A. Papen relates,

> It is a well-established fact that in Western Canada, Michif French speakers were discriminated against by everyone, including French-Canadians, the French-speaking Catholic clergy, missionaries, and nuns, and schoolteachers... Métis children were regularly punished if they spoke their dialect on the school grounds... and it is not surprising that many Francophone Métis have abandoned their heritage language in favour of English.

As a result, Papen estimates that there remain less than five thousand fluent "Michif French speakers in the Canadian provinces west of Ontario."

While much culture is lost when language is lost, a Métis person does not lose his status so long as he continues to identify as Métis. It is only when people assimilate into another culture that they lose their ancestral culture. Some Louisiana Cajuns have lost their French language; however, they still maintain a strong cultural identity. They are proud of their French ancestry, Catholic religion, music, and dances. The same can be said of many English-speaking Métis people.

While French was always the dominant language of the Métis, in most cases, in the French-Canadian Métis variant, a smaller number spoke Michif-Cree or French-Cree. Although fewer than a thousand people maintain these mixed languages—and Bungi, an English dialect with influence from Scottish English, Orcadian Scots, Norn, Scottish Gaelic, French, Cree, and Ojibwe, has gone extinct—their speakers had a linguistic connection to the Métis people. Michif, however, only developed in the early nineteenth century. What is more, "it was arguably never the language of the majority of Métis, much less a *lingua franca*." "What is depicted as Michif," writes Malette, "was, in fact, spoken in isolated segments of the communities in the vicinity of the Red River, mostly in relation to small groups of Bison hunters." "In fact," he continues, "there is no historical evidence that Michif ever served as a nationally unifying language." As noted by Robert A. Papen,

> Michif has unfortunately become a handy political tool for the MNC and its provincial affiliates. By declaring Michif to be the historical and official language of the Métis, these organizations have succeeded in obtaining federal and provincial financing, which they have devoted exclusively to the hybrid language, to the detriment of the other Métis languages such as Michif French... These efforts, however, have not significantly increased the number of speakers.

Historically, many Métis spoke Indigenous languages on top of French and English, languages they learned from their First Nations mothers and grandmothers or interacting with other Indigenous nations. Bilingualism, trilingualism, and multilingualism are Métis cultural markers. As such, it is not unusual to find Métis people who are polyglots.

6) A Métis is a Métis by History, Family, Kinship, and Community

Societies consist of families, and families consist of individuals. Ultimately, to be a Métis is a matter of individual identity. As a result of discrimination and racism, many Métis were not openly raised as Métis. In some cases, their parents, and grandparents, preferred to pass as French or English Canadians. Some, darker in skin colour, claimed that they were of Spanish ancestry. Just like Jewish people did not tattoo the star of David on their foreheads for fear of persecution, neither did the Métis brand themselves with the infinity flag. If and when possible, many African Americans passed for white due to Jim Crow laws, segregation, racism, and discrimination. People cannot be faulted for trying to protect their children from harm. Métis children whom non-Métis parents adopted have a right to humbly reconnect with their heritage at any stage of their lives. Some Métis come from families that emphasized their French-Canadian or Scottish side and minimized or denied their Indigenous one. Those people have the right to reconnect with their roots in the same way as any Italian American or Lebanese American who was raised in an English-speaking home.

To be a Métis, one must come from a bona fide Métis family that goes back generations. Proving a connection to a historic Métis community, in a specific geographic location is problematic, as majority Métis communities were small and scattered. In most cases, they were mixed communities that consisted of First Nations, Métis people, Europeans, and, in some cases, even Africans, as in the case of Kaskaskia in Illinois. As Malette and Marcotte note,

> The Métis of the Outaouais never regrouped in homogeneous "villages" or even "reserves" defined by geographic clusters. Instead, they were comprised of a regional community whereby individuals socialized with fellow Métis but also participated in the larger society in interaction with settler and Indigenous communities.

As they note by comparing the ethnic composition of Baskatong Lake, Sault Ste. Marie, Ontario, the Red River, and even Labrador, historical Métis communities were "mixed or multiethnic." Consequently, "it would be a mistake to seek a historical community that is 'purely' Métis both ethnically and culturally homogeneous."

To claim that one cannot be Métis unless one proves that one's ancestors came from a majority Métis community demonstrates ignorance of Métis history and reality. It is like denying a person is Jewish American unless they can prove that they came from a majority Jewish American community. In many cases, the Métis were minorities living among other populations. They lived with or in proximity to First Nations and French-Canadians. This does not change the fact that they viewed themselves and were considered by others as distinct. Having an ancestor who lived in a historical Métis-majority community makes it easier to establish a racial, ethnic, genealogical, linguistic, and cultural connection; however, it cannot serve as a litmus test. Since there was no single ethnogenesis of the Métis people but rather a series of micro-geneses, it is important to frame Métis identity on a larger "continuum that spans geographic boundaries linking the East to the West." As Siomonn Pulla summarizes,

> The research is clear that, historically, Métis were present across the many regions of North America, and they "expressed their distinct

identity as a claim for both their French and Indian heritage" (Malette and Marcotte 2017: 42). In its landmark *Powley* decision, the Supreme Court of Canada (2003) recognized the diversity of Métis communities in Canada who "exhibit their own distinctive traits and traditions (para 11)." The notion of Métis diversity was further recognized by the court in its more recent 2016 *Daniels* decision. The *Daniels* decision highlighted that there is "no exclusive Métis people in Canada" (2016, para 17), stressing the notion that identity formation is a fluid process (2016, para 48-49).

NOTES ON SOURCES

PREFACE

More histories... have been written about Riel (Reid 2); *"Sir John A. MacDonald:" O Dieu Puissant! Daignez protéger les métis / Que déjà les Anglais ont presqu'anéantis* (Riel, vol. 4: 239); WASPS are ... becoming a minority (Todd n. page); It's a bit late to ask (Todd n. page); freeze all immigration (Todd n. page); oblivious to Indigenous issues (Todd n. page); freed all races (Riel, vol. 2: 369); colored people (Riel, vol. 2: 374); *cette sensibilité aux prejugés de race* (Campbell, vol. 4: note 63).

CHAPTER 1: LOUIS RIEL AND THE NAME MÉTIS

1.2 Métis, the First Name of a New First People: *Et je désire que ce nom distinctif soit le nom Métis que nous avons toujours porté. Je crois que le nom Métis est de nature à favoriser la fondation d'une puissante nationalité dans le Manitoba et le Nord-Ouest* (Riel, vol. 2: 120); *C'est un nom qui signifie mélange. Jusqu'ici il a servi à designer la race issue du sang mêlé des européens et des Sauvages, mais il est également propre de dénommer une race d'hommes, qui se recruterait du mélange de tous les sangs, entre eux; et qui, tout en passant dans le moule canadien-français, conserverait le souvenir de son origine, en s'appelant Métisse* (Riel, vol. 2: 120);

Le nom Métis serait agréable à tout le monde, parce qu'il n'est pas exclusif et qu'il a l'avantage de mentionner d'une manière convenable, le contingent pour lequel chaque nation contribuerait à fonder le peuple nouveau. Et à ce point de vue je crois qu'il serait difficile de donner comme base à notre nationalité dans le Manitoba et le Nord-Ouest, une idée plus large et plus forte que l'idée Métisse (Riel, vol. 2: 120);

The Métis dispersed (Redbird 27); nowhere ... to retreat (Sealy and Lussier 181); little choice but to integrate (Sealy and Lussier 179); Although all Métis are by definition persons who consider themselves Métis (Slobodin 151); 46% of Métis applicants (Slobodin 150); did not self-identity as readily (Slobodin 151-152); differences in histories (Slobodin 151); the shallow genealogies (Slobodin 155); do not identify themselves as such (Lusty 4); Many Métis families (Malette and Marcotte 2021: 312); adopted whatever identity (Gagnon 2021: 17); Hiding one's identity (Richardson 2006: 60); shifting and contested meaning (Fagan et al. 261); accusations of recent opportunism (Malette 2021:

53); not all western Métis people endorse (Malette 2021: 318); Many Métis in the Red River (Malette 2021: 318); there are no universal pan Métis definitions of Métis identity (Larivière 101); universal rights (Larivière 108); as they see fit (Larivière 108); to accept and acknowledge (Larivière 108); Recognition of the Métis Nation (White 12).

CHAPTER 2: LOUIS RIEL AND MÉTIS UNITY

2.2 *Sauvages*: *"Révélation contre Beauport" Connaissez-moi: Presque tout mon sang vient de la France; j'en ai de l'Irlande; et j'ai du sang sauvage* (Riel, vol. 2: 72); *"Le Sang Sauvage en moi rayonne" Le Sang Sauvage en moi rayonne / et je louange mes aïeux* (Riel, vol. 4 : 178); *"Pétition à Alexander Morris" nous faisons tout notre possible pour parler du mieux qu'on peut à toutes les nations sauvages pour agir en droit et en justice* (Riel, vol. 1: 483); Riel described Indigenous people as *sauvages* (Riel, vol. 2: 120); *peuple sauvage* (Riel, vol. 4: 123); *"Notes sur le métissage des peuples"* (Riel, vol. 2: 409-410); *langues sauvages* (Riel, vol. 4: 322); [Indian blood] of the Métis (Riel, vol. 4: 322); *"Le peuple Métis-Canadien-Français" Les Métis et les Cris se traitent comme doivent se traiter de bons amis et de bons parents* (Riel, vol. 3: 84); "Memorandum" (Riel, vol. 3: 21-22); *les tribus sauvages* (Riel, vol. 3: 358); *"Lettre aux Métis Anglais et Français"* (Riel, vol. 3: 69); *nos parents les sauvages* (Riel, vol. 3: 65); *"Journal"* (vol 3: 393, 394, 488); Riel wrote about "Indians" (Riel, vol. 3: 90-91); *chefs sauvages* (Riel, vol. 3: 118); *"Mémoire se rapportant au Nord-Ouest"* (Riel, vol. 3: 308); *"Manifeste à mes concitoyens américains"* (Riel, vol. 3: 309); *"Révélation se rapportant à l'annexation américaine du Nord-Ouest" les sauvages... dans le Nord-Ouest* (Riel, vol. 3: 312).

2.3 Natives / Indians: A native of the Northwest Territory (Riel, vol. 3: 179); *la droiture indienne* (Riel, vol. 4: 326); *les défauts de notre sang Indien* (Riel, vol. 4: 326).

2.4 Aboriginals: As [an] aboriginal (Riel, vol 3: 319, 320).

2.5 Original Half-Breeds / Aboriginal Half-Breeds: The fur traders (Jackson 278, note 1); Original Half-Breeds (Riel, vol 3: 53); The Aboriginal Half-Breeds (Riel, vol. 3: 53).

2.6 Whites: White people in general (Bakker 65); The white men married to Indian women (Riel, vol. 2: 259); Montana has a pretty numerous (Riel, vol 3: 5); Métis culture was syncretic (Barnholden 31); I remembered that Half-Breed meant white and Indian (Riel, vol. 3: 525); Indian and white (Hitlermann n. page); Prior to 1981 (Hitlermann n. page).

2.7 French: The French-speaking population (Riel, vol. 1: 22); *Ma mère est de race guerrière. / Elle vient du pur-sang français. / Son nom est Lagimodière* (Flanagan 1996: 124), see also 5); *"Compte rendu incomplet de la convention de novembre-décembre 1869"* (Riel, vol. 1: 23-31); *la langue de nos chers aïeux* (Riel, vol. 4: 324); the respect and cooperation of the Indians (Gray 42).

2.8 French-Canadians: *"Programme National des Métis Canadiens Français" ces généreux Canadiens Français, nos pères et nos frères, qui sont ainsi dire l'ami et la force de la Nation Métisse et qui parmi les Métis paraissent en vérité plus Métis que les Métis eux-mêmes, nous appuyons de toutes nos forces réunies la noble démarche que nos représentants ont fait dans l'hiver de '71, en demandant pour chacun d'eux et les anciens colons de sang non-Métis un octroi de 160 acres de terre* (Riel, vol. 1: 291);

"Discours à l'occasion de la fête de la saint Jean-Baptiste" Vos enfants se réunissant sous le drapeau de la St. Jean-Baptiste que nous adoptons comme notre fête nationale, viennent vous saluer. Ça doit être un grand bonheur... de voir dans la fondation d'un peuple nouveau fêtant ici sa nationalité... Les Métis Canadiens Français tendant la main à leurs frères les Canadiens Français, veulent continuer ici la belle œuvre qui se poursuit depuis longtemps par la généreuse et noble province de Québec (Riel, vol. 1: 267);

"Lettre à C.-J. Coursel" Je félicite les Canadiens-Français de célébrer comme peuple notre fête nationale d'une manière aussi digne, aussi grandiose... Je sais que le noble cœur des Canadiens Français aime les Métis Canadiens de Manitoba et du Nord-Ouest. Et puis qu'en travaillant pour les Métis, pour mes chers compatriotes, je suis un de ceux qui a le plus à se féliciter des sympathies canadiennes françaises, et je tiens à vous assurer au nom des Métis que je suis uni de cœur et d'esprit avec vous pour fêter ce beau jour (vol. 1: 368); *"Le peuple Métis Canadien Français"* (vol. 4: 321); He praised the qualities of French-Canadians (vol. 4: 321-322); his love for the French language (vol. 4: 324); French-Canadians becoming French-Canadian Métis (vol. 4: 324-325); "brings Métis 'civilization' to the Canadians" (343).

2.9 *Bois-Brûlés* [Burnt Wood]: The Algonquin tribes (Redbird 1); The term *Bois-Brulés* (Kohl 260; Taché 1863; 1884: 215; Stuart 4; Tocqueville 1865: 244; Foxcrurran et al. 2016: 176; Malette 2021: 42); The term was also used in 1899 (Foxcurran, Bouchard, and Malette 2016: 389); *nation métisse* (Riel, vol. 4: 90); Bois-Brûlés du Nord (Riel, vol. 4: 91); *"Pendant que les Métis semaient" Les chefs zélés / De tous les Bois-Brûlés* (Riel, vol. 4: 123);

"Chanson de la Grenouillère" Voulez-vouz écouter chanter / Une chanson de vérité? / Le dix-neuf de juin la bande des Bois-Brûlés / Sont arrivés comme des braves guerriers. / En arrivant à la Grenouillère / Nous avons pris trois prisonniers; / Trois prisonniers des Arkanays / Qui sont ici pour piller notr' pays / Étant sur le point de débarquer / Deux de nos gens se sont mis à crier: / Deux de nos gens se sont mis à crier: / Voilà l'Anglais qui vient nous attaquer ! (Bouchard et al. 2020: 80); the term *Bois-Brûlés* (Bouchard et al. 2020, 82); *Bois-Brûlés* formed a distinct group (Bouchard et al. 2020: 82).

2.10 Métis Canadien [Canadian Métis]: *"Lettre à 'Monsieur le Redacteur'" Population Métis Canadienne de la Rivière Rouge* (Riel, vol. 1: 18-19); *Deux habitants Métis Canadiens de la Rivière-Rouge* (Riel, vol. 1: 20).

2.11 Half-Breeds: American Half-Breed citizens (Riel, vol. 2: 257); Half-Breed American citizens (Riel, vol. 2: 258); "Assiniboine Half-Breed" (Riel, vol. 2: 303); "Note about the Half-Breed Vote" (Riel, vol. 2: 360); numerous half-breed families (Riel, vol. 4: 285); "Speech at Prince Albert" (Riel, vol. 3: 499); "Petition 'To His Excellency the Governor-General-in-Council" (Riel, vol. 3: 33); "Statement to G.H. Young's Diary" (Riel, vol. 3: 90-91); "Interview with C.B. Pitblado" (Riel, vol. 3: 519); "Address to the Jury" (Riel, vol. 3: 519, 524, 531, 532, 533, 534, 547, 549, 556); When he wrote to J.W. Taylor (Riel, vol. 3: 37); "Interview with a Correspondent of the *Toronto Globe*" (Riel, vol. 3: 581).

2.12 English Half-Breeds: "Agreement of Surrender" (Riel, vol. 1: 34); "To the English Half- Breeds" (Riel, vol. 3: 53, 59).

2.13 Métis Anglais [English Métis]: *"A nos frères les Métis Anglais et Français du Lac Qu'Appelle et des environs"* (Riel, vol. 3: 62); "Letter to 'Dear Relatives'" (Riel, vol. 3: 66); *"Chers parents et amis"* (Riel, vol. 3: 69); The Métis whom Louis Riel championed (Flanagan 1992: 3).

2.14 Métis Français [French Métis]: "Mémoire ayant trait aux difficultés de la Rivière-Rouge" *les Métis Français* (Riel, vol. 1: 198); "Programme National des Métis Canadiens Français" *nous Métis français ... notre droit d'indien aux terres du pays* (Riel, vol. 1: 290*); "Lettre à 'Nos Parents:'" Les Métis Français ont pris les armes en masse. Il n'y a personne de nos gens contre. Dites à nos parents les sauvages de se tenir prêts à venir nous aider, s'il le faut* (Riel, vol. 3: 65).

2.15 Métis-Celte: "Révélation contre Beauport: " *j'en ai de l'Irlande* (Riel, vol. 2: 72); "Ode à ma sœur :" *J'aime... cet esprit Métis-Celte* (Riel, vol. 4: 233).

2.16 Métis: The term "Métis" (Bouchard, Malette, and Pulla 2021: xiv); *"Lettre à William Dease" Je ne demande pas de recompense; rien que le support et le soutien de tous les Métis* (Riel, vol. 1: 52); *les Métis ne font plus qu'un* (Riel, vol. 1: 53); *"Lettre à 'Chers amis'" les Métis* (Riel, vol. 1: 99); *"Lettre à A.-A. Taché" faible peuple des Métis* (Riel, vol. 1: 105); he referred to his people as the "Métis" (Riel, vol. 1: 106-107); *"Pétition des Métis et autres habitants du Manitoba au lieutenant-gouverneur A.G. Archibald" Métis* (Riel, vol. 1: 151); *"Adresse des habitants de St. Vital à Robert Cunningham"* We are the foundators (Riel, vol. 1: 272); when writing to John McDougall (Riel, vol. 1: 294); *"Lettre à 'Mes chers amis'"* (Riel, vol. 1: 292); They were used throughout North America (Marcotte 2021: 187).

2.17 Métis Canadiens Français [French-Canadian Métis]: *"Programme National des Métis Canadiens Français"* (Riel, vol. 1: 289); *"Lettre à C.-J. Coursel" Les Métis Canadiens Français du Nord sont une branche de l'arbre Canadien Français; ils veulent grandir comme cet arbre, avec cet arbre, ne point se détacher de lui, souffrir et se réjouir avec lui* (Riel, vol. 1: 368); *"Révélations que Jésus Christ a daigné faire à son serviteur, pauvre et inutile, Louis 'David' Riel" Métis Canadiens Français"* (Riel, vol. 2: 140);

"Lettre à Paul Proulx" Je voudrais qu'avec le secours de Dieu, nous travaillions à faire du peuple Métis Canadien Français un peuple assez grand pour mériter de recueillir l'héritage du Bas Canada [i.e. Québec], comme un bon fils reçoit et fait profiter les biens qui lui ont été légués par ses parents...

Et si vous me demandez pourquoi je ne veux pas que notre peuple s'appelle Canadien Français, tout court, je vous répondrai que ce nom-là étant déjà son nom de famille, il convient de lui en donner un autre qui le désigne particulièrement et qui soit en quelque sorte son nom de baptême comme peuple. Et je désire que ce nom distinctif soit le nom Métis que nous avons toujours porté. Je crois que le nom Métis est de nature à favoriser la fondation d'une puissante nationalité dans le Manitoba et le Nord-Ouest.

C'est un nom qui signifie mélange. Jusqu'ici il a servi à designer la race issue du sang mêlé des Européens et des Sauvages, mais il est également propre de dénommer une race d'hommes, qui se recruterait du mélange de tous les sangs, entre eux; et qui, tout en passant dans le moule Canadien-Français, conserverait le souvenir de son origine, en s'appelant Métisse.

Le nom Métis serait agréable à tout le monde, parce qu'il n'est pas exclusif et qu'il a l'avantage de mentionner d'une manière convenable, le contingent pour lequel chaque nation contribuerait à fonder le peuple nouveau. Et a ce point de vue je crois qu'il serait difficile de donner comme base à notre nationalité dans le Manitoba et le Nord-Ouest, une idée plus large et plus forte que l'idée Métisse.

Pour mieux achever l'exposition de ma pensée, je comparerai la fondation du peuple Métis Canadien-Français à une pièce d'étoffe que nous aurions à faire... Et quand l'étoffe sera finie, ce sera de l'étoffe française, parce que les ouvriers du beau métier de France y auront travaillé. Ce sera de l'étoffe vraiment canadienne; parce que nos tisserands étaient des Canadiens du moral. Ce sera de l'étoffe Métisse Canadienne-Française...

Soyons donc sans inquiétudes. Français, Canadiens et Métis, travaillons ensemble non seulement sans méfiance mais encore avec beaucoup d'amitié, selon que Dieu veut se servir de nous tous pour fonder le peuple Métis-Canadiens-Français (Riel, vol. 2: 120-121);

Je me suis marié depuis plus d'un an [1881]. J'ai pris une fille de la Prairie-du-Cheval-Blanc, une Métisse Canadienne-Française. Elle s'appelle Marguerite (Riel, vol. 2: 254);

"Notes sur le Métissage des peuples" toute la race sauvage de l'Amérique du Nord ferait place à une race nouvelle, la race Métisse, qui varierait selon les pays; dans le Manitoba, elle serait Métisse Canadienne-Française (Riel, vol. 2: 409-410);

"Le peuple Métis Canadien Français" J'aime sans mesure et j'admire / Les Métis Canadiens Français / Ce peuple nouveau qui se mire. / Déjà dans de brillants succès. / Il fait connaitre sa gloire / Aux Indiens du Minnesota. / Il a toujours gagné victoire / Sur les tribus du Dakota... / Le Manitoba si précoce / Est grand, parce

qu'il l'a fondé / Sous le beau frein du Sacerdoce / Qui l'a toujours si bien guidé... Si le trait d'union se place / Entre Métis et Canadien; / Assure, l'une et l'autre race / N'en sera que plus apte au bien... / Métis, la grande différence / Que nous tenons du sang indien / Se rendant jusques à l'outrance; / Et tout de même, Canadien... /

Dotons notre langue française / De mots étrangers qui soient beaux; /Afin que plus riche elle plaise / Plus en ces parages nouveaux. / Empruntons aux langues sauvages / Un certain choix d'expressions; / Quelques-unes de leurs images, / Quelques belles locutions. / Ces nouveautés rendront plus forte / La langue de nos chers aïeux. / Embellissons-la de la sorte / Suivant le goût de notre mieux. / Métis et Canadiens ensemble / Français, si nos trois éléments / S'amalgament bien, il me semble / Que nous serons un jour plus grands. /

Les trois feuilles du trèfle peuvent / Exister sur le même pied. / Toutes les trois, jolies, se meuvent / A l'unisson, comme il leur sied. / Le clergé qui nous édifie / Nous unira bien surement, / Comme le trèfle identifie / Ses trois fleurs admirablement. / Son grand cœur prend beaucoup de peine / A consolider, je le sais, / La nation manitobaine / Des Métis-Canadiens-Français. (Riel, vol. 4. 319-325);

"Lettre à J.-V. Grandin" Bénissez-nous, particulièrement, nous les Métis Canadiens Français. Bénissez-nous avec les Métis de toutes autre origines (Riel, vol. 3:23); *Choisissez-vous d'une manière particulière tous les Métis-Canadiens-Français et faites-en votre peuple de prédilection* (Riel, vol. 3: 49); "Lettre à Valentin Vegreville. Batoche" *les intérêts des Métis Canadiens Français* (Riel, vol. 3: 81);

"Formule No. 1 Serment pour les gardes" Faites-vous serment devant Dieu que vous serez fidèle au mouvement des Métis Canadiens Français et à leur Gouvernement Provisoire (Riel, vol. 3: 507); *"Journal" nos cœurs Métis Canadien Français* (Riel, vol. 3: 406); *Les Membres de l'Exovidat Métis Canadien Français de Saskatchewan* (Riel, vol. 3: 83);

"Lettre à A.-A. Taché" Vous les Métis, particulièrement avec tous les Métis Canadiens Français (Riel, vol. 3 138); he repeatedly wrote about the French-Canadian Métis (Riel, vol. 3: 293; vol. 3: 369; vol. 3: 375; vol. 4: 346); French-Canadians to come and help us there today (Riel, vol. 3: 556); *Le Manitoba deviendra tout Métis Canadien Français. Dans cinq cents ans d'ici, sa population Métisse Canadienne française sera de quarante millions d'âmes* (Riel, vol. 3: 490); The idea of a French-Canadian Métis Nation (Malette and Marcotte 2021: 313); a series of legislative acts (Malette and Marcotte, 2021: 313).

2.18 Identified as white (Flanagan 1985: 189-190).

CHAPTER 3: LOUIS RIEL AND THE MÉTIS NATION

3.2 Métis Diversity: *les Métis de toutes autres origines* (vol. 3: 125); There were *Bois-Brulés* long before (Howard 41); there was a Métis identity in the Great Lakes Region by 1757 (Bouchard, Malette, Pulla 2021: xv); a sizeable portion of Métis (Peterson 41); is contemporaneous with that of the western Métis (Bouchard, Malette and Pulla 2021: xvii-xviii); the Old Northwest (Flanagan 1985: 188); Métis settlements (Peterson and Brown 44;45); is one of the regions of North America (Bouchard, Malette, and Marcotte 2020: 7); it is well established that the history of the Métis (Gagnon 2021: 11); A shared ethnicity (Foxcurran, Bouchard, and Malette 2016: 389); Historical evidence (Gagnon 11-12); the Métis arrived in the Pacific Northwest (Jackson 7); a significant Detroit *coureur-de-bois* family (Gagnon 7); the retreating mixed bloods (Jackson 8);

Many of the Métis who settled in the Pacific Northwest (Jackson 132); a sampling of Métis origins (Jackson 132); these Eastern Métis bachelors took native American wives (Jackson 132); several of them were related to kinsmen (Jackson 94-95); These 115 trail-worn Red River Métis (Jackson 111); The Pacific Northwest mixed bloods (Jackson x); eastern Métis decorative arts (Jackson 200); The patterns of and symbols of their clothing (Jackson 200); an old Métis recipe (Jackson 228);

"French half-breed Oregonians" (Jackson 201); there were roughly 300 Métis (Jackson 227); belonged to the same race as those from the Red River and the Winnipeg Basin (Jackson 228); many Métis opted to identify publicly as French-Canadians while others retreated to Indian reservations (Jackson 229); The children of the trade (Jackson 229); Métis names are found on most tribal rolls (Jackson 229). Assimilation is a hard nut of concession and surrender (Jackson 229); the voyageur tradition (Slobodin 152); The Red River Métis (Bumsted 10); Although the acts are often cited as clear evidence of the establishment of a Métis "Nation" (DesJarlait n. page)

3.3 The Métis Race: *Jusqu'ici il a servi à designer la race issue du sang mêlé des Européens et des Sauvages* (Riel, vol. 2: 120); the Indian race (Riel, vol. 3: 179); the greater part of my... blood was white (Riel, vol. 3: 525); *la race Métisse* (Riel, vol. 2: 120); *race à trois-sangs* (Riel, vol. 4: 326); It is a truism that all human populations are "mixed" (Slobodin 1); the Métis are distinctly not the hybrids of two or more homogeneous races (Slobodin 1); The Métis of Canada are "mixed" genotypically and in cultural traditions (Slobodin 1); The risk of cultural essentialism (Malette 2021: 40);

The genesis of the Plains Métis (Sperry 20); To move beyond the current understanding of Métis peoplehood (Gagnon 2021: 9); Not all of us fit a formula (Green 169; Malette 2021: 41); The very polyvalent nature of Métis-ness (Turner 12); David Bouchard (MNBC 7); The Métis nationality (Slobodin 12); Many men formed marital unions with Cree women (Sutherland n. page); one First Nations grandparent on his father's side and none on his mother's side (Bouchard, Malette, and Marcotte 2020: 246, note 5); Disqualifying the authenticity of ethnic identity (Bouchard, Malette, and Marcotte 2020: 246, note 5); settled by Métis from Ontario and the Great Lakes regions (Sperry 23); many Métis settlers in Pembina (23).

3.4 The Métis People: *"Lettre à A.-A. Taché:" faible peuple des Métis* (Riel, vol. 1: 105); *"Discours à l'occasion de la fête de la saint Jean-Baptiste:" peuple nouveau* (Riel, vol. 4: 324); *"Du Dieu du ciel la Providence" peuple Métis* (Riel, vol. 4: 207); *"Le peuple Métis Canadien Français"* (Riel, vol. 4: 324); "Memoir to Ulysses S. Grant" (Riel, vol. 2: 6); *petit peuple Métis* (Riel, vol. 1: 449, 453); Julie Riel (Riel, vol. 1: 467); *"Lettre à Ignace Bourget"* (Riel, vol. 1: 476, 451); *"Lettre à Paul Proulx"* (Riel, vol. 2: 120-121); *"Pendant que les Métis semaient"* (Riel, vol. 4: 123); *"Consécration des Métis au Sacré-Cœur de Jésus"* (Riel, vol. 3: 49); "Notes Diverses:" *Mon Dieu ! Prenez en pitié les groupes éparpillés de mon peuple; du peuple que vous m'avez donné, de ce peuple qui est à vous entre tous les peuples de la terre. Mon Dieu, souvenez-vous que vous n'avez eu un aussi bon peuple que le peuple Métis* (Riel, vol. 3: 197); *"Prophéties de Regina" le peuple Métis Canadien Français est le peuple des Élus, le peuple de la Sainte Trinité* (Riel, vol. 3: 315).

3.5 The Métis Flock: *"Lettre à Paul Proulx" le petit troupeau Métis* (Riel, vol. 2: 121); Exoveed (Riel, vol. 3: 67); I prefer to be called one of the flock (Riel, vol. 2: 534); I believe I am the prophet of the New World (Riel, vol. 2: 534).

3.6 The Métis Tribe: to protect, to defend, [and] to sustain... all our tribes (Riel, vol. 3: 66); *les tribus sauvages* (Riel, vol. 3: 358).

3.7 The Métis Country: *"Programme National des Métis Canadiens Français:"* the lands of the country (Riel, vol. 1: 290); *"La Métisse"* (Riel, vol. 4: 88; 453-454); *"Pendant que les Métis semaient:" chaque Métis... loin de son cher pays* (Riel, vol. 4: 123); *"Lettre à R.B. Deane, à Edgar Dewdney, et à John A. MacDonald:" Monsieur Dumont va se préparer secrètement à déclarer, tout d'un coup, son pays libre* (Riel, vol. 3: 119); *"Mémoire sur la question du Nord-Ouest" Je déclare mon pays libre* (Riel, vol. 3: 269); *"Mémoire se rapportant au Nord-Ouest:" En ma qualité de citoyen américain je pense que, sans léser, en aucune manière le droit international, je fais partie de la république avec mes gens, les Métis et avec mon pays indien, comme tant d'autres chefs sauvages américains qui font partie des Ètats-Unis avec leurs tribus et leurs terrains, même avant d'avoir traité avec le gouvernement de Washington* (Riel, vol. 3: 307).

3.8 The Métis of the Northwest: *Les Métis ont pour ancêtres paternels les employés que la compagnie de la Baie d'Hudson et la compagnie du nord-ouest avaient à leur service, et pour ancêtres maternels des sauvagesses indiennes appartenant aux diverses tribus* (Riel, vol. 3: 272; see also 278);

Le nom de Métis rend bien l'idée du mélange du [sang]. Le nom français, Métis, convient mieux à cette race d'homme que le mot anglais Half-Breed. Car tout approprié que ce nom fut à la première génération du mélange de sang, maintenant que le sang indien et européen sont mêlés à tous les degrés, l'idée qu'elle rend n'est pas assez général.

Ce mot métis, qui semble être un dérivé du mot latin mixtus, *exprime ce mélange d'une manière aussi générale que possible, et devient un nom convenable de race...*

Il y a beaucoup de gens très polis et très gentils qui souvent diront à un Métis, mais vous n'avez pas l'air d'avoir grand sang sauvage; "on dirait que vous êtes blancs. Oh ! vous n'avez presque pas de sang sauvage." Ces personnes parlent sous l'influence des préjuges qu'ils ont vis-à-vis des indiens, et leurs compliments semblent partir de l'idée qu'un Métis devrait rougir de ses ancêtres indiens et c'est probablement pour lui aider à porter le poids de sa honte qu'on se dépêche de luis dire: "oh ! vous n'avez pas presque pas de sang sauvage."

Les Métis sont chrétiens. Quand même leur origine indienne est humble, ils tiennent à honorer leurs mères autant que leurs pères. Le Métis s'en tient à son nom de race. Il ne s'occupe à quel dégré de mélange ils possèdent son [sang] indien et son sang européen. Pour peu qu'il ait de l'un ou de l'autre, il dit, je suis Métis, et c'est fini, ses enfants le sont jusqu'à [toujours]... (Riel, vol. 3: 272);

C'est vrai que notre origine sauvage est humble, mais il est juste que nous honorions nos mères aussi bien que nos pères. Pourquoi nous occuperions-nous à quel degré de mélange nous possédons le sang européen et le sang indien ? Pour peu que nous ayons de l'un ou de l'autre la reconnaissance et l'amour filial, ne vous font-ils pas une loi pour dire: "Nous sommes Métis" (Riel, vol. 3: 278);

Ce passage contient probablement un élément personnel. Riel qui n'avait qu'un huitième de sang indien et qui avait une apparence très caucasienne devait souvent avoir entendu de telles remarques de la part d'amis québécois bien intentionnés (Flanagan, vol. 2: 292, note 3).

3.9 The Métis Nation: "La Métisse" *Je suis une Métisse et je suis orgueilleuse / D'appartenir à cette nation* (Riel, vol. 4: 88; 453-454); "Programme National des Métis Canadiens Français" *la Nation Métisse* (Riel, vol. 1: 289, 291); the national holiday of the Métis (Riel, vol. 1: 368); *Saint Pierre, bénissez la nation Métisse. C'est la plus jeune de toutes les nations du monde. Elle est toute petite. Elle aime la Saint Vierge. Bénissez-la comme nation catholique. Et au milieu de votre famille composée de tous les autres peuples, la nation Métisse sera votre joie* (Riel, vol. 1: 476); Mr. President (Riel, vol. 2: 6); *que le Bon Dieu conserve, fasse grandir la petite Nation Métisse et qu'elle soit fidèle à sa mission. Car elle en a une et une belle. Les épreuves auxquelles elle est en lutte en sont la preuve* (vol. 1: 467) (Riel, vol. 1: 467); *nation menacée* (Riel, vol. 4: 207); *La Nation Métisse est neuve* (Riel, vol. 4: 208); *la fête de la Nation Métisse* (Riel, vol. 2: 287); "Lettre à L-.A. Prud'homme [1853-1941]" it was the national celebration of the Métis (Riel, vol. 2: 289); our nation (Riel, vol. 3: 66) ; "Journal" *ma nation* (vol. 3: 407); "Prophéties de Regina" *peuple Métis Canadien Français* (Riel, vol. 3: 315) ; *une nationalité fraiche et nouvelle* (vol. 3: 315) ; *La Nation Métisse est neuve... / De son esprit, clair comme un fleuve / Il arrosera tous le Nord* (Riel, vol. 3: 402); *nation menacée* (Riel, vol. 3: 407); *peuple Métis Canadien Français* (Riel, vol. 3: 315); It was in Western Canada (Sealy and Lussier 3); Louis Riel explicitly recognized (Malette and Marcotte 2021: 312).

3.10 Métis Self-Rule: *"Les Métis du Nord-Ouest:"Comme peuple primitif, simple, de bonne foi, et placé dans une heureuse abondance de biens, et d'ailleurs sans beaucoup d'ambition les Métis n'avaient presque pas besoin de gouvernement. Cependant quand ils allaient à la chasse du bison par caravanes de plusieurs centaines de familles, il se faisant naturellement, au milieu d'eux une pression d'intérêts. Et tant pour maintenir l'ordre dans leurs rangs que pour se tenir en garde contre les vols de chevaux et même contre des attaques d'ennemis: ils s'organisaient et se composaient un champ. (Tout chasseur était soldat. Les soldats se groupaient par dizaine. Et chaque dizaine se choisissait un capitaine.)*

Un chef était élu; on élisait aussi douze conseillers, un crieur public, et des guides. Tout chasseur était soldat. Le premier commençait par se choisir un capitaine. Et lorsque neuf de ceux autres qui approuvaient ce choix venaient se ranger librement sous le capitaine qui se trouvait ainsi à la tête d'une dizaine d'hommes d'autant mieux décidés à le suivre partout que sa charge au-dessus d'eux était un effet de leur choix. Le conseil des chasseurs avait des règlements. On les appelait "les lois de la Prairie." Le conseil était un gouvernement provisoire; c'était un tribunal que prenait connaissance des infractions aux règlements et de tous les différends. Les capitaines exécutaient les ordres et les jugements du conseil. Dans les affaires ordinaires le conseil agissait d'après son autorité telle qu'elle lui avait été confiée. (Riel, vol. 3: 274-275);

3.11 Métis Nationhood: *Je ne peux pas te le dire. Je suis Voyageur—je suis Chicot, monsieur. Je reste partout. Mon grand-père était Voyageur: il est mort en voyage. Mon père était Voyageur: il est mort en voyage. Je mourrai aussi en voyage, et un autre Chicot prendra ma place. Such is our course of life* (Kohl 26); *"Lettre à Joseph Riel:" Nous sommes au grand détour de la Rivière au Lait. Il y a là environ 150 familles Métisses. On m'a fait l'honneur de m'élire chef du camp* (vol. 2: 210); "I Can Sing in My Poetry:" numerous Half-Breed families (Riel, vol. 4: 285); I have been amongst the Half-Breeds for about two years (Riel, vol. 2: 240). The large seasonal hunting camps (Sperry 51); part of *La Nation Métisse* (Riel, vol. 4: 262); There is in Montana a certain number of Half-Breeds (Riel, vol. 3: 3); broke from Riel (Zion 27); The Spring' Creek band's Métis roots (Foster 185);

"Lettre à R.B. Deane, à Edgar Dewdney, et a John A. MacDonald:" Quant aux provinces canadiennes de l'Est, beaucoup de Métis y vivent méprisés sous le costume indien. Leurs villages sont des villages d'indigence. Leur titre indien au sol est pourtant aussi bon que le titre indien des Métis du Manitoba.

Pour leur faire avoir un jour leur septième des terres, ou un revenu adéquat les Allemands des États-Unis seront invités à projeter l'invasion des deux Canadas et des provinces maritimes. Si l'entreprise avait à être couronnée de succès, la compensation des Allemands serait d'occuper toute la région du Lac Supérieur et du

Lac Huron depuis la ligne américaine jusqu'à la mer, du côté du Nord; et de fonder ainsi une Allemagne, à eux, dans le Nouveau Monde (Riel, vol. 3: 121).

Il voudrait que je fusse reconnu comme l'homme en tête des Métis, dans toute l'Amérique Britannique du Nord. Lui-même serait à la tête des Métis du Nord-ouest en deçà et au-delà des Montagnes-de-Roche, jusqu'à la Mer. Son dire est que les Métis du Manitoba ont eu le septième des terres de la province: que les Métis de la Colombie Anglaise ont également droit à leur septième des terres, puisque leur titre est absolument le même (Riel, vol. 3: 120-121); *"Prière:" Joseph ayez pitié de la grande famille métisse répandue sur les terres et mers* (Riel, vol. 2: 83); *Le plan au sujet de la Colombie Anglaise, est de l'offrir en partage aux corporations Belges, Bavaroises, Danoises, Suédoise et Norvégiennes, à la condition, lorsqu'elles pourront s'en emparer, de laisser le septième des terres, aux Métis* (Riel, vol. 3: 121) (Riel, vol. 3: 545);

The people described by Riel were merely mixed-blood First Nations (O'Toole 36); Language of co-proprietor of the soil with the Indians (Riel, vol. 3: 547); It is constitutionally acknowledged (Riel, vol 3: 547); The Métis were the mixed-blood descendants (Stanley 1964: 5); observed that few people living in Sault Ste. Marie (Sealy and Lussier 3); It indicated that there were five thousand Métis (Lusty 14-15); These very same statistics (Sealy and Lussier 193); The map shows the major population belts (Sealy and Lussier 193); it includes a list of Métis associations (Lusty 23); If we could obtain the number of Métis in Canada (Havard 317; qtd. Malette and Marcotte 2021: 317: note 9); The political activism of the Métis in eastern Canada (Michaux 2021: 133); In his list of post-Riel Métis organizations (Redbird 31); upward of ten thousand non-status and Métis people (Daniels 36); The Acadians were the first white settlers in New Brunswick and Nova Scotia (Daniels 37); the development of a mixed-blood population (Daniels 37); the ethnogenesis of the Acadian Métis (Bouchard, Malette, and Pulla 2021: xviii);

The forces that maintained their distinct and separate identity (Bouchard, Malette, and Pulla 2021: xviii); the ancestors of the Acadians (O'Connell 111); Métis communities had developed in the region (O'Connell: 111). *Métissage* did occur in colonial Acadia (O'Connell 126); the ethnogenesis of the Acadian Métis (126); This process took place (O'Connell 117-119); The root ancestors (O'Connell 122); They lived in family clusters (O'Connell 128); intimately linked to the fur trade (O'Connell 128); The Acadian Métis acted collectively (O'Connell 126); Despite of the discrimination" (O'Connell 125-126); If the Métis of the Maritimes (Daniels 39-44); Almost all of the rioters are Métis (Michaux 2021: 142); The rioters are Métis (Michaux 2021: 142); these Acadian Métis (New York Times 1886: 5);

Nowhere in Canada (Daniels 47); the Métis were found throughout the Great Lakes (Bouchard and Mager 2021: 230-231); identities could overlap (2021: 239); in and around Nipissing (Pulla 2021: 223); the real effervescence (Michaux 2021: 133); The Métis populations of Canada (Michaux 201: 134); The onus on an individual (Narine: n. page); Since the Powley case (St. George 318); sick kind of politics (Narine: n. page); that leaves out the vast, vast majority (Narine: n. page); Neither Belcourt nor Campbell have a connection to the Red River (Narine: n. page); For Belcourt (n. page); they do have their own rich Métis history (Narine: n. page); I don't want to take anything away from Red River people (Narine: n. page); we have our own cultures (Narine: n. page);

They are found in "different parts of the country" (Narine: n. page); They are "who we are" (Narine: page); It's not up to (Narine: n. page); It frightens me (Narine: n. page); *Le plan au sujet de la Colombie Anglaise, est de l'offrir en partage aux corporations Belges, Bavaroises, Danoises, Suédoise et Norvégiennes, à la condition, lorsqu'elles pourront s'en emparer, de laisser le septième des terres, aux Métis* (Riel, vol. 3: 121); *jusqu'à par de la des Montagnes Rocheuses* (Riel, vol. 3: 148); He was willing to offer Vancouver Island (Riel, vol. 3: 148); on the other side of the mountains (Riel, vol. 3: 556); To ensure the survival of the French in North America (Benoit 117-118); Our young men (Hartai n. page); the civil government of New France (Benoit 118); Nine months after (Sealy 1: Redbird 1);The Indian wife (Schreiber 189); More than 400 years ago (Howse 4-5); the offspring of the fur trade (Driben 19); These trading posts (Esarey 13; Anson 41); Scattered clusters of Mixed Bloods (Germain 132); Throughout North America (Ens 12-13); The crystallization (Ens 15); In Western Canada (Ens 17); The contact period (Howse 29); the first Métis emerged from the fur trade (Malette and Marcotte 2021: 302); The Métis have plied the waters (Malette and Marcotte 2021: 302);

Even if the majority (Bouchard, Malette, and Marcotte 2020: 228); conclusively demonstrates (Bouchard, Malette, and Marcotte 2020: backcover); The first Half-Breeds in the West were Eastern Métis (Redbird 2); the union of a French trader and an Iroquois woman (Driben 56); The senior governing body (Thistle 11); the French river system fur trade (Thistle 11); *Là nation métisse est sortie du mélange des races rouge et blanche. Au cours du premier siècle ou s'opèrent ces alliances, c'est-à-dire de 1650 jusqu'à la cession du Canada à l'Angleterre, la nation métisse n'était naturellement qu'en voie de formation... C'est surtout durant le siècle qui suivit, c'est-à-dire de 1760 à 1860, et même dans le premiers cinquante ans, soit de 1760 à 1810, que se cristallisèrent les divers éléments de la nation métisse...* (Trémaudan 46);

By the beginning of the nineteenth century (Rivard and Littlejohn 6-7); We were very aware of our distinctiveness (Rivard and Littlejohn 7); aspired to nationhood (Sealy 2); *leurs frères d'Acadie ou du Québec se fusionnèrent avec les éléments prépondérants du people canadien [français]* (Trémaudan 47); It was in these residential (Ens and Sawchuck 65-66; qtd. Bouchard, Malette, and Pulla 2021: xv); Métis families (Elsey 260); deep ancestral ties (Elsey 261); a larger national narrative (Esley 261); lived and observed (Elsey 261).

3.12 Métis Nation or Métis Reservation? lived with the Indians in true Indian fashion (Esarey 9); were no better, perhaps no worse (Esarey 23); White Indians (Allison 21); worse than the Indians (Allison 21-22); Indianized Frenchmen (Rafert 24); the French element persisted in the Miami and other western tribes (Rafert 35); While new sovereignties (Rafert 35); Richardville (Rafert 84); Métis identities emerged (Bouchard, Malette, and Pulla 2021: xi); *"Lettre à Joseph Riel:" Il y a de la chasse par ici. Si les Métis ne peuvent plus habiter notre chère Province, qu'ils s'en viennent tout droit dans le Montana avec leurs charrues et leurs animaux, leurs bêtes à cornes. Peut-être que ce sera plus avantageux pour eux par ici qu'ailleurs. Pour moi, je deviens citoyen américain. J'en ai déclaré mon intention suivant la loi. Et j'en ai mon papier depuis le 17 de mai. Je pense que je pourrai mieux aider aux Métis de cette façon-là qu'autrement (Riel, vol. 2: 222)*

We ask the government to set apart a portion of land as a special reservation (Riel, vol. 2: 224-225); two small Half-Breed counties in the crow reservation (Riel, vol. 2: 227); On behalf of the Métis hunters (Riel, vol. 2: 219); A considerable number of Half-Breeds (Riel, vol. 2: 375); *"L'avenir des chefs Métis Canadiens Français dans les États-Unis:" Louis est le seul qui puisse amener les Pieds-Noirs, les Corps-Beaux, les Gros-Ventres, les Pendants d'Oreilles, les Têtes-Plates, etc.* (Riel, vol. 2: 214); An Indian-Métis republic in the West (Flanagan, vol. 2: 257, note 3); Over the winter of 1879-80 (Flanagan 1992: 15); Riel could not make his radical view of aboriginal rights prevail (Flanagan vol. 2: xxxix); Only the French Métis followed Riel on his radical path (Flanagan 1992: 18); If a Métis reservation had been formed in Montana (Flanagan 1985: 190).

3.13 The Future of the First Nations, Colonization, and Mass Immigration: *"Notes sur le Métissage des peuples:" Je crois que dans un espace de temps relativement court, cette manière de procéder vis-à-vis des sauvages aurait pour effet de les faire disparaitre sans secousse et degré par degré. Les tribus réunies dans le Manitoba s'amalgameraient avec les Métis et les Canadiens Français de cette province. Et les tribus rassemblées dans le Nord-Ouest se mêleraient avec les Italiens, les Irlandais, les Bavarois, les Polonais.*

Ainsi, toute la race sauvage de l'Amérique du Nord ferait place à une race nouvelle la race Métisse qui varierait selon les pays; dans le Manitoba, elle serait Métisse Canadienne-Française. Dans la nouvelle Italie elle serait Métisse Italienne. Dans la nouvelle Irlande, elle serait Métisse Irlandaise; dans la nouvelle Bavière, elle serait Métisse Bavaroise; dans la nouvelle Pologne, elle serait Métisse Polonaise.

Et toutes ces nations apprendraient de Washington l'art de gouverner comme les nations Européennes ont jadis appris de l'empire romain l'obéissance et le commandement. (Riel, vol. 2: 409-410) ;

race that is going and has gone (Smith 2008: 109-110); he devoted the remainder of his life to fighting for the working class and the Indigenous people of North America (Smith 2021: n. page); 80% of the Canadian population will be non-European in less than a century (Collacott 2017, n. page);

Canada is undergoing the fastest rate of ethnic change of any country in the Western world (Collacott 2017, n. page); population replacement and genocide (Paradis 2019, n. page); he was opposed to Asian immigration (Riel, vol. 2: 369-371); With their good qualities (Riel, vol. 2: 369).

3.14 Confederation or Separation? *amener le Gouvernement d'Ottawa* (Riel, vol 3: 85); *"Lettre à A.-A. Taché:" extinction du titre indien des Métis* (Riel, vol. 3: 148); *Il s'adressera aux Sociétés incorporées et connues par leur hostilité au Canada. Il leur dira tout court que le gouvernement Canadien est engagé, par foi de traité, à octroyer aux Métis du Nord-ouest un bon septième des terres, pour l'extinction de leur droit indien au sol... Monsieur Dumont va se préparer secrètement à déclarer, tout d'un coup, son pays libre* (Riel, vol. 3: 119); ineffective in the cause of creating and legitimizing a Métis nation (Barnholden 24); *Bien des années avant la confédération* (Riel, vol. 3: 118); *Profita-t-il de son séjour pour rendre visite à ses frères, les Métis du Québec, qui vécurent, les uns dans des réserves, les autres en hommes libres, mais selon la description qu'en avait naguère donné Louis Riel, "méprisés sous le costume indien"? Cela est fort possible- Riel avait notamment de la famille paternelle dans l'Outaouais* (Combet and Toussaint 206); *Ce n'était pas la première fois, en 1885, que les Métis français ont fait trembler, et tant que nous aurons une goutte de sang français et indien dans les veines, nous revendiquerons les droits pour lesquels nous avons combattu et pour lesquels ils ont assassiné juridiquement feu Louis Riel* (Combet and Toussaint 238).

3.15 The Birth of the Métis Nation: *"Lettre à R.B. Deane, à Edgar Dewdney, et à John A. MacDonald:" Bien des années avant la confédération, Monsieur Gabriel Dumont était dans le Nord-ouest à la tête d'un conseil Métis. Ce conseil s'appelait le conseil de lois de la Prairies.... Tous les chefs sauvages même les plus insignifiants ont été reconnus d'une manière ou d'une autre, avec leurs petits camps. Mais Monsieur Gabriel Dumont a été tout à fait ignoré. Il a toujours été froissé de cela dans l'âme (Riel, vol. 3: 118).*

3.16 Conclusions: They fused two identities ... into a single Métis one (Ferguson 26).

CHAPTER 4: LOUIS RIEL AND THE INDIANS

4.2 A Name is a Name is a Name: Louis Riel... referred to the First Nations as *sauvages* (Riel, vol. 1: 483; vol. 3: 21-22, 69, 118, 308, 312, 358, 393, 394, 488; vol. 4: 123, 322); proud of being part Indian (Riel, vol. 2: 72); described the First Nations as "Indians" (Riel, vol. 3: 90-9); *les Tribus indiennes* (Riel, vol. 4: 360); the Wood Indians (vol. 3: 64, 67); the Cree (vol. 3: 84, 548); little sister (vol. 3: 547).

4.3 The People of the Red River Will Not Allow the Indian Nations to be Mistreated: *Pour prouver aux nations sauvages que le peuple de la Rivière Rouge ne veut pas les laisser maltraiter par le Canada; nous avons dit au Gouvernement*

Canadien que nos consentirions à entre avec lui: 1. Si la terre de Rupert et le Nord-Ouest entrent dans la Confédération Canadienne avec tous les droits communs aux autres provinces. 2. Si des traités sont conclus entre le Canada et les différentes tribus Indiennes de la terre de Rupert et du Nord-Ouest, par l'avis et la coopération de la Législature du pays (Riel, vol. 1: 65).

4.4 Ban the Booze: Waged a struggle (Martel, vol. 2: xli); the nomadic way of life (Riel, vol. 2: 248); demoralized and impoverished them (Riel, vol. 2: 248); Riel was trying to gain acceptance (Riel, vol. 2: 276); the sale of liquor (Martel, vol. 2: 276).

4.5 Organize the Indian Movement: Riel wanted to conscript (Martel, vol. 2: xxxix; Riel, vol. 4: 222); *Riel rêvait d'une grande confédération de Métis et de tribus indiennes de l'Ouest du Canada qui y établiraient une république indigène indépendante* (Campbell, vol. 4: 224; see also Flanagan 101); *Ces quatre années et demie de vie et de luttes métisses au Montana sont d'une importance considérable pour notre connaissance de Riel. Pour la première fois de son existence, Riel connait de l'intérieur et partage la vie du Métis des plaines, chasseur de bisons* (vol. 2: xlii); organize an "Indian movement" (Martel, vol. 2: xlii ; 197 note 1); an alliance against Canada (Martel, vol. 2: xliii); Riel... tried to convince the Indians (Martel, vol. 2: 220, note 4).

4.6 Feed the Indians: *"Memorandum preparé par Riel et montré à Mgr. Grandin" Que le gouvernement Canadien nourrisse les Sauvages. Qu'on ne donne pas à la chrétienté le spectacle navrant de les faire mourir par la faim. Si la civilisation de notre siècle le permettait, et si la Puissance le veut; que le gouvernement fasse travailler les Indiens autant que Pharaon a fait travailler les Juifs, mais à tout prix, qu'il ne les laisse pas en proie aux hallucinations, au délire de la faim. On ne veut pas que les gens parlent pour ces Sauvages; mais les Sauvages accablent les établissements métis. Les Métis et autres colons dépensent plus pour les Sauvages que le gouvernement. Et on veut défendre au peuple de mentionner cet état de choses. Ce n'est pas ainsi que le gouvernement Fédéral devrait administrer les affaires indiennes* (Riel, vol. 3: 21-22 ; see also vol. 2 : 377, note 2); the Indians are so reduced (Riel, vol. 3: 33); *"Petition à 'votre excellence en conseil'" Le moyen de contenter les Indiens est de leur donner ce qui leur appartient, en leur payant la valeur de leurs terres* (Riel, vol. 3: 27).

4.7 Métis-First Nations Relations: Crow Indians (Riel, vol. 2: 215); Gros Ventre Indians (Riel, vol. 2: 215); Pend d'Oreilles Indians (Riel, vol. 2: 216); *ces gens-là... reconnaissent le domaine absolu de Dieu sur toutes choses. Ils s'adressent franchement à Lui dans leurs épreuves d'ici-bas; et leur recours naturel au Maitre de la vie donne à leur conduite une mesure de charité et de bon sens, beaucoup plus moral qu'on ne l'imagine. Ils rompent en deux leur bouchée de pain, pour en faire part à l'indigent. Ils ont grand égard aux liens de parenté. Ils ne sont pas attachés aux richesses. Ils sont affectionnés aux biens de la vie. Eux-mêmes font connaitre quel est le caractère de cette affection lorsqu'ils disent qu' "ils n'aiment rien:" exprimant par la que leur estime des biens matériels ne va pas jusqu'à leur faire mettre ces biens avant l'amour du au prochaine* (Riel, vol. 2: 217);

I have been amongst the Half-Breeds (Riel, vol. 2: 240); The Cree have a very good chief in Big Bear (Riel, vol. 2: 240); too civilized (Riel, vol. 3: 272); they cannot stay (Riel, vol. 3: 272); As regards the whites (Riel, vol. 3: 272); "Les Métis du Nord-Ouest" *Les Métis par leur supériorité en tout sur les tribus indiennes les dominaient, mais sans aucun abus de force. Les rapports humains et doux qu'ils avaient avec elles les civilisaient plus au moins. (Quelquefois ceux-ci refusaient aux Métis le droit de chasse, et cherchaient à les [faire] reculer par la guerre). Ils étaient charitables pour eux. Quelquefois à la chasse, les Indiens déclaraient la guerre aux Métis, ou leur volaient des chevaux. Satisfaction était demandée. En cas de refus, jamais en agression; mais toujours à sa propre défense, ou à la défense de ses droits, la nation métisse entrait en guerres aves les malveillants. Mais qu'on le remarque bien; elle n'a jamais fait de luttes agressives, ses combats étaient toujours ceux de la défense ou de la protection du droit. Il n'y a pas eu de circonstance ou elle ait eu le dessous. Grace en soit rendues à Dieu, la nation métisse a toujours eu l'honneur de vaincre ses ennemis indiens. Les avantages qu'elle réclamait de ses victoires étaient la paix d'abord et la liberté de communication et de traite avec la tribu vaincue* (Riel, vol. 3: 274);

the terminology of the dominator (DesJarlait 2018: n. page); Métis people are the true Natives of Canada (Sealy 9); only ethnic groups indigenous to the continent (Redbird 53); forgive and forget (Campbell 1979: 25); *"Mémoire sur les Métis: Les trois principaux défauts des Métis du Montana" 1. Les Métis manquent d'économie. 2) Ils sont insoucieux du lendemain. 3) Ils sont indolents* (Riel, vol. 3: 406);

"Les Métis Canadiens-Francais" Les Métis Canadiens-Français ont au moral, plusieurs avantages sur les blancs: 1. Ils croient plus simplement et plus véritablement en Dieu. 2. Leurs espérances de chrétiens sont plus fermes. 3. Ils sont plus charitables de beaucoup. 4. Ils sont plus modestes dans leurs habits. 5. Ils sont plus francs dans leurs relations sociales. 6. Leur politesse est plus naturelle et plus cordiale. 7. Ils sont moins sacreurs, moins jureurs et moins blasphémateurs. 8. Ils sont paisibles et plus doux dans leurs rapports avec tout le monde. 9. Ils sont plus patients dans la misère et dans les difficultés de toutes sortes. 10. Leurs manières de penser et de juger sont plus droites et plus justes. 11. Leur vie est plus conforme à la nature; elle est plus réglée. 12. Ils pardonnent plus facilement les injures; ils excusent plus volontiers leur prochain. 13. Ils sont plus soumis. 14. Ils savent se contenter de peu. 15. Ils sont plus respectueux. 16. Ils parlent moins. Ils sont meilleurs juges d'hommes. Ils ont plus la connaissance des hommes (Riel, vol. 2: 297);

Au physique 1. Ils ont plus vigoureux. 2. Ils résistent mieux à différents maux et aux privations. 3. Ils ont le corps plus dispos. 4. Ils ont la vue plus prime, plus claire et plus forte. 5. Ils sont en général mieux faits. 6. Ils ont le pas plus sûr. 7. Leur figure exprime plus de bonté. 8. Ils ont meilleure santé (Riel, vol. 2: 297-298); *Quant aux biens de l'esprit, les blancs ont sur les Métis Canadiens-Français l'avantage d'être 1. plus savants. 2. plus artistes. 3. plus expérimentés; 4. plus travaillants; 5. plus constants; 6. plus tempérants 7. plus économes 8. plus disciplinés, plus soigneux. Ils ont plus la connaissance des choses. Sous le rapport du physique, les blancs sont: 1. d'un teint plus clair. 2. Ils sont mieux habillés; 3. Ils sont mieux logés; 4. Ils sont mieux nourris; 5. Ils sont plus riches.* (Riel, vol. 2: 297-298) ; score a direct hit (Dumont 84) ; a huge crime against humanity (Dumont 84).

4.8 The Joint Ownership to the Land : Métis-First Nations Relations: Joint Ownership of the Land: *le sang indien de leurs veines établissait le droit ou le titre qu'ils avaient à la terre. Ils avaient la propriété du sol conjointement avec les Sauvages* (Riel, vol. 3: 279); ownership (Howard 37-38).

4.9 The Indians are Sell-Outs: *La Puissance a eu soin de faire les traités avec les sauvages du Nord-Ouest, elle a reconnu tous les petits camps sauvages avec leurs chefs. C'est vrai qu'en reconnaissant ces pauvres indiens, elle a eu la finesse, de ne leur reconnaitre ni le droit ni d'estimer leurs terres ni d'en faire le prix... C'est vrai qu'elle a calomnié le Gros Ours et sa tribu de toute la civilisation parce que le Gros Ours et ses cris sans être assez éclairés pour demander la valeur de leurs terres, avaient néanmoins assez de bon sens et de connaissance des choses pour prétendre à une compensation réelle* (Riel, vol. 3: 276); the Indians who took treaty (Riel, vol. 3: 521); No treaty has been made with us (Riel, vol. 2: 521); more civilized (Riel, vol. 23: 29); the destruction of game (Riel, vol. 3: 374).

4.10 And the First Nations Shall Become Métis: *"Notes sur le métissage des peuples" Je crois que dans un espace de temps relativement court, cette manière de procéder vis-à-vis des sauvages aurait pour effet de les faire disparaitre sans secousse et degré par degré. Les tribus réunies dans le Manitoba s'amalgameraient avec les Métis et les Canadiens Français de cette province. Et les tribus rassemblées dans le Nord-Ouest se mêleraient avec les Italiens, les Irlandais, les Bavarois, les Polonais. Ainsi, toute la race sauvage de l'Amérique du Nord ferait place à une race nouvelle, la race Métisse qui varierait selon les pays; dans le Manitoba, elle serait Métisse canadienne-française. Dans la nouvelle Italie elle serait Métisse italienne. Dans la nouvelle Irlande, elle serait Métisse irlandaise; dans la nouvelle Bavière, elle serait Métisse bavaroise; dans la nouvelle Pologne, elle serait Métisse polonaise. Et toutes ces nations apprendraient de Washington l'art de gouverner comme les nations Européennes ont jadis appris de l'empire romain l'obéissance et le commandement (Riel, vol. 2: 409-410).*

4.11 Indian Rights: *Journal: L'Esprit de Dieu m'a fait voir la grandeur des droits que l'Indien possède au sol du Nord-ouest. Oui la profondeur des droits indiens, la grandeur de la cause indienne sont bien au-dessus de tous les autres intérêts. Le Sauvage est debout sur le bord d'un abyme, dit-on. Ce n'est pas lui qui est sur le bord d'un abyme: ses réclamations ne sont pas fausses. Elles sont justes... Chaque démarche que fait l'indien renferme un profond aperçu de droit* (Riel, vol. 3 : 409).

CHAPTER 5: LOUIS RIEL AND THE JEWS

5.2. Louis Riel, the Jew: Louis Riel believed himself to be David Mordecai (Littmann 1978: 451); *"Le Juif de Marseille" Né sur la plage de Marseille / Je fus privé de tout parent... / On m'instruisit du Judaïsme: / Longtemps mon âme le servit. / J'abhorrais le christianisme. / Juif: ennemi de Jésus-Christ* (Riel, vol. 4: 62); *Dans une lettre adressée à Mgr. Taché, il avoue s'être 'dit Juif' quand il était 'jeune encore' ... En plus, le docteur Daniel Clark, aliéniste torontois qui a témoigné au procès de Riel, raconte que Riel écrivait à un ami en 1865 qu'il n'était pas Louis Riel mais plutôt David Mordecai, un juif né à Marseille, venu au Canada alors qu'il était encore enfant* (Riel, vol. 4: 63, note 1); the Spirit of God (Riel, vol. 4: 38, 41, note 14).

5.3. Louis Riel and the Jewish Indians: Series of revelations (Riel, vol. 2: 33, note 1); "Lettre à Ignace Bourget" *le Saint Esprit m'a révélé, que les Sauvages d'Amérique du Nord sont Juifs et du plus pur-sang d'Abraham, à l'exception des Esquimaux qui viennent du Maroc* (Riel, vol. 2: 39); Lost Tribes of Israel (Riel, vol. 2: 39-45); *"Prophéties" Les Sauvages du nord de notre continent sont d'origine juive* (Riel, vol. 3: 488); *Les sauvages du Sud de ce continent sont des Égyptiens* (Riel, vol. 3: 488); a second David (Flanagan 1996: 127).

5.4. Louis Riel, the Hebrew Prophet: Rise up (Littmann 1978: 452; see also Riel, vol. 3: 322-323); on Hebrew examples (Flanagan 1996: 203); Elijah was with him (Flanagan 1996: 156); As the first Chosen People (Flanagan 1996: 203); an ingenious genealogical similarity (Flanagan 1996: 83); By the Indian blood (Flanagan 1996: 83); the practice of polygyny (Riel, vol. 4: 146, 150-153, 154, 155); *"Révélations se rapportant aux lois de l'Ancien Testament" Les lois de Moïse sont les lois de la vie, parce qu'elles viennent de Dieu immuable. C'est pour le monde entier qu'elles ont été faites* (Riel 1985, vol. 4: 154); *Dieu veut la polygamie... La polygamie est agréable à Dieu sans aucun doute* (Riel, vol. 2: 146); the Saturday Sabbath (Flanagan 1996: 198).

5.5 Louis Riel, the Jewish Messiah: The earthly messiah (Flanagan 1996: 203); *Tu es le David des temps chrétiens, dont l'ancien n'était que la figure. Tu es le Messie de gloire humaine que la maison de Jacob s'attendait de trouver dans le verbe incarné. Mais ce Messie, elle n'a pas pu le trouver dans la personne de Jésus Christ dont le royaume est de l'éternité et qui est venu enseigner aux hommes la perfection, et la pratiquer selon sa nature humaine...*

Les Juifs, il est vrai, ont manqué comme nation de reconnaitre le premier avènement, à cause de leur corruption qui les a empêchés de suivre le fils de Dieu caché dans le mystère de sa douceur et de son humilité parfaite. Mais selon la miséricorde des prophéties dont ils sont encore en possession, et selon qu'ils espèrent toujours la venue d'un Messie humainement glorieux, ils trouveront en toi celui qu'ils appellent de tous leurs vœux (Riel, vol. 2: 44-45);

"Venez-vous demander, en regardant ma mise" Venez-vous demander, en regardant ma mise / Si Dieu peut envoyer un prophète en chemise. / O fils de Chanaan, je

reviendrai chez vous (Riel, vol. 4: 147); *Les juifs occupent ... une place spéciale dans les croyances millénaristes. Riel qui s'appelle le Messie des juifs croit que le salut de ceux-ci fera partie du salut de toutes les nations. Lors de l'Apocalypse, ils devraient être réunis avec les chrétiens* (Riel, vol. 4: 148, note 2); I have good friends (Riel, vol. 4: 283); 1876 years (Campbell, vol. 4: 287, note 7);

"Lettre à Ignace Bourget" *Un tiers du peuple hébreux va se convertir maintenant. Par le moyen de Henri V le triomphateur et le Victorieux tu donneras la Pologne à la maison de Jacob, afin que... je considère encore le trône de David* (Riel, vol. 4: 39); *"Calepin" O Vierge Reine Immaculée des Hébreux, bénissez le peuple* Juif (Riel, vol. 3: 358).

5.6 Louis Riel and the Jewish State: Monsieur Dumont (Riel, vol. 3: 120); *"Lettre à R.B. Deane, à Edgar Dewdney, et à John A. MacDonald" Il n'ignore pas que les Juifs sont riches; qu'ils souffrent amèrement d'être sans patrie; et que s'ils pouvaient se préparer à en laisser une à leurs enfants, ils se mettraient à l'œuvre avec un patriotisme inouï* (Riel, vol. 3: 122); "Lettre à A.-A.Taché:" *Ne serait-ce pas charmant de voir, sur la terre ferme, vis-à-vis d'Elle, surgir une nouvelle Judée, en faveur des Juifs qui consentiraient à reconnaitre Jésus-Christ pour l'Unique Messie et à vous reconnaitre, Monseigneur, pour le guide autorisé de la foi ?* (Riel, vol. 3: 148); on the other side of the mountains (Riel, vol. 3: 556); If the Jews will help us (Riel, vol. 3: 545); one eighth Indigenous (vol. 62: note 2); We know that all religious aspiration (Nerburn 83).

5.7 Conclusions: Riel's infatuation with the Jews (Flanagan 1996: 203); the French-Canadian Métis Exovedate (Flanagan 1996: 155); the first and only Canadian politician (Arnold 2016: n. page).

CHAPTER 6: LOUIS RIEL AND ISLAM

6.1 Introduction: In the wake of Riel's execution in 1885 (Basson 2006: n. page; *Alarm*, 28 November 1885: p. 3); posthumous exoneration (Kilpatrick 2020: n. page); every record has been destroyed or falsified (Orwell 1982, p. 103); counterpart to Ayatollah Khomeini (Flanagan 1986: 227; Braz 2003: 10-11); Thomas Flanagan (Basson 2006: n. page); Historians... cease to be historians (Flanagan, vol. 3: xxviii).

5.2. The Image of Islam in the Works of Louis Riel: The young Riel excelled (Stanley 2013: n. page); lost interest in the priesthood (Stanely 2013: n. page);

"Révélations se rapportant aux nations de la terre" Les quatre grands empires de Mahomet, de Photius, de Luther et du colosse Anglais, ont paru devant mes yeux comme les quarte étincelles que vous verriez sortir ensemble de quatre mouches à feu perdues dans la nuit (Riel, vol. 2: 131); *"La force que Dieu me donne" La force que Dieu me donne / Peut renverser déjà la plus ferme colonne. / Je suis plus grand que Samson. / Et mon génie en veut aux succès de Nelson. / Dans la méditerranée / Je m'en viens le chercher encore cette année. / Voilà soixante et six ans / Que je*

veux en finir avec les protestants. / Je déteste leur commerce / Parce qu'il me trahit. L'avare qui l'exerce, / Prend la cause du Sultan / Comme si j'étais, moi, pour le mahométan (Riel, vol. 4: 143);

Prophète, Pontife infaillible, Prêtre-Roi (Riel, vol. 2: 68, 85, 165; vol. 4: 126, 132); prophet of the New World (Riel, vol. 3: 559*); Le tigre de Byzance... Voilà la Turquie: est-elle donc immense?* (Riel, vol. 4: 144); *La chrétienté se met / Par le libéralisme, au joug de Mahomet. / Un Dieu creuse la mère morte /Pour y faire une place à la sublime Porte. / Le Seigneur dit aux tyrans / Qu'il va mettre en lambeaux tous leurs maudits corans; / Que les Czars tombent par mille. / Jésus-Christ seul est Roi; la loi, c'est l'Évangile. / J'accomplis tout ce qu'il faut. / La vérité de Dieu, Sa Sainteté l'affiche. / Je viens des pays d'en Haut. / Suivez-moi, vous vivrez: car je suis pauvre et riche* (Riel 1985, vol. 4: 144); two other sources of inspiration (Campbell, vol. 4: 144-145);

Riel attaque les ennemis de la foi catholique qui sont, selon lui, les libéraux, les protestants, les tyrans musulmans, et d'autres qu'il énumère de façon précise. Contre tous ces adversaires, le poète luttera car Dieu lui a donné la force nécessaire pour les vaincre. Il a une mission à accomplir, dit-il, et il invite le lecteur à la suivre (Campbell 1985, vol. 4: 145); Even the Russians (Campbell, vol. 4: 145, note 5); bad dog (Campbell 1985, vol. 4: 145, note 4); Joseph II (Campbell, vol. 4: 145, note 4); Bismarck (Campbell 1985, vol. 4: 145, note 7); Victor-Emmanuel II (Campbell, vol. 4: 145, note 8); The extreme ultramontanes (Voisine 2006: n. page); *Chez les Métis l'état, l'église / de tout temps, n'ont jamais fait qu'un* (Riel, vol. 4: 207); a strong passion for intoxicating drinks (Riel, vol. 3: 273);

"La tempérance" *S'il faut le dire / Le turc est tempérant. / Mais son empire / Aussi fut grand. / Ses terribles brigades / Se sont montrées partout. / L'Europe en huit croisades / N'en put venir à bout* (Riel, vol. 4: 294); *Les Turcs seldjoukides conquirent Jérusalem en 1098. Pour libérer la ville et pour protéger les pèlerins, les chrétiens européens entreprirent une série de guerres de religion (les Croisades) qui durèrent environ deux cents ans* (Campbell, vol. 4: 296, note 3);

O Mecque Ancienne / Votre sobriété, / Vertu chrétienne, / En vérité, / Vous a fait régner fort / Douze cent soixante ans. / Votre sublime Porte / S'ouvrait à deux battants (Riel, vol. 4: 295); *Construite en 1478, la Sublime Porte d'Istanbul se trouvait à l'entrée du palais du grand vizir. Cette porte monumentale devint par la suite synonyme de la puissance ottomane. Étant donné que le calife, successeur de Mahomet, siégeait dans la ville turque, Riel implique ici que la Sublime Porte serait l'entrée véritable au monde musulman* (Campbell, vol. 4: 296, note 5);

Vous êtes née / Du Coran hasardeux / Pendant l'année / Six cent vingt-deux. / Comme Puissance sobre / Je vous fais mes adieux. / Vous mourez sans opprobre / Juste en quatre-vingt-deux (Riel, vol. 4: 295); *parce que Mahomet, pour se sauver, dut s'échapper de La Mecque* (Campbell, vol. 4: 296, note 6); *L'apocalypse / A bien décrit le cours / De votre ellipse; / Compte vos jours. / Vous êtes la comète, / Ce bel astre écarté / Qui passe et qui nous jette / Aussi lui sa clarté* (Riel, vol. 4: 297-

296); *parle de 622, an premier de l'ère musulmane, ou hégire. (Le 22 juillet 622, Mahomet dut fuir les Mecquois qui voulaient l'assassiner.) A partir de cette date, La Mecque régna 1260 ans... Le numéro 1260 a aussi une grande signification; le poète le considère sacré car Jean dans son Apocalypse (11:2) y fait allusion. Nous voyons donc pourquoi, d'après ses calculs (622+1260=1882), Riel insiste tellement sur la date qu'il écrit quatre fois sur l'ébauche* (Campbell, vol. 4: 295, note 1);

Je ne veux induire personne en erreur. Dieu m'a donné un génie bien plus grand que celui de Mahomet. Je le sais, je peux fonder sans l'autorisation, une religion et des empires bien plus fameux que les siens (Riel, vol. 2: 397);

"Système philosophico-théologique: Le transfert de la papauté" 64. Dieu m'a donné un génie bien plus grand que celui de Mahomet. Et je peux fonder une religion et des empires bien plus fameux que les siens, même si je voulais travailler comme lui, sans me mettre en peine d'autorisation divine. 65. Mais cette gloire ne me tente pas. J'aime mieux être sans influence et obéir à Dieu que de me faire une grandeur dans les égarements de l'orgueil, au détriment de la soumission que je dois à mon créateur (Riel, vol. 2: 396);

"Révélation de la Sublime Porte" L'esprit de Dieu s'est choisi un prophète. La charité infinie s'est reposée dans son plus petit, dans son plus indigne serviteur. Voici les paroles que le Verbe Incarné daigne prononcer par ma bouche: /

Terre d'Amérique! Reçois le salut de ton Dieu. Voici des jours pleins de salut pour toi. O ma fille bien-aimée! Tes traits sont couverts d'une voile de différentes couleurs: fais-le disparaitre afin que je contemple ta beauté! /

"C'est la première fois que la voix de Dieu resonne à tes oreilles par l'entremise d'un prophète, mais on va te porter envie; car le prophète que je me suis élu est tellement rempli de mon esprit et je le rends si fort, que ses mugissements retentiront d'un pôle à l'autre et du couchant à l'aurore. /

J'étends ma vue sur tous les points du monde à la fois, mais en même temps j'arrête mes regards du côté du Levant. Écoutez-moi: /

Les forces musulmanes ont travaillé et se sont dépensées sans m'appeler à leurs secours. Elles ont travaillé contre moi. La sollicitude que j'ai prise de les tenir en contact avec la Croix ne les a pas touchées, elles que j'avais laissés comme héritières de la Judée, pendant que mon peuple est errant sans patrie et qu'il boit à longs traits la honte des nations. La Judée captive ne les a pas instruites. Le torrent de ses eaux desséchées n'a pas été compris. La Judée toujours environnée de prophéties et que trois milles ans et plus ont émaillée de leçons n'a pas pu se faire entendre. /

Je me suis tenu moi-même près la Porte comme un ami. J'ai fait durer ma patience mille ans et plus. Mes caresses de gloire ont été méconnues ainsi que mes menaces. Comment se fait-il que mes corrections salutaires soient devenues une cause d'endurcissement! Ne les donne-je pas à ceux que j'aime pour les guérir du plus grand mal! /

Les forces musulmanes n'ont pas voulu être guéries du péché. Enfin le père en moi fait place au juge. /

Je frappe à la Sublime Porte. Ma colère est allumée. Le feu de ma colère va réduire en cendres les serrures et les cadenas puissants, les verrous et les barres d'acier, les fortes pentures et les gonds de la Sublime Porte. Mes deux pieds foulent dans le sable les liens et les entraves que les sultans ont mis sur mon chemin. /

La Sublime Porte est renversée. Qui est-ce qui prendra l'empire de Mahomet sous sa protection? /

Le fils de l'homme abandonne au jour de sa vengeance, le grand empire de Mahomet dans le désert du Sahara au milieu des sables brûlants, pour qu'il devienne la proie de la tempête. /

Jésus-Christ le prive à jamais des services du dromadaire et lui ôte pour toujours ses beaux chevaux arabes qu'il prête à d'autres mains. /

Le Coran s'efface devant mes regards irrités. Je le mets parmi les iniquités, les grandes iniquités de la Mer Morte. /

J'ouvre la Sublime Porte, j'ouvre la Porte de l'Orient. Déjà l'aube du jour parait. /

Puisque Dieu est Dieu, Mahomet n'est pas son prophète. /

La plus grande partie du grand empire de Mahomet passe à la Russie. J'en fais une seconde part pour la maison d'Autriche, et je donne le reste à l'Angleterre. /

Parce que la maison d'Autriche est de ma seule Église catholique, apostolique et romaine, je lui confie l'honneur et le soin de composer l'armée qui doit combattre les Ottomans et de partager leur empire, selon mon bon plaisir. /

J'ai un ennemi remarquable entre tous les autres. Il me fait la guerre à la vue du monde entier: ne suis-je pas contraint de me défendre, de me défendre à la vue de tous les hommes? Cet ennemi, c'est le grand rouge de nom Allemand. /

Le grand empire d'Allemagne charge de châtier, de châtier surtout la fille ainée de l'Église, le grand empire d'Allemagne comblé de gloire, comblé de richesses et qui ne s'est pas mis en peine de se tourner ensuite contre le Pontife Infaillible, est devenu plus abominable à mes yeux que le Croissant. /

Je ne veux point que ses forces entre en ligne dans la guerre qui se prépare contre la Turquie. Je le rejette. Je ne veux point me servir du grand rouge de nom Allemand. En ma qualité de Seigneur des Seigneurs, je désavoue d'avance toutes les prétentions qu'il pourrait faire valoir dans le partage du butin musulman. A partir de ce jour, le concours de ses armes devient une source de malédictions pour tous ceux qui feront alliance avec lui. /

Si le grand rouge de nom allemand ose encore me braver dans la sentence que je porte ici contre lui, quoiqu'il soit loin de moi, moi qui suis le lion de la tribu de Juda, je me jetterai sur lui en ne faisant que quatre bonds au lieu de sept ou dix, au lieu de douze ou quinze. /

La maison d'Autriche est avertie, je ne veux point qu'elle s'étende avec le grand rouge de nom allemand. /

O mon fils Joseph! Obéis-moi et je suis avec toi pour te soutenir contre tes ennemis. Souviens-toi des temps miraculeux d'Isaïe et de Jérémie, d'Ézéchiel et de Daniel.

Considère que j'ai rempli moi-même à la lettre chacun de leurs décrets divins contre les empires du monde ancien. /

Est-ce que mon fils bien-aimé, que j'ai chargé par ma grâce de gouverner l'Autriche, est-ce que mon fils Joseph va m'obéir? /

O mon fils Joseph, ne me désobéis pas. Car ta mauvaise volonté et ton respect humain seront suivis de terribles conséquences, de châtiments redoutables pour ton peuple et pour toi. /

Et s'il y a dans le monde un Czar de Russie, je lui conseille, après avoir entendu la voix de son Dieu, de s'appliquer à l'écouter pour en connaitre la douceur; de s'appliquer à la méditer pour s'y attacher; de s'appliquer à la mettre en pratique pour consolider et révéler les degrés de son trône. S'il y a dans le monde un Czar de Russie et qu'il lui soit permis de caresser la pensée d'agrandir tous les jours l'empire de Pierre le Grand, je lui demande d'examiner pourquoi le fils de Dieu fait homme n'aurait-il pas de même à cœur de voir s'étendre jusqu'aux extrémités du monde, le royaume de celui qui est en vérité Pierre le Grand... /

Dieu veut que l'Autriche préside entre toutes les Puissances au règlement des difficultés qui vont ruiner le gouvernement Turque. /

Dieu ne veut pas que le Grand Rouge de nom allemand prenne aucune part quel qu'indirectement et moindrement que ce puisse être à la croisade qui est en frais de s'organiser contre la Turquie. Comme preuve que telle est la volonté divine, Jésus-Christ prédit au monde par son prophète, aujourd'hui le dixième jour de Mars, 1876, que la Sublime Porte perdra trois grandes batailles dont la première le 19 mars, dont la seconde, le 19 avril et dont la... (Riel, vol. 2, pp. 30-33);

The spirit of God has chosen a prophet. Infinite charity has rested upon his smallest, most unworthy servant. Here are the words that the Word Incarnate deigns to pronounce by my mouth:

"Land of America! Receive God's salvation. These are days filled with blessings for you. O my beloved daughter! Your traits are covered with a veil of different colours: cast them off so I can contemplate your beauty!

"This is the first time that the voice of God resonates in your ears through a prophet; however, you will be subject to envy for the prophet that I have appointed is so filled with My spirit, making him so strong, that his roars will resonate from one pole to another and from dusk to dawn.

"My vision extends to every point in the world simultaneously, but, at the same time, I focus My eyes on the Levant. Listen to me:

"The Muslim forces have worked, exerted, and exhausted themselves without calling me for help. They have worked against Me. The care that I took to keep them in contact with the Cross did not affect them, those that I left as heirs in Judea, while My people were wandering without a nation and while they quaffed the shame of other nations. Captive Judea did not instruct them. The torrent of its dried-up waters was not understood. Judea, surrounded by prophecies and which delivered lessons for three thousand years and more, could not make itself heard.

"I stood next to the Porte like a friend. My patience lasted for over one thousand years. My strokes of glory went unrecognized, as did my threats. How is it possible that my salutary corrections became a source of insensitivity and the hardening of hearts? Do I not give to those I love the most harm so that I can heal them?

"The Muslim forces did not want to be healed from sin. At last, the father in me gives way to the judge.

"I knock on the Sublime Porte. My wrath is ignited. The fire of my wrath will reduce to ashes the powerful locks and padlocks, the bolts and bars of steel, the strong hinges, and the handles of the Sublime Porte. My two feet tread upon the sand that the shackles and the obstacles that the sultans have placed on my path.

"The Sublime Porte is overthrown. Who will place the empire of Mahomet under his protection?

"On the day of his vengeance, the Son of Man abandons the great empire of Mahomet in the Sahara Desert in the middle of burning sands, so that is consumed by the storm.

"Jesus-Christ forever deprives it of the services of the dromedary and forever removes its best Arab horses, which he turns over to other hands.

"The Koran erases itself in the face of my irritated eyes. I place it among the iniquities, the great iniquities of the Dead Sea.

"I open the Sublime Porte. I open the Door to the Orient. Dawn already starts to rise.

"Since God is God, Mahomet is not His Prophet.

"The largest part of the great empire of Mahomet passes to Russia. I allocate a second part for the House of Austria and the rest I give to England.

"Since the House of Austria is my only Catholic, Apostolic, and Roman Church, I grant it the honour and the care of forming the army that must fight the Ottomans and divide up their empire, according to my goodwill and pleasure.

"I have a remarkable enemy among all others. He openly wages war against me in front of the entire world. Am I not obliged to defend myself, to defend myself in the sight of all men? That enemy is the great, German-named, redhead.

"The great empire of Germany seeks to punish, to punish, above all, the elder daughter of the Church, the great empire of Germany crowned with glory and crowned with riches, has not hesitated to turn against the Infallible Pontiff, and has become more abominable in my eyes than the Crescent.

"I do not want his forces to join the war that is being prepared against Turkey. This, I reject. I do not want to employ the great German-named redhead. In my quality as Lord of Lords, I disavow all the pretensions that he may have regarding a share in the Muslim booty. From this day forward, the assistance of his weapons is a source of malediction for all who ally themselves with him.

"If the great, German-named, redhead dares to defy the judgment that I bring upon him, even though he be far from me, I, the lion of the tribe of Judah, shall cast myself upon him in as little as three leaps, instead of seven or ten, and instead of twelve or fifteen.

"The House of Austria is warned, and I do not want it to expand with the great, German-named, redhead.

"O my son Joseph! Obey me and I will be with you to support you against your enemies. Remember the miraculous times of Isaiah, Jeremiah, Ezekiel, and Daniel. Consider that I fulfilled myself, to the letter, each of their divine decrees against the empires of the ancient world.

"Will my beloved son, the one I charged with governing Austria; will my son Joseph obey me?

"O my son, Joseph, do not disobey me for your ill will, and your human respect will be followed by terrible consequences and dreaded punishments for your people and yourself.

"And if there is a Czar of Russia in the world, I advise him, after having heard the voice of God, to apply himself to meditate upon it; to apply it to the letter in practice to consolidate and reveal the degrees of his throne. If there is a Czar of Russia in the world and if it allowed for him to cherish the thought of expanding every day the empire of Peter the Great, I ask him to examine why the son of God made man would not himself desire to see the kingdom, which is truly that of Peter the Great, spread to the farthest reaches of the world...

"God wants Austria to preside over all powers when settling the difficulties that will ruin the Turkish government.

"God does not want the great, German-named, redhead to play any part, even indirectly or slightly, in the crusade that is starting to be organized against Turkey. As proof that this is the divine will, Jesus Christ predicts to the world through his prophet, on this tenth day of March 1876, that the Sublime Porte will lose three great battles, the first of which is March 19, the second of which is April 19, and the..." (Riel, vol. 2, pp. 30-33);

A series of revelations (Martel, vol. 2: 33, note 1); *folies des grandeurs* (Martel 1985, vol. 2: 33, note 1 ; Campbell vol. 4 : 113, note 6); *"Riel est-il fou?"* (Martel, vol. 2: 33, note 1); the Ottoman empire (Martel: 33: note 1); The Koran erases itself (Riel, vol. 2: 31), Mahomet is not His Prophet (Riel, vol. 2: 31); waging war against God (Martel, vol. 2: 34, note 4); the Lion of Judah (Martel, vol. 2: 34, note 6); the successor of saint Peter (Martel, vol. 2: 34, note 6, 9); *Journal: L'Esprit de Dieu m'a dit en parlant du croissant des Turcs: 'Ils ont choisi quelque chose de beau'* (Riel, vol. 3: 485).

Il n'y a de dieu que Dieu, bien certainement; mais Mahomet n'est pas son prophète; et en associant à cette vérité ce mensonge, tu détruis la première (Montandon: 42); *Dieu est grand... et Mahomet n'est pas son prophète* (Raffenel 219); *Dieu seul est Dieu, mes frères; Mahomet n'est pas son prophète* (Loüis 281); *Allah n'est pas Allah, et Mahomet n'est pas son prophète* (Guyot 17-18); *Dieu est Grand! Et Mahomet n'est pas son prophète!* (Trobriand 105); Thomas Jefferson (Morrow 2021: 133-135; Morrow 2021: 198-210; Morrow 2020: n. page); half-breed Mahdi (Kodó n. page).

6.3 Conclusions: Bahai Revelation (Smith 2008: 103); associate his ideology with Islam (Basson, n. page: note 8); under Qur'anic law (Riel, vol. 2: 230).

CHAPTER 7: LOUIS RIEL'S PSYCHO-SPIRITUAL STATE

7.2. Riel's Mental State: his heart ... was inconsolable (Flanagan 1996: 13); He believed himself to be David Mordecai (Littmann 1978: 451); brain fever (Stanley, vol. 5: 79; Littmann 1978: 455); the foundation of his prophetic mission (Stanley, vol. 5: 84); mystical experiences (Stanley, vol. 5: 85); Rise up (Littmann 1978: 452); divine Providence (Stanley, vol. 5: 84); bellow, howl or roar at night (Martel, vol. 2: 33, note 2); Riel is committed (Stanley, vol. 5: 84); he struggles violently (Stanley, vol. 5: 85); he writes prolifically (Stanley 1985, vol. 5: 85); Quand je vous parle (Riel, vol. 4: 146); intense spiritual experiences (Stanley, vol. 5: 88); communications with God (Riel, vol. 2: xxxv; vol. 2: 73, note 1; vol. 3: 261); a leader like the Biblical David (Riel 1985, vol. 4: xxxix); Rome to Montreal (Campbell, vol. 4: xxxix); sanctified polygyny (Riel, vol. 2: 145-145);

"Révélations se rapportant aux lois de l'Ancien Testament" Un homme a-t-il retardé se marier jusqu'à l'âge de quarante ans ? Si alors une de ses sœurs, ayant été mariée, devient veuve; il peut la demander en mariage, à condition qu'il regarde les enfants de sa sœur comme s'ils étaient les siens propres. Une fille a-t-elle atteint l'âge de trente ans sans avoir été mariée ? Qu'elle voie alors si son frère a les cinq femmes qu'il lui est permis d'avoir. S'il en a moins, elle a le droit de lui présenter la main, car c'est la volonté de Dieu que son frère la prenne en mariage. Tous les mariages que Notre Seigneur Jésus Christ permet sont gros de bénédictions (Riel, vol. 2: 152);

la loi mosaïque condamnait très sévèrement cette forme d'inceste... la situation ici evoquée par Riel fut exactement la sienne (Martel, vol. 2: 162, note 23); Flanagan 1996: 95; Riel was released (Stanley, vol. 5: 85); the Book (Martel, vol. 2: xl); bits and pieces (Martel, vol. 2: 229-239); *Le* Massinahican *aurait donc été une vaste synthèse englobant à la fois une cosmogénèse et une histoire politico-religieuse de l'humanité divisée en trois époques: religion mosaïque, religion romaine, religion nouvelle du Nouveau Monde, de type œcuménique, dans laquelle les Métis, et en particulier les Métis Canadiens-Français auraient un rôle privilégié* (Martel, vol. 2: xliii);

theocratic utopia (Martel, vol. 2: xxvi); In a prayer to the Virgin Mary (Riel, vol 2: 340); *la peur, la crainte et l'épouvante* (Riel, vol. 2: 346); Riel's *Massinahican* has never been discovered (Martel, vol. 2: xxvi); visions, revelations, and prophecies (Flanagan, vol. 3: xli); "*Partie du* Massinahican:" *Les dénominations religieuses du Nouveau Monde ont besoin d'être reliées ensemble, d'une manière droite... les catholiques du Mont Royal, les catholiques épiscopaliens, les catholiques méthodistes, les catholiques Luthériens, les catholique universalistes, etc., tous selon leur croyance feraient partie de cet ordre religieux que je voudrais voir* (Riel, vol. 3 : 231);

hell was not eternal (Flanagan, vol. 3: 82, note 1); the example of Jesus and Moses (Flanagan, vol. 3: 82, note 1); a prophet like Joshua (Littmann 1978: 456); subjected to insults of all kinds (Flanagan, vol. 3: 82, note 1); renaming the days of the weeks (Littmann 1978: 461); He insisted that they only take mass from him (Dumont 94); recanted his "heresies" (Stanley, vol. 5: 94; Riel 1985, vol. 3: 170-172; Flanagan 1985, vol. 3: xliv); his retraction was "only exterior" (Flanagan, vol. 3: xliv; 173, note 1); his writings were divinely inspired (Flanagan, vol. 3: xliv); The Spirit told me (Flanagan, vol. 3: xliv); heated liquid (Flanagan, vol. 3: xliv); prophet of the New World (Riel, vol. 3: 559);

maybe I am a prophet (vol. 3: 541); Up to this moment (Riel, vol. 3: 540); Riel related his revelations with apparent pride (Riel, vol. 2: 567); an inveterate masturbator (Flanagan 1996: 15-16); All that was required to lock Riel up in a madhouse (Flanagan 1996: 64); Riel's sanity (Stanley, vol. 5: 94); the commission submitted its reports (Stanley 1985, vol. 5: 94); the death penalty on grounds of high treason (Stanley, vol. 5: 95); political expediency (Littmann 1978: 461); Paranoid schizophrenia (Littmann 1978: 461); If I am insane (Riel 1985, vol. 4: 531-533); fifty percent of people suffering from schizophrenia (Murray et al: n. page); Creativity and schizophrenia (Kaufmann and Paul n. page), see also Brandt and scores of other studies; a role for the supernatural (Murray et al.: n. page); highly probably "narcissistic" (Perrota: n. page); as much as 60% percent (Murray et al.: n. page); They only want to convert the world to make money (Dumont 95); *A cette époque, nous étions ignorants, et la parole des prêtres était synonyme de vérité; mais depuis, nous avons compris certaines choses et nous savons qu'ils peuvent très bien nous mentir* (Combet and Toussaint 207); Sane and insane are relative (Upton 2020: n. page); Creative people are more likely (Legg n. page); Louis Riel believed that on 8 December 1875 (Flanagan 1996: backcover).

7.3 "I know the Good Lord wants me to die" (Dumont 93) "I will not lay down my arms" (Dumont 89).

CHAPTER 8: LOUIS RIEL AND QUEBEC

8.1 *Depuis mon départ de Batoche, après la guerre, j'ai toujours eu envie de venir dans cette Province de Québec, chez nos gens, comme on dit là-bas.* (Combet and Toussaint 196).

8.2 Quebec: The Mother of the Métis: Québec! *"O Québec" Québec! Mère Colonie! / Tu fus de nos aïeux sans cesse les amours ! / Et durant toute ma vie, / J'aimerai ton doux nom, le prononçant toujours. / Québec ! Province chérie ! / Oublieras-tu jamais tes Métis-Canadiens ! / De Manitoba trahie / Tes enfants, O Québec, sont pourtant les soutiens ! / Des ennemis fort à craindre / Menaçant le berceau de tes enfants chéris. / Mais ils ne pourront atteindre, / O Québec! Malgré toi, jamais notre pays ! / Que la sainte Providence / Inspire à notre égard tes hommes d'Ottawa. / Souviens-toi combien la France / Te fit mal ! O Québec ! Lorsqu'elle t'oublia ! / Noble pays ! Ton courage / Te rend superbe après un siècle de combats ! / Accepte le beau présage / De l'Immortel Pie-Neuf bénissant tes soldats ! / Toi qui fournis des zouaves / A l'Église, jamais aurais-tu la douleur /de voir écraser tes braves / Tes fiers enfants du Nord, héritiers de ton Cœur !* (Riel, vol. 4: 95-96); *La Province de Québec, comme c'était son droit et son devoir, se mit en tête du mouvement, et l'on vit pendant un certain temps, comme aux beaux jours de nos glorieuses luttes politiques du passé, régner l'union parmi les descendants de la grande famille française et catholique* (Ouimet 3).

8.3 Quebec: A Source of Cultural Inspiration: *"Lettre à Ignace Bourget" la province du Québec exerce sur le peuple Métis toute son influence et la lui fait subir. Les Métis du Manitoba ne peuvent se défendre de copier le Bas Canada* (Riel, vol. 1: 451)

8.4 Quebec: A Fountain of Catholic Inspiration: "To the Catholic program" (Riel, vol. 1: 453); *"Le peuple Métis Canadien français" Le clergé qui nous édifie / Nous unira bien surement* (vol. 4: 324); *"De bons français venus d'outremer sont nos hôtes" Le Métis est charitable. / Et le Canadien traitable. / Le bon français a vieilli / A défendre l'église. Elle est belle sa page / D'histoire ! Il faut qu'il propage / Sa foi qui n'a pas failli* (Riel, vol. 4: 326).

8.5 Quebec: The Political Defender of the Métis: "Lettre 'Aux Electeurs du District de Provencher et à mes compatriotes du Manitoba'" *La province du Québec s'est levée pour nous défendre et elle a fait entendre ses voix les plus éloquentes en notre faveur. Son généreux et puissant concours a été pour nous d'un prix inestimable et c'est par elle j'en ai le ferme espoir, que justice nous sera rendue un jour* (Riel, vol. 1: 461); *qui est tout notre appui, qui nous aime et que nous aimons: c'est le pays de nos pères* (Huel, vol. 1: xlvi; vol. 1: 196); Given the bond (Huel, vol. 1: xlvi).

8.6 The Nation of Quebec: The Precursor of the Métis Nation: *"Lettre à Paul Proulx" Je voudrais qu'avec le secours de Dieu, nous travaillions à faire du peuple Métis canadien-français un peuple assez grand pour mériter de recueillir l'héritage du Bas Canada, comme un bon fils reçoit et fait profiter les biens qui lui ont été légués par ses parents* (Riel, vol. 2: 120).

CHAPTER 9: LOUIS RIEL AND THE FRENCH-CANADIANS

9.2 The French-Canadians and the Métis: All for One and One for All: *"Lettre à N.-J. Ritchot" Quand les Canadiens Français s'occupent de la question du Nord-Ouest, en se disant et en montrant qu'ils ne veulent pas en faire une question de race et de religion, le fanatisme orangiste d'Ontario reprend son vacarme ordinaire... La Province de Québec n'aurait qu'à accepter franchement la question de race et de religion et dire à Ontario: 'Tu m'attaques comme telle, je me défends comme telle'* (Riel, vol. 1: 397);

Je disais à Monsieur Royal de prendre cela, dans sa tête et dans son cœur; l'autonomie du peuple Métis, d'appeler toute l'émigration canadienne française possible au Manitoba, avec l'idée bien arrêtée et tout avouée de conserver, de faire grandir le peuple Métis fondé dans le nord-ouest par la Province de Québec. Que cela aura le grand avantage de faire disparaitre beaucoup de défiance ente les Métis et un certain noyau de Canadiens français, de rendre l'arrivée des Canadiens chez nous tout à fait heureuse, et de faire adopter aux Métis satisfaits une plus grande somme des mœurs, des traditions canadiennes françaises de telle sorte que tout en nous appelant le peuple Métis, nous soyons de fait, sans effort de la meilleure grâce du monde, identifiés à la Province de Québec, par l'éducation. Ce qui est très désirable, ce me semble (Riel, vol. 1: 398-399).

9.3 French-Canadian: The Family Name of the Métis: *"Lettre à Paul Proulx" Et si vous me demandez pourquoi je ne veux pas que notre peuple s'appelle canadien-français, tout court, je vous répondrai que ce nom-là étant déjà son nom de famille, il convient de lui en donner un autre qui le désigne particulièrement et qui soit en quelque sorte son nom de baptême comme peuple* (Riel, vol. 2: 120); *le petit troupeau Métis* (Riel, vol. 2: 121); a fabric that was yet to be quilted (Riel, vol. 2: 120);

Et quand l'étoffe sera finie, ce sera de l'étoffe française, parce que les ouvriers du beau métier de France y auront travaillé. Ce sera de l'étoffe vraiment canadienne; parce que nos tisserands étaient des Canadiens du moral. Ce sera de l'étoffe Métisse canadienne-française... Soyons donc sans inquiétudes. Français, Canadiens et Métis, travaillons ensemble non seulement sans méfiance mais encore avec beaucoup d'amitié, selon que Dieu veut se servir de nous tous pour fonder le peuple Métis-Canadien-Français (Riel, vol. 2: 121);

three-bloods (Riel, vol. 4: 326); *"De bons Français venus d'outremer sont nos hôtes" les bonnes qualités canadienne-françaises / corrigent les défauts de notre sang Indien* (Riel, vol. 4: 326); *Dans la race a trois-sangs, est-ce le Canadien, / Est-ce le français, ou le Métis dont l'exemple / Mérite plus qu'on le contemple ? / Quel est celui des trois qui fait le plus de bien ?* (Riel, vol. 4: 326);

"Le peuple Métis Canadiens Français" J'aime sans mesure et j'admire / Les Métis-canadiens-français / Ce peuple nouveau qui se mire. / Déjà dans de brillants succès (Riel, vol. 4: 319); *Il fait connaitre sa gloire / Aux indiens du Minnesota. / Il a toujours gagné victoire / Sur les tribus du Dakota* (Riel, vol. 4: 319); *Le Manitoba si précoce / Est grand, parce qu'il l'a fondé / Sous le beau frein du Sacerdoce / Qui l'a toujours si bien guidé* (Riel, vol. 4: 319-320); *Si le trait d'union se place / Entre Métis et Canadien; / Assure, l'une et l'autre race / N'en sera que plus apte au bien* (Riel, vol. 4: 321);

they learned from Anglo-Saxon rule (Riel, vol. 4: 321); the English constitution (Riel, vol. 3: 555); It was due to Anglo influence (Riel, vol 4: 321); *Métis et Canadiens ensemble / Français, si nos trois éléments / S'amalgament bien, il me semble / Que nous serons un jour plus grands* (Riel, vol. 4: 324); *Les trois feuilles du trèfle peuvent / Exister sur le même pied. / Toutes les trois, jolies, se meuvent / A l'unisson, comme il leur sied* (Riel, vol. 4: 324); *Son grand cœur prend beaucoup de peine / A consolider, je le sais, / La nation manitobaine / Des Métis Canadiens Français* (Riel, vol. 4: 325); to come and help us (Riel, vol. 3: 556); the Fathers of the Métis (Riel, vol. 3: 24); *fidèle au mouvement des Métis Canadiens Français et à leur Gouvernement Provisoire* (Riel, vol. 3: 507);

9.4 French-Canadian Métis Unity: *"Lettre à Pierre Lavallée" Que les Métis et les Canadiens Français cessent à tout prix de se reprocher malicieusement leurs défauts les uns aux autres. La bonté des Métis et la générosité des Canadiens Français sont appelées à s'entraimer; de telle sorte que les Métis deviennent plus Canadiens par les vertus canadiennes, et que les canadiens devienne plus Métis par les admirables vertus que les Métis possèdent comme peuple primitif. Il le faut; soyons Métis-Canadiens* (Riel, vol. 2: 301).

CHAPTER 10: LOUIS RIEL AND THE FRENCH LANGUAGE

10.2 Louis Riel's French-Canadian French: *Ses grands-parents Lagimodière venaient tous les deux du Québec. Leur fille, Julie, mère de Louis Riel, avait appris sa langue de ses parents. Louis Riel, père, avait été élevé dans l'Est et avait fait deux années d'études chez les oblats nouvellement arrivés de France. Il nous est permis de croire que dans ce milieu familial, on parlait un français un peu plus châtié que celui des autres familles de la Rivière-Rouge. Il n'en était pas toujours ainsi pour les petits camarades de Louis, qui, issus de mariages mixtes, parlaient souvent les langues de leurs pères et de leurs mères, et que dans le milieu bilingue, les langues s'influençaient mutuellement pour produire un dialecte français possédant sa propre identité* (Motut, vol. 5: 50-51);

Rien dans les écrits de Louis Riel, sauf peut-être, quelques mots et quelques expressions... ne transperce de cette connaissance qu'avait Louis Riel de la langue des Métis (Motut, vol. 5: 53); *S'il se disait Métis, c'est qu'il appartenait à ce peuple par d'autres liens que ceux de la langue parlée. Il semblerait même, que les Riel avaient la fierté de bien parler français* (vol. 5: 53); *parlent un jargon français qui est bien laid à entendre* (Motut, vol. 5: 54); Louis Riel had a sound mastery... (Motut, vol. 5: 54); His grades... (Motut, vol. 5: 54);

Le lecteur qui aura pris la peine de lire l'œuvre entière de Louis Riel, telle que commentée et exposée dans les pages écrites en français, des quatre volumes, se sera vite rendu compte que Louis Riel possédait bien sa langue maternelle. Il la possédait au point de pouvoir l'utiliser pour s'exprimer en vers, avec tout ce que la versification française comprend de difficultés stylistiques dans la composition afin que le message soit clair et compréhensible (Motut, vol. 5: 48).

10.2 French: The Language of the Métis: *Dotons notre langue française / De mots étrangers qui soient beaux; / Afin que plus riche elle plaise / Plus en ces parages nouveaux / Empruntons aux langues sauvages / Un certain choix d'expression; / Quelques-unes de leurs images, / Quelques belles locutions. / Ces nouveautés rendront plus forte / La langue de nos chers aïeux. / Embellissons-la de la sorte / Suivant le goût de notre mieux* (Riel, vol. 4: 324);

Louis Riel ... did not speak Michif... (Papen 90, note 24); "Lettre à Pierre Lavallée:" *Soyons fiers d'être français. La langue française est l'une des plus belles langues du monde, et certainement, la plus polie de toutes. Aimons beaucoup les Français. Soyons Métis-Canadiens-Français* (Riel, vol. 2: 301).

CHAPTER 11: LOUIS RIEL AND THE IRISH

11.2 Irish Pride: I don't abandon my ancestors (Riel, vol. 3: 557); originality, wit, and unsurpassed courage (Riel, vol. 2: 361); *"Partie du* Massinahican": *Aussi est-il difficile de trouver un peuple aussi attaché à sa religion que le peuple irlandais* (Riel, vol. 2 : 230).

11.3 The Feinians: With a strong Irish movement (Riel, vol. 2: 7, 11); an Irish province (Riel, vol. 2: 13); Irish Land League (Riel, vol. 3: 126); the establishment of land rights for the Métis (Flanagan, vol. 3: 129, note 14); negotiate an accord with the Fenians (Campbell vol. 4: 252, note 33; Stanley et al. vol. 5; Martel, vol. 2: 197, note 1); *"John A. MacDonald" Les nombreux rejetons de l'Irlande indomptable / Ne sont pas, sans dessein, dans les États-Unis. / Le jour qu'ils se mettront sous un chef acceptable / Et qu'ils voudront marcher dans des chemins bénis, / Les canadiens français et les métis sincères / Marcheront avec eux comme avec des bon frères* (Riel, vol. 4 : 325).

CHAPTER 12: LOUIS RIEL AND THE UNITED STATES

12.1 Introduction: He even threatened (Martel, vol. 2: xxxix; vol. 3: 122-123; Riel, vol. 4 : 249).

12.2 Louis Riel: The Métis Ambassador to the United States: Not a single pledge (Riel, vol. 1: 117); The Métis people... entered (Riel, vol. 2: 6); Mr. President... (Riel, vol. 2: 6).

12.3 Louis Riel: The American Citizen: *"Lettre à Joseph Riel" Pour moi, je deviens citoyen américain. J'en ai déclaré mon intention suivant la loi. Et j'en ai mon papier depuis le 17 de mai. Je pense que je pourrai mieux aider aux Métis de cette façon-là qu'autrement* (Riel, vol. 2: 222); Historically (Daniels 33); Louis Riel became an American citizen (Stanley, vol. 3: xxvii; Riel, vol. 2: 266-267);

[L]orsque j'étais sujet anglais je l'étais avec mon droit au sol... mes papiers de naturalisation américaine ont effacé la ligne entre le N.O. et les États-Unis (Riel, vol. 3: 307); *En ma qualité de citoyen américain je pense que, sans léser en aucune manière le droit international, je fais partie de la république avec mes gens, les Métis et avec mon pays indien, comme tant d'autres chefs sauvages américains qui font partie des États-Unis avec leurs tribus et leurs terrains, même avant d'avoir traité avec le gouvernement de Washington* (Riel, vol. 3: 307); It is constitutionally acknowledged... (Riel, vol. 3: 547); Who starts the nations? (Riel, vol. 3: 547).

12.4 Louis Riel: The American Activist: *"L'avenir des chefs Métis Canadiens Francais dans les États-Unis" Louis est le seul qui puisse amener les Pieds-Noirs, les Corps-Beaux, les Gros-Ventres, les Pendants d'Oreilles, les Têtes-Plates, etc.* (Riel, vol. 2: 214); war of extermination (Flanagan: vol. 3: xli); They consider that the American authorities (Riel, vol. 2: 219); I have the honor (Riel, vol. 2: 219); *"Dans l'état du Minnesota" Je veux aller quérir des nations cruelles* (Riel, vol. 4 : 222).

Tout au long de cet hivernement de 1879, Riel reste en contact non seulement avec une forte concentration de Métis, mais aussi avec une importante population d'Indiens de multiples tribus, dont plusieurs sont venues des Territoires du Nord-Ouest canadien. Il tente, mais en vain, d'organiser une alliance avec ces Indiens contre le Canada (Martel, vol. 2: xl); We ask the government (Riel, vol. 2: 224-225); two small half breed... (Riel, vol. 2: 227); Dakota ought not to allow (Riel, vol. 3: 284); immoral... (Riel, vol. 2: 364-365).

12.5 Louis Riel: The American Imperialist? The cause of the United States (Riel, vol. 2: 369); the United Moral States (Riel, vol. 2: 370-371); *"Manifeste à ses concitoyens americains" En ma qualité de citoyen américain je prie le gouvernement de Washington d'effacer la ligne international depuis le Lac Supérieur jusqu'à l'océan Pacifique, de me délivrer de la tyrannie et de soustraire tout le [Nord] Ouest à l'oppression* (Riel, vol. 3: 309); protect New France (Flanagan 1996: 186);

"Révélation se rapportant à l'annexation américaine du Nord-Ouest" Annexez le Nord-Ouest depuis le Lac Supérieur jusqu'à l'Océan Pacifique; Placez les Métis et les Sauvages des États-Unis dans le Nord-Ouest; Garantissez aux Métis un septième des Terres du Nord-Ouest; Prenez pour vous un septième des Terres du Nord-Ouest; Organisez dans le Nord-Ouest des Territoires nommés d'après les nationalités dont nous sommes originaires (Riel, vol. 3: 312); Riel went to Indianapolis... (Huel, vol. 1: 474, note 1); proposed that the land be divided (Riel, vol. 3: 309).

12.6 Conclusions: Wrote to J.W. Taylor (Flanagan: vol. 3: xliii); to investigate the claims (Riel, vol. 3: 163); alleged United States citizenship (Harrison 2); asking for American annexation (Flanagan: vol. 3: xliii).

CHAPTER 13: LOUIS RIEL AND WOMEN

13.2 Barefoot, Pregnant, and Pious: *"Révélations se rapportant aux lois de l'Ancien Testament" Notre Seigneur Jésus Christ permet qu'un homme épouse désormais jusqu'à cinq femmes. Il veut qu'il en soit ainsi: 1. pour qu'un plus grand nombre de filles se marie; 2. pour que les femmes, étant plusieurs ensembles à rechercher les faveurs de l'époux, se sentent plus d'émulation dans le ménage et dans l'éducation chrétienne qu'elles doivent donner à leurs enfants; 3. pour enseigner de nouveau aux femmes que leur seul moyen d'être agréable à Dieu, de plaire à leur mari et d'être longtemps honorées dans le monde, c'est de pratiquer sincèrement la modestie, l'économie et les amabilités de la vertu* (Riel, vol. 2: 150-151);

in the mind... (Riel, vol. 2: 151); a limit of five wives (Riel, vol. 2: 150); a total of fifteen (Riel, vol. 2: 161); *une jeune fille, tout en étant chaste, peut avoir des inclinations, sans les avouer aux autres* (Riel, vol. 2: 148); he complimented... (Riel, vol. 4: 233); *"Si mon amour vous plait: si mes joies vous conviennent" Plus votre vie est exemplaire, / Plus aussi savez-vous me plaire* (Riel, vol. 4: 215); *Montrez-vous ferme et sage entre toutes les femmes* (Riel, vol. 4: 215); *La femme est grande avec des aspirations / qui lui donnent le gout des saintes actions* (Riel, vol. 4: 214); *Vous qui voulez servir votre Dieu, vous savez / Ce qu'il faut de sagesse à la femme chrétienne / Pour échapper au monde ainsi qu'à ses dangers* (Riel, vol. 4: 213); *Je cherche une femme de bien* (Riel, vol. 4: 211)

CHAPTER 14: LOUIS RIEL AND LIBERALISM

14.1 Liberalism: Riel's political ideas were an exaggerated form of ultramontane thought (Flanagan 1996: 102);

14.2 *"La force que Dieu me donne" La chrétienté set met / par le libéralisme, au joug de Mahomet* (Riel, vol. 4: 144); Riel's religious teachings were mostly devoid of syncretism (Flanagan 1996: 198); there is no record of this (Flanagan 1996: 198); *Jésus-Christ seul est Roi; la loi, c'est l'évangile* (Riel, vol. 4: 144); *Conduisez-nous, tous les Métis, et par le gouvernement de votre esprit et par celui de votre main. Nous ne réclamons plus la liberté de professer des opinions contraires à votre manière de voir. La libre pensée est fatale. Elle est la mère du libertinage ou du libéralisme. C'est l'obéissance à la Sainte hiérarchie de l'église de Saint Pierre qui conduit les particuliers, les familles et les peuples à la vie* (Riel, vol. 4: 158; vol. 2: 90);

"Lettre à A.-A Taché" les gouvernements mondains ne sont pas conservateurs de la loi évangélique, ils sont tous Libéraux. Je sais que les gouvernements constitutionnels sont des gouvernements de servitude et d'esclavage. Je vois clairement que le gouvernement représentatif est le gouvernement des sauterelles dont l'apôtre

Saint Jean fait la description dans le chapitre neuvième de son apocalypse depuis le verset 3ieme jusqu'à douzième (Riel, vol. 2: 90-91); *"L'homme du cercle catholique" Le prêtre ... c'est La Liberté. / Il possède son catéchisme. / C'est assez pour vaincre l'erreur / Il en veut au libéralisme / Dont il se montre la terreur* (Riel, vol. 4: 181); *Le libéralisme était un des grands ennemis de la foi catholique selon Riel et les ultramondains. Le Cercle catholique avait certainement attaqué cette doctrine politique au cours de ses discussions* (Riel, vol. 4: 182*);*

"Oh! Que j'ai fait attention" Mon Dieu: délivrez-moi du noir libéralisme. / Et de tous les maux qu'il produit (Riel, vol. 4: 190*); Défenseur de la pensée ultramontaine, Riel considérait le libéralisme comme l'un des plus grands péchés* (Campbell, vol. 4: 191); *Je voudrais sauver cette partie du peuple Métis du malheur des idées libérales* (Riel, vol. 1 : 451); *"Lettre à Ignace Bourget" le bon Dieu vous choisit entre tous les évêques du monde ! Sa Providence vous a conservé afin qu'en ces temps malheureux ou le libéralisme est introduit partout, partout, partout* (Riel, vol. 2: 37*); Quoi! ... mes prophètes et mes souverains Pontifes ne seraient pas infaillibles, quand le doctorat du libéralisme se pose avec une infaillibilité à Lui pour gouverner et soigner à sa manière* (Riel, vol. 2: 67);

La lutte des ultramontains, et en particulier de Mgr Bourget, contre le libéralisme battait son plein. Le premier février 1876, Mgr Bourget avait publié sa fameuse lettre pastorale contre le libéralisme (voir Mandements, lettres pastorales, circulaires et autres documents publiés dans le diocèse de Montréal, *Montréal: Chancellerie de l'Archevêché, sans date, 7:299-310)* (Martel, vol. 2: 69); *"Révélations contre Beauport" Quel est cet homme qui chante à pleine tête, les Psaumes de l'Église ? Mais qui a les deux mains attachées et toujours enveloppées avec du gros cuir rouge, avec le gros cuir rouge du libéralisme?* (Riel, vol. 2: 75);

"Prière:" Seigneur ! Jésus Christ ! O Dieu vivant ! Il y a bien des camps et des postes avances de libéralisme dans le monde. Daignez n'en abattre que 45 maintenant (Riel, vol. 2: 83); *"Lettre à A.-A Taché" Les gouvernements mondains de toutes les formes et de toutes les couleurs ne sont bons qu'à mettre les hommes hors la loi de Dieu, qu'à leur faire la guerre, qu'a les persécuter, qu'a les expatrier, qu'a les jeter en prison, qu'a les juger sataniquement et qu'a les condamner à mort. Quand ils ne peuvent pas faire autrement, ils pardonnent au juste d'avoir été juste. Mais ils font attention de lui pardonner le moins qu'ils peuvent. Les générosités qu'ils font semblant de pratiquer sont mal inspirées. Les grâces qu'ils se piquent d'accorder sont aussi imparfaites que possible quand elles ne sont accompagnées de quelque insulte ou de quelque dérision* (Riel, vol. 2: 91);

he chastised Mastaï-Ferreti... (Riel, vol. 2: 112); he also condemned... (Riel, vol. 2: 112); it was the will of God (Riel, vol. 2: 137); *"Révélations se rapportant aux lois de l'Ancien Testament" Je ne serais jamais abandonné au libéralisme! Ce libéralisme qui consiste à tourner le dos à Dieu, à fuir les œuvres de la vertu persévérante, pour l'amour de ses aises, de la mollesse et des plaisirs sensuels* (Riel, vol. 2: 146); Mosaic law... (Martel, vol. 2: 161, note 1); Riel even believed that his physical ailments... (Martel, vol. 2: 162, note 29); He also condemned... (Martel, vol. 2: 163, note 36).

14.3 Conclusions. Union of church and state (Flanagan 1996: 103); *Les Canadiens-français et Irlandais libéraux m'ont fait beaucoup de bien* (Martel, vol. 2: 309, note 8).

CHAPTER 15: LOUIS RIEL AND MÉTIS UNITY

15.2 United We Stand, Divided We Fall: "Proclamation aux Peuples du Nord-Ouest" *Restons unis, et nous serons heureux.... Si jamais nous laissons arriver le jour d'une division comme celle que des étrangers ont tenté de répandre parmi nous, ce jour sera le signal de tous les désastres que nous avons eu le bonheur d'éviter* (Riel, vol. 3: 81); Riel counseled... (Huel, vol. 1: xlvi-xlvii; vol. 1: 292); our politics... (Riel, vol. 1: 62)

GENERAL CONCLUSIONS

From a historical point of view (Flanagan 1985: 184); During the winter of 1879-80... (Flanagan 182-183); "Letter to the Editor of the St. Paul Pioneer Press" Our is a battle for homes and human rights (Riel, vol. 3: 509); *"L'avenir des chefs Métis-Canadiens-français" les chrétiens libéraux qui ne veulent pas obéir à personne ; pendant que Jésus-Christ a été obéissant jusqu'à la mort.* (Riel, vol. 2 : 218)

APPENDIX: WHAT MAKES A MÉTIS?

1. A Métis is a Métis: the old genocidal system (Hitt n. page); the American Kennel Club (Hitt n. page); I don't like being talked about (Jarvis n. page); Many Canadians have mixed Aboriginal / non-Aboriginal ancestry (Standing Senate Committee 14); A lot of Indians haven't looked "Indian" for quite a while (Hitt n. page); The colour of the skin makes no difference (Nerburn 76).

3. A Métis is a Métis by Identity. Increased Indigenous self-identification (Hitt n. page); This diasporic sense of community (MacLeod 2013: 103); Ethnic identity is at the intersection of ethnic self-definition (Sperry 6); identity is neither black nor white (Sperry 6); used no less than thirty-five different ethnonyms (Malette: 2021: 42); The fact that the Métis (Bouchard, Malette, and Marcotte 2020: 228); there are many Métis peoples in Canada (O'Connell 113); There is no one exclusive Métis people (Gaffney, Gould, and Semple 62; O'Connell 113); an open-ended diaspora culture (Bouchard, Malette, and Marcotte 2020: 228); a people in motion (Sperry 16); ethnically dynamic (Sperry 85); Métis identity is not limited to just one region of Canada (Foxcurran, Bouchard, and Malette 2016: 390); The Métis, Cree and Chippewa people of Montana (Sperry 10); other communities can legitimately claim a Métis identity of their own (Foxcurran, Bouchard, and Malette 2016: 390); pan-continental (Foxcurran,

Bouchard, and Malette 2016: 389); the Métis exist today (Bouchard, Malette, and Marcotte 2016: 228); I am part white (Jarvis n. page).

5. A Métis is a Métis by language: It is a well-established fact that in Western Canada, Michif French speakers were discriminated against by everyone (Papen 74); Michif French speakers (Papen 75); it was arguably never the language of the majority of Métis (Papen 80); Michif has unfortunately become a handy political tool (Papen 88);

6. A Métis is a Métis by History, Family, Kinship, and Community: The Métis of the Outaouais (Malette and Marcotte 2021: 305); mixed and multiethnic (Malette and Marcotte 317: note 3); ethnically and culturally homogenous (Malette and Marcotte 2021: 317, note 3); a continuum that spans geographic boundaries (Elsey 271); The research is clear (Malette and Marcotte 2017: 42).

WORKS CITED

Allison, Harold. 1986. *The Tragic Saga of the Indiana Indians*. Paducah, KY: Turner Publishing.

Anson, Bert. 1970. *The Miami Indians*. Norman: University of Oklahoma Press.

Arnette, Travis R. No date. "Where the Buffalo Roam: Migration of the French Red River Métis to Lewiston, Montana." Internet: https:// www.montana.edu

Arnold, Abraham. 2016. "Wilfrid Laurier and Canada's Jews." *Canada History* (September 6). Internet: https://www.canadashistory.ca

Bailey, Alfred. 1937. *The Conflict of European and Eastern Algonkian Cultures, 1504-1700: A Study in Canadian Civilization*. Saint John: New Brunswick Museum.

Bakker, Peter. 1997. *A Language of Our Own: The Genesis of Michif, the Mixed Cree-French Language of the Canadian Métis*. Oxford: Oxford University Press.

Barnholden, Michael, trans. 2009. *Gabriel Dumont Speaks*. Vancouver: Talonbooks.

Basson, Lauren L. 2005. "Savage Half-Breed, French-Canadian or White US Citizen? Riel and US Perceptions of Nation and Civilization." *National Identities* 7.4. Internet: https://www.tandfonline.com

Benoit, Virgil. "French Presence in the Red River Valley Part I: A History of the Métis to 1870." 1987. *L'Héritage Tranquille: The Quiet Heritage*. Ed. Clarence A. Glasrud. Moorhead: Concordia College. 116-133.

Bonnycastle, Richard Henry. 1846. *Canada and the Canadians in 1846*. London: Henry Colburn.

Bouchard, Michel, Sébastien Malette, and Siomonn Pulla, eds. 2021. *Eastern Métis: Chronicling and Reclaiming a Denied Past*. Lanham, MD: Lexington Books.

Bouchard, Michel, Sébastien Malette, and Siomonn Pulla. 2021. "Introduction." *Eastern Métis: Chronicling and Reclaiming a Denied Past*. Ed. Michel

Bouchard, Sébastien Malette, and Siomonn Pulla. Lanham, MD: Lexington Books. ix-xxiv.

Bouchard, Michel, and Tiana Mager. 2021. "The Voyageur Métis of Penetanguishene: An Examination of the Ethnohistory of the Métis in Ontario." *Eastern Métis: Chronicling and Reclaiming a Denied Past.* Lanham, MD: Lexington Books. 229-257.

Bouchard, Michel, Sébastien Malette, and Guillaume Marcotte. 2020. *Bois-Brûlés: The Untold Story of the Métis of Western Quebec.* Vancouver: UBC Press.

Bouchard, Russel. 2005. *La communauté métisse de Chicoutimi, fondements historiques et culturelles.* Chicoutimi: Cegep de Chicoutimi. Internet: http://classiques.uqac.ca

Brandt, Michelle L. 2005. "More Evidence of Association Between Bipolar Disorder and Artistic Creativity." *Stanford News* (November 16). Internet: https://news.stanford.edu

Braz, Albert Raimundo. 2003. *The False Traitor: Louis Riel in Canadian Culture.* Toronto: University of Toronto Press.

Bryce, George. 1885. *The Old Settlers of Red River.* Winnipeg: ManitobaDaily Free Press.

Bumsted, J.M. 2001. *Louis Riel v. Canada: The Making of a Rebel.* Winnipeg: Great Plains Publications. Internet: https://archive.org

Campbell, Glen, ed. 1985. *The Collected Writings of Louis Riel / Les Écrits complets de Louis Riel. Vol. 4. Poetry / Poésie.* Edmonton: The University of Alberta Press.

Campbell, Maria. 1979. *Halfbreed.* Toronto: Seal Books.

Collacott, Martin. 2017. "Opinion: Canada Replacing its Population a Case of Willful Ignorance, Greed, Excess Political Correctness." *Vancouver Sun* (June 5). Internet: https://vancouversun.com

Combet, Denis Paul, and Ismène Toussaint. 2009. *Gabriel Dumont : souvenirs de résistance d'un immortel de l'Ouest.* Québec: Cornac.

Daniels, Harry W. 1979. *The Forgotten People: Métis and Non-Status Indian Land Claims.* Ottawa: Native Council of Canada.

Dickason, Olive Patricia. 1985. "From 'One Nation' in the Northeast to 'New Nation' in the Northwest: A Look at the Emergence of the Métis." *New Peoples: Being and Becoming Métis in North America.* Ed. Jacqueline Peterson and Jennifer Brown. Winnipeg: University of Manitoba Press. 19-36.

DesJarlait, Robert. 2018. "The Métis: A Question of Race." *Anishinaabe Perspectives* (November 30). Internet: https://anishinaabeperspectives.weebly.com

Driben, Paul. 1985. *We are Métis: The Ethnography of a Half-Breed Community in Northern Alberta*. New York: AMS Press. Internet: https://archive.org

DuLong, John P. 2002. "Jean Baptiste dit Lirlande. " *Habitant.org* (February 13). Internet: https://habitant.org

Dumont, Gabriel. 2009. *Gabriel Dumont Speaks*. Trans. Michael Barnholden. Vancouver: Talonbooks.

Elsey, Christine. 2021. "The Story of French-Canadian Métis Voyageur Joseph Dussault." *Eastern Métis: Chronicling and Reclaiming a Denied Past*. Ed. Michel Bouchard, Sébastien Malette, and Siomonn Pulla. Lanham, MD: Lexington Books. 259-273.

Ens, Gerhard John. 1996. *Homeland to Hinterland: The Changing Worlds of the Red River Métis in the Nineteenth Century*. Toronto: University of Toronto Press. Internet: https://archive.org

Ens, Gerhard John, and Joe Sawchuk. 2016. *From New Peoples to New Nations: Aspects of Métis History and Identity from the Eighteenth to Twenty-First Centuries*. Toronto: University of Toronto Press.

Esarey, Logan. 1970. *A History of Indiana: From its Exploration to 1850*. Indianapolis: Hoosier Heritage Press.

Fagan, Kristina, Bryce Donaldson, Robyn Moore, Stephanie Danyluk, Amelia Horsburgh, Martin Winquist. 2009. "Reading Reception of Maria Campbell's *Halfbreed*." *The Canadian Journal of Native Studies* 29 1&2: 257-281. Internet: http://www3.brandonu.ca

Ferguson, Robert. 2016. "Politics as Métis Ethnogenesis in Red River: Instrumental Ethnogenesis in the 1830s and 1840s in Red River." *Constellations* 8(1): 26–51. Internet: https://doi.org

Flanagan, Thomas. 1996. *Louis "David" Riel: Prophet of the New World*. Toronto: University of Toronto Press.

Flanagan, Thomas. 1992. *Louis Riel*. Ottawa: The Canadian Historical Association.

Flanagan, Thomas. 1986. "Louis Riel: Icon of the Left." *Transactions of the Royal Society of Canada, 5th Series*, 1: 219-228.

Flanagan, Thomas, ed. 1985. *The Collected Writings of Louis Riel / Les Écrits complets de Louis Riel*. Vol. 3. Edmonton: The University of Alberta Press.

Flanagan, Thomas. 1985. "Louis Riel and the Dispersion of the American Métis." *Minnesota History* (Spring). Internet: http://collections.mnhs. org

Foster, Martha Harroun. 2006. "'Just Following the Buffalo:' Origins of a Montana Métis Community." *Great Plains Quarterly*. Internet: https://digitalcommons.unl.edu

Foxcurran, Robert, Michel Bouchard, and Sébastien Malette. 2016. *Songs Upon the River: The Buried History of the French-Speaking Canadiens and Métis from the Great lakes and the Mississippi across to the Pacific*. Montreal: Baraka Books.

Gaffney, Ronald E., Gary P. Gould, and Alan J. Semple. 1984. *Broken Promises: The Aboriginal Constitutional Conferences*. Fredericton: New Brunswick Association of Métis and Non-Status Indians.

Gagnon, Denis. 2021. "Symbolic Violence against the 'Other Métis.' The Making of a New Forgotten People in Canada." *Eastern Métis: Chronicling and Reclaiming a Denied Past*. Lanham, MD: Lexington Books. 3-21.

Gagnon, Denis, and Suzanne Gagné. 2007. "L'étude des langues métisses et les programmes de révitalisation du Mitchif." *Recherches Amerindiennes au Québec* 37. 2-3: 77-87.

Germain, Georges-Hebert. 2003. *Adventurers in the New World: The Saga of the Coureurs des Bois*. Hull: Canadian Museum of Civilization.

Glasrud, Clarence A., ed. 1987. *L'Héritage Tranquille: The Quiet Heritage*. Moorhead: Concordia College.

Gough, Barry, and Laird Christie. 1991. *New Dimensions in Ethnohistory: Papers of the Second Laurier Conference on Ethnohistory and Ethnology*. Ed. Barry Gough and Laird Christie. Ottawa: Canadian Museum of Civilization.

Gray, Ralph. 1989. *The Hoosier State: Readings in Indiana History*. Bloomington and Indianapolis: Indiana University Press.

Green, Joyce. 2011. "Don't Tell us Who We Are (Not): Reflections on Métis Identity." *Aboriginal Policy Studies* 1.2: 166-170.

Guyot, Yves. 1883. *La morale*. Paris: Octave Doin.

Hamon, M. Max. 2017. *The Many Worlds of Louis Riel: A Political Odyssey from Red River to Montreal and Back, 1840-1875*. Doctoral dissertation. Montreal: McGill University. Internet: https://escholarship.mcgill.ca

Harrison, Benjamin. 1889. "Message from the President of the United States, Transmitting in Response to Senate Resolution of February 11, 1889, a Report Upon the Case of Louis Riel." Washington: State Department. Internet: https://archive.org

Hart, Michael H. 1992. *The 100: A Ranking of the Most Influential Persons in History*. 2nd ed. New York: Hart Publishing.

Hartai, Katie. 2014. "Who are the Métis?" *Ottawa Life* (December 15). Internet: https://www.ottawalife.com

Havard, V. 1880. "The French Half-Breeds of the Northwest." *Annual Report of the Board of Regents of the Smithsonian Institution, Showing the Operations,*

Expenditures, and Condition of the Institution for the Year 1879. Washington: Government Printing Office. 309-327.

Hitt, Jack. 2005. "The Newest Indians." *The New York Times* (August 21). Internet: https://www.nytimes.com

Howard, Joseph Kinsey. 1965. *Strange Empire: The Story of Louis Riel*. Toronto: Swan Publishing.

Howse, Jennifer. 2008. *The Métis*. Calgary: Weigl. Internet: https://archive.org

Huot, Pascal. 2010. "Les Métis de la Boréalie. Une présence autochtone au Québec." *Rabaska: Revue d'ethnologie de l'Amérique française* 8: 77-92. Internet: https://www.erudit.org

Ignatiev, Noel. 2008. *How the Irish Became White*. New York: Routledge.

Jackson, John C. 1996. *Children of the Fur Trade: Forgotten Métis of the Pacific Northwest*. Missoula: Mountain Press.

Jaenen, Cornelius. 1991. "Miscegenation in Eighteenth Century New France." *New Dimensions in Ethnohistory: Papers of the Second Laurier Conference on Ethnohistory and Ethnology*. Ed. Barry Gough and Laird Christie. Ottawa: Canadian Museum of Civilization: 79-116.

Jarvis, Brooke. 2017. "Who Decides Who Counts as Native American?" *New York Times* (January 18). Internet: https://www.nytimes.com

Jean, Denis. 2011. *Ethnogenèse des premiers métis canadiens (1603-1763)*. PhD dissertation. Moncton: Université de Moncton.

Karahasan, Devrim. 2006. *Métissage in New France: Frenchification, Mixed Marriages, and Métis as Shaped by Social and Political Agents and Institutions, 1508-1886*. PhD dissertation. Fiesole: European University Institute.

Kaufmann, Eric. 2018. *Whiteshift: Immigration and the Future of White Minorities*. New York: Harry N. Abrams.

Kaufman, Scott Barry, and Elliot S. Paul. 2014. "Creativity and Schizophrenia Spectrum Disorders Across the Arts and Sciences." *Front Psychol.* 5: 1145. Internet: https://www.ncbi.nlm.nih.gov

Kilpatrick, Sean. 2020. "Manitoba Métis Federation Says Streets, Schools Named after Colonial Figures Should Stay." *The Globe and Mail* (June 18). Internet: https://www.theglobeandmail.com

Kodó, Krisztina. 2021. "The Story Behind the Story, or the Untold Story? John Coulter's Perceptions of a Canadian Tragic Hero, Louis Riel." *On the Other Side(s) of 150: Untold Stories and Critical Approaches to History, Literature, and Identity in Canada*. Ed. Linda M. Morra and Sarah Henzi. Waterloo: Wilfred Laurier University Press.

Kohl, Johann Georg. 1985. *Kitchi-Gami: Life Among the Lake Superior Ojibway*. St. Paul, MN: Minnesota Historical Society.

Kohl, Johann Georg. 1860. *Kitchi-Gami: Wanderings Round Lake Superior*. London: Chapman and Hall.

Larivière, Peter. 2015. *Métis Identity in Canada*. Master's thesis. Ottawa: Carleton University. Internet: https://curve.carleton.ca

Lavallée, Guy. 2003. *The Métis of St. Laurent, Manitoba: Their Life and Stories, 1920-1988*. Winnipeg: Guy.

Lawrence, Bonita. 2004. *"Real" Indians and Others: Mixed-Blood Urban Native Peoples and Indigenous Nationhood*. Lincoln: University of Nebraska Press.

Legg, Timothy J. 2019. "Bipolar Disorder and Creativity." *Healthline* (December 6). Internet: https://www.healthline.com

Littmann, S.K. 1978. "A Pathology of Louis Riel." *Canadian Psychiatric Association Journal* 23: 449-462. Internet: https://journals.sagepub.com

Loüis, Gustave. 1867. *Physiologie de l'opinion*. Paris: E. Dentu.

Lusty, Terry. 1973. *Métis Social-Political Movement*. Calgary: Métis Historical Society.

MacLeod, Katie K. 2021. "Situating Nova Scotia Métis Identities in a Colonial Past." *Eastern Métis: Chronicling and Reclaiming a Denied Past*. Ed. Michel Bouchard, Sébastien Malette, and Siomonn Pulla. Lanham, MD: Lexington Books. 97-109.

Marcotte, Guillaume. 2021. "'The Lowest Race of Any in Canada': Mitifs from the Fur Trade and the Voyageurs Parishes of St. Lawrence Valley." *Eastern Métis: Chronicling and Reclaiming a Denied Past*. Ed. Michel Bouchard, Sébastien Malette, and Siomonn Pulla. Lanham, MD: Lexington Books. 171-192.

Malette, Sébastien. 2021. "Political Ontologies in Turmoil: Métis 'Neo-Nationalism' and the 'Other Métis.'" *Eastern Métis: Chronicling and Reclaiming a Denied Past*. Ed. Michel Bouchard, Sébastien Malette, and Siomonn Pulla. Lanham, MD: Lexington Books. 23-64.

Malette, Sébastien and Guillaume Marcotte. 2021. "'This Hero Whom the Métis Nation at Large Must Be Proud:' Private Patrick Riel of Maniwaki." *Eastern Métis: Chronicling and Reclaiming a Denied Past*. Ed. Michel Bouchard, Sébastien Malette, and Siomonn Pulla. Lanham, MD: Lexington Books. 301-324.

Manitoba Métis Federation. 2022. "The Red River Métis—la Nouvelle Nation." Manitoba Métis Federation. Internet: https://www.mmf.mb.ca

Martel, Gilles. 1986. "L'idéologie messianique de Louis Riel et ses sentiments sociaux." *Transactions of the Royal Society of Canada, 5th Series*, 1: 229-238.

Martel, Gilles, ed. 1985. *The Collected Writings of Louis Riel / Les Écrits complets de Louis Riel. Vol. 2. Prose.* Edmonton: The University of Alberta Press.

Michaux, Emmanuel. 2021. "*Métissage* and Métis Identity in the Gaspé Peninsula from its Origins to the 1886 Paspébiac Riots." *Eastern Métis: Chronicling and Reclaiming a Denied Past.* Ed. Michel Bouchard, Sébastien Malette, and Siomonn Pulla. Lanham, MD: Lexington Books. 133-150.

Montandon, Augustin Laurent. 1845. *Étude élémentaire du décalogue: Première esquisse des devoirs de la religion.* Paris: L-R. Delay.

Morrow, John Andrew. 2021. *The Messenger of Mercy: The Covenants of Coexistence from the Prophet of Pluralism.* New Delhi: Sanbun Publishers.

Morrow, John Andrew. 2020. "Thomas Jefferson and the Covenants of the Prophet Muhammad." *The Islamic Interfaith Initiative: No Fear Shall be Upon Them.* Newcastle upon Tyne: Cambridge Scholars Publishing. 198-210.

Morrow, John Andrew. 2020. "Thomas Jefferson and the Covenants of the Prophet Muhammad." *The Maydan* (January 9). Internet: https://themaydan.com

Motut, Roger. 1985. "La langue écrite de Louis Riel et quelques aspects de la langue parlée par les Métis." *The Collected Writings of Louis Riel / Les Écrits Complets de Louis Riel.* Vol. 5. Ed. George F.G. Stanley, Thomas Flanagan, and Claude Rocan. Edmonton: The University of Alberta Press. 47-60.

Murray, Evan D. et al. 2012. "The Role of Psychotic Disorders in Religious History Considered." *The Journal of Neuropsychiatry* 24.4. Internet: https://neuro.psychiatryonline.org

Narine, Shari. 2021. "Métis Must Gain Belonging from Community, Not Government, Says Belcourt." *Toronto Star* (September 28). Internet: https://www.thestar.com

Nerburn, Kent, ed. 1999. *The Wisdom of the Native Americans.* Novato, CA: New World Library.

O'Connell, Seán. 2021. "The Acadian Métis on the Geographic and Social Margins." *Eastern Métis: Chronicling and Reclaiming a Denied Past.* Ed. Michel Bouchard, Sébastien Malette, and Siomonn Pulla. Lanham, MD: Lexington Books. 111-131.

O'Toole, Darren. 2017. "Y a-t-il des communautés métisses au Québec? Une perspective juridique." *Nouveaux Cahier du Socialisme* 18 (Fall). Internet: https://www.erudit.org

Orwell, George. 1982. *Orwell's Nineteen Eighty-Four: Texts, Sources, Criticism.* Ed. David Levin and Irving Howe. San Diego: Harcourt Brace Jovanovich.

Ouimet, Adolphe. 1889. *La vérité sur la question métisse.* Montreal. Internet: http://classiques.uqac.ca

Papen, Robert A. 2021. "The Languages of the Métis in Canada." *Eastern Métis: Chronicling and Reclaiming a Denied Past.* Ed. Michel Bouchard, Sébastien Malette, and Siomonn Pulla. Lanham, MD: Lexington Books. 67-94.

Paradis, Jean-François. 2019. "What is White Genocide?" *Geopolitica* (January 16). Internet: https://www.geopolitica.ru

Perrotta, G. 2019. "The Psychopathological Profile of the Biblical God Called Yhwh (Yahweh): A Psychological Investigation into the Behaviour of the Judaic-Christian God Described in the Biblical Old Testament." *Journal of Neuroscience and Neurological Surgery* 4.5 (September 27). Internet: www.researchgate.net

Peterson, Jacqueline, Jennifer S.H. Brown, eds. 1985. *The New Peoples: Being and Becoming Métis in North America.* Lincoln, NE: University of Nebraska Press.

Peterson, Jacqueline. 1978. "Prelude to Red River: A Social Portrait of the Great Lakes Métis." *Ethnohistory* 25.1 (Winter): 41-67. Internet: https://www.jstor.org

Philpot, Robin. 2021. "L'histoire macabre des pensionnats autochtones au Canada: Une conséquence de la 3e conquête britannique en Amérique." *Defend Democracy Press* (July 20). Internet: http://www.defenddemocracy.press

Pratt, Beverly M., Lindsay Hixson, and Nicholas A. Jones. 2015. "Measuring Race and Ethnicity Across the Decades: 1790-2010." United States Census Bureau. Internet: https://www.census.gov

Pulla, Siomonn. 2021. "Understanding the Impacts of a Transitional and Mixed Regional Economy on the Emergence of the Historic Métis of Mattawa." *Eastern Métis: Chronicling and Reclaiming a Denied Past.* Lanham, MD: Lexington Books. 195-227.

Rafert, Stewart. 1996. *The Miami Indians of Indiana: A Persistent People.* Indianapolis: Indiana Historical Society.

Raffenel, Anne. 1856. *Nouveau voyage dans le pays des nègres.* Paris: Napoléon Chaix.

Rameau de Saint-Père, François-Edme. 1888. "Remarques sur les registres de Belle-Isle-en-Mer." *Le Canada français, collection de documents inédits sur le Canada et l'Amérique—documents sur l'Acadie.* vol 1. Québec: L.-J. Demers. 135-136.

Rameau de Saint-Père, François-Edme. 1877. *Une colonie féodale en Amérique (l'Acadie, 1604-1710).* Paris: Didier.

Read, Geoff, and Todd Webb. 2021. "'The Catholic Mahdi of the Northwest:' Louis Riel and Métis Resistance in Transatlantic and Imperial Context." *Canadian Historical Review* 102.1 (June): 265-284.

Redbird, Duke. 1980. *We are Métis: A Métis View of the Development of a Native Canadian People*. Willowdale: Ontario Metis & Non-Status Indian Association.

Reid, Jennifer. 2008. *Louis Riel and the Creation of Modern Canada: Mythic Discourse and the Postcolonial State*. Albuquerque: University of New Mexico Press.

Riel, Louis. 1985. *The Collected Writings of Louis Riel / Les Écrits complets de Louis Riel*. Ed. George F.G. Stanley, Raymond Huel, Gilles Martel, Thomas Flanagan, and Glen Campbell. 5 vols. Edmonton: The University of Alberta Press.

Riel, Louis. 1985. *The Collected Writings of Louis Riel*. Vol. 1. Ed. Raymond Huel. Edmonton: University of Alberta Press.

Riel, Louis. 1985. *The Collected Writings of Louis Riel*. Vol. 2. Ed. Gilles Martel. Edmonton: University of Alberta Press.

Riel, Louis. 1985. *The Collected Writings of Louis Riel*. Vol. 3. Ed. Thomas Flanagan. Edmonton: University of Alberta Press.

Riel, Louis. 1985. *The Collected Writings of Louis Riel*. Vol. 4. Ed. Glen Campbell. Edmonton: University of Alberta Press.

Richardson, Cathy. 2006. "Métis Identity Creation and Tactical Responses to Oppression and Racism." *Variegations* 2: 56-71.

Rivard, Etienne. 2020. "À l'invisible nul n'est tenu: les conditions spatiales de l'identification métisse au Canada au XIXe siècle." *Espaces, Populations, Sociétés* 1-2: Internet: https://journals.openedition.org

Rivard, Etienne. 2004. *Prairie and Quebec Métis Territoriality: "Interstices Territoriales" and the Cartography of in-Between Identity*. Vancouver: University of British Columbia. Internet: https://open.library.ubc.ca

Rivard, Ron, and Catherine Littlejohn. 2003. *The History of the Métis of Willow Bunch*. Np: Saskatoon. Internet: https://archive.org

Sealy, Bruce D. and Antoine S. Lussier. 1975. *The Métis: Canada's Forgotten People*. Winnipeg: Manitoba Métis Federation Press.

Schaefli, Laura M. 2012. *Indigenous People and Quebec Identity: Revelations from the 2007 Bouchard-Taylor Commission on Reasonable Accommodation*. Master's thesis. Kingston: Queen's University. Internet: https://qspace.library.queensu.ca

Schreiber, June. 1988. *Alberta's Métis: People of the Western Prairie*. Edmonton: Reidmore Books. Internet: https://archive.org

Slobodin, Richard. 1996. *Métis of the Mackenzie District*. Ottawa: Canadian Research Center for Anthropology.

Smith, Donald B. 2021. "Honoré Jaxon: Madman or Visionary?" *Calgary Herald* (December 11). Internet: https://calgaryherald.com

—. *Honoré Jaxon: Prairie Visionary*. 2008. Regina: Coteau Books.

Sperry, Elizabeth. 2007. *Ethnogenesis of Métis, Cree, and Chippewa in Twentieth Century Montana*. Master's thesis. Missoula: University of Montana. Internet: https://scholarworks.umt.edu

St. Georges, Darlene. 2020. *Embodied Landscapes: A Creation-Research Indigenous Métissage*. PhD thesis. Montreal: Concordia University.

St-Onge, Nicole, and Carolyn Podruchny. 2012. "Scuttling along a Spider's Web." *Contours of a People: Métis Family, Mobility, and History*. Ed. Carolyn Podruchny, Brenda Macdougall, and Nicole St-Onge. Norman, OK: University of Oklahoma Press. 59-92.

Standing Senate Committee on Aboriginal Peoples. 2013." '*The People Who Own Themselves:' Recognition of Métis Identity in Canada*." Internet : https://publications.gc.ca

Stanley, George F.G. 2013. Louis Riel. *The Canadian Encyclopedia* (online ed.). Historica Canada.

Stanley, George F.G. 1963. *Louis Riel*. Toronto: The Ryerson Press.

Stanley, George F.G., Thomas Flanagan, and Claude Rocan, eds. 1985. *The Collected Writings of Louis Riel / Les Écrits complets de Louis Riel. Vol. 5. Reference*. Edmonton: The University of Alberta Press.

Stuart, Andrew, and David Stuart. 1830. *Rapport des commissaires nommé pour l'exploration du pays, borné par les rivières Saguenay, Saint-Maurice et Saint-Laurent*. Québec: Chambre d'Assemblée.

Sutherland, Donna. 2021. "First nations and Métis People of the Red River Settlement (Pre and Post Confederation)." *Red River North Heritage*. Internet: https://redrivernorthheritage.com

Taché, Joseph-Charles. 1863. *Forestiers et voyageurs*. Québec: Brousseau & Frères.

—. *Forestiers et voyageurs*. 1884. Montréal: Librairie Saint-Joseph, Cadieux et Derome.

Thistle, Jesse. 2016. "'We are Children of the River:' Toronto's Lost Métis History." *Revue Your Review* 1: 11-23. Internet: https://yourreview.journals.yorku.ca

Todd, Douglas. 2021. "What do Indigenous Voices Say About Immigration?" *Vancouver Sun* (October 24). Internet: https//:vancouversun.com

Toqueville, Alexis de. 1865. *Mélanges*. Vol. 8. Paris, Michel Lévy.

Trémaudan, Auguste-Henri de. 1979. *Histoire de la nation métisse dans l'Ouest canadien.* Saint-Boniface: Les Éditions du Blé.

Trobriand, Régie de, and Marie Caroline Post. 1910. *The Life and Memoirs of Comte Régie de Trobriand.* New York: E.P. Dutton.

Turner, Tara J. 2010. *Re-Searching Métis Identity: My Métis Family Story.* Doctoral dissertation. Saskatoon: University of Saskatchewan. Internet: https://citeseerx.ist.psu.edu

Upton, Charles. 2020. "Regarding Riel." Email (September 29).

Vermette, David. 2018. *A Distinct Alien Race: The Untold Story of Franco-Americans.* Montreal: Baraka Books.

Voisine, Nive. 2006. "Ultramontanism." *The Canadian Encyclopedia.* Internet: https://www.thecanadianencyclopedia.ca

White, Robin. 2014. *Louis Riel, Justice, and Métis Self-Identification: Literary Politics for Survival in the Evolution of Canadian Nationhood.* Doctoral dissertation. London: University of London.

Wilcox, Michael. "Orange Order in Canada." *The Canadian Encyclopedia* (June 6, 2007). Internet: https://www.thecanadianencyclopedia.ca

Zion, Candi. 2021. *In Between People: The Métis of Central Montana.* Montana: Snowy Mountain Development Corporation and the Montana Memory Project. Internet: https://www.mthistory.org

"I have nothing but my heart and I have given it long ago to my country." Louis Riel

INDEX

ALSO FROM BARAKA BOOKS

ᐙᔂᓂᐱᔅ
Waswanipi
Jean-Yves Soucy
with an Afterword by Romeo Saganash

Songs Upon the Rivers
The Buried History of the French-Speaking Canadiens and Métis from the Great Lakes and the Mississippi across to the Pacific
Foxcurran, Bouchard Malette

A Distinct Alien Race
The Untold Story of Franco-Americans
David Vermette

Montreal, City of Secrets
Confederate Operations in Montreal During the American Civil War
Barry Sheehy

Mussolini Also Did a Lot of Good
The Spread of Historical Amnesia
Francesco Filippi

After All Was Lost
The Resilience of a Rwandan Family Orphaned on April 6, 1994 when the Rwandan President's Plane was Shot Down
Alice Nsabimana

The Einstein File
The FBI's Secret War on the World's Most Famous Scientist
Fred Jerome

The Plains of Abraham
Battlefield 1759 and 1760
Hélène Quimper
(Translated by Katherine Hastings)

MIX
Paper
FSC® C100212

Printed by Imprimerie Gauvin
Gatineau, Québec